D1294965

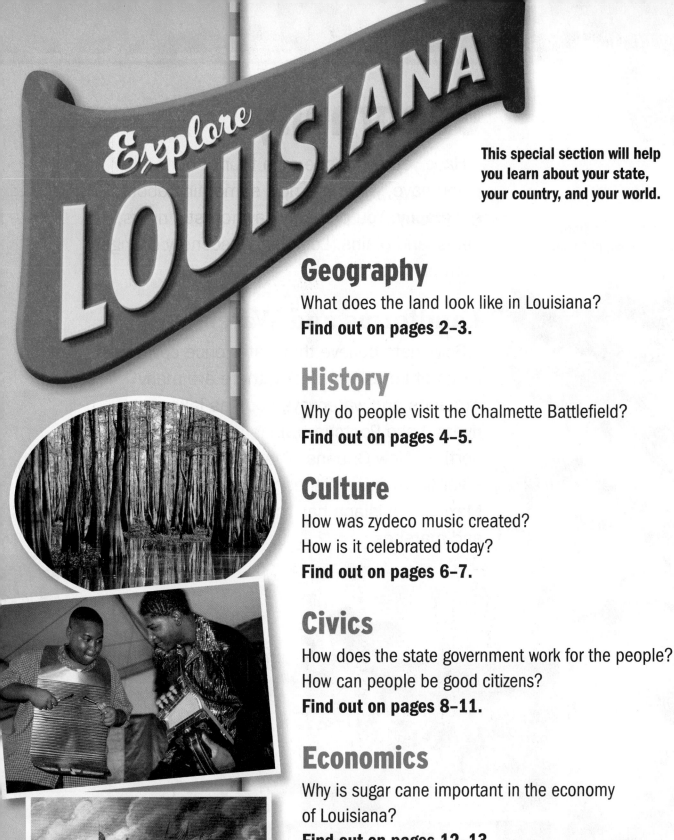

Explore LOUISIANA

This special section will help you learn about your state, your country, and your world.

Geography

What does the land look like in Louisiana?
Find out on pages 2–3.

History

Why do people visit the Chalmette Battlefield?
Find out on pages 4–5.

Culture

How was zydeco music created?
How is it celebrated today?
Find out on pages 6–7.

Civics

How does the state government work for the people?
How can people be good citizens?
Find out on pages 8–11.

Economics

Why is sugar cane important in the economy of Louisiana?
Find out on pages 12–13.

Science and Technology

How did the introduction of railroads change Louisiana?
Find out on pages 14–15.

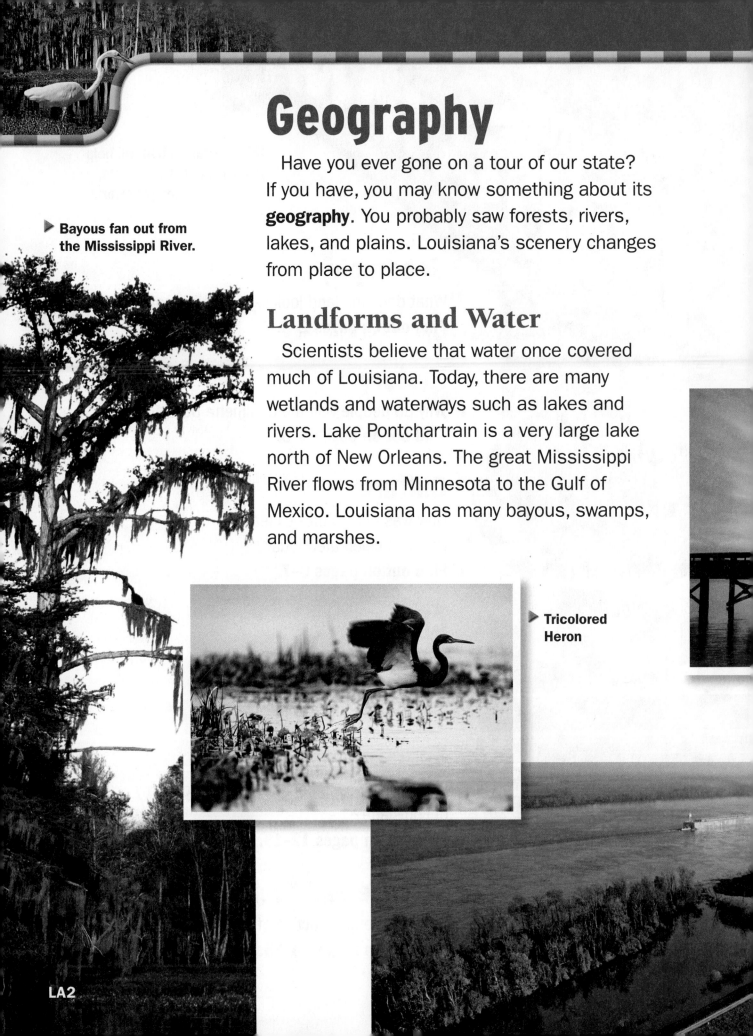

Geography

Have you ever gone on a tour of our state? If you have, you may know something about its **geography**. You probably saw forests, rivers, lakes, and plains. Louisiana's scenery changes from place to place.

Landforms and Water

Scientists believe that water once covered much of Louisiana. Today, there are many wetlands and waterways such as lakes and rivers. Lake Pontchartrain is a very large lake north of New Orleans. The great Mississippi River flows from Minnesota to the Gulf of Mexico. Louisiana has many bayous, swamps, and marshes.

▶ Bayous fan out from the Mississippi River.

▶ Tricolored Heron

Lowland is a good word to describe Louisiana. The lowest point in the state is in the south at New Orleans. Driskill Mountain in the north is the highest point. There are forests on Driskill Mountain and in many parts of Louisiana. The Kisatchie National Forest is in Louisiana. There are also treeless prairie lands, or plains. The land is good for farming.

REVIEW Compare two landforms or bodies of water in Louisiana.

Vocabulary

geography the study of land surface and how people live on and use the land

▶ Lake Pontchartrain is near New Orleans.

▶ Mount Driskill is the highest point in Louisiana.

▶ Louisiana has both swamplands (left) and plains (below).

▶ The Mississippi River flows to the Gulf of Mexico.

LA3

History

The United States and Great Britain were at war in 1812. The last important battle of the war took place in Louisiana on January 8, 1815. It was called the Battle of New Orleans.

The Chalmette Battlefield

American generals knew that Chalmette would be a good place to fight. The British had to march between a swamp and a river to reach Chalmette. Both sides had trouble seeing because of fog, but the Americans won the battle. New Orleans was safe from capture by the British.

▶ **General Andrew Jackson led American troops.**

▶ **Many Louisianians helped the United States win the Battle of New Orleans.**

The Battlefield Today

Today, the National Park Service takes care of the historic battlefield. Each year, actors dress like American and British soldiers so that visitors can see what the battle was like. Visitors can climb steps to the top of a **monument** and view the battlefield from there. There is a cemetery next to the battlefield for American **veterans**.

The hurricanes of 2005 caused damage to the battlefield. Hurricane Katrina destroyed the visitor center. Trees fell in the cemetery. The battlefield and cemetery were closed for a while to make repairs and build a new visitor center.

REVIEW Why is the Chalmette Battlefield important to American history?

Vocabulary

monument building or statue that honors a person or event

veterans people who fought in their country's wars

▶ **Chalmette Battlefield and monument**

Culture

Many people came to Louisiana from different countries and brought unique styles of music from their **heritage**. Through the years, people learned these different styles. They also blended the styles and created new music. Today, bands play new styles of music at festivals.

Southwest Louisiana Zydeco Music Festival

One popular style of music is called zydeco. It is a blend of different styles such as Cajun and African American Creole. Each year people come to hear bands play zydeco music at the Southwest Louisiana Zydeco Music Festival. The festival is held near Opelousas in St. Landry Parish.

▶ Clifton Chenier is known as the King of Zydeco.

▶ The rubboard and accordian are important instruments in Zydeco music.

Opelousas has become a zydeco music capital. Clifton Chenier was born in Opelousas. He played zydeco music on his accordion and helped to make zydeco popular all over the world.

A zydeco band has a number of instruments. The accordion is an important zydeco instrument. Another important instrument is the rubboard. The rubboard is like a washboard. Other zydeco instruments include the guitar, the saxophone, and the drums.

Vocabulary

heritage something that is passed on from one generation to the next

REVIEW How does the music created in Louisiana reflect its culture?

home of the
SOUTHWEST LOUISIANA
ZYDECO MUSIC FESTIVAL

SATURDAY BEFORE
LABOR DAY

SAT
SEPT. 2

Civics

Louisiana has three branches, or parts, of state government. The branches are the executive, legislative, and judicial. Louisiana parishes and towns have governments too. All of these governments provide services to citizens.

State Government

The **governor** leads the executive branch. The governor works with the legislative branch to make new laws. Judges in the judicial branch help decide if a law is fair under the constitution. A **constitution** is a written plan for government.

▶ **Many departments within the Executive Branch help provide services.**

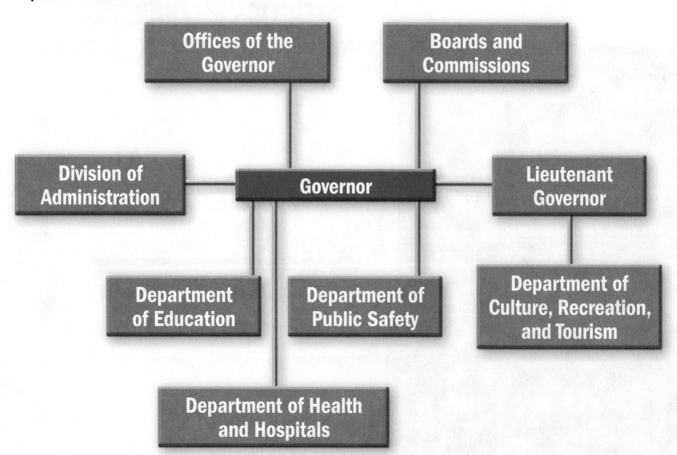

Citizens receive important services from the executive branch. But the governor cannot do all the work alone. Many departments provide these services. Some of the departments that might help you are the Department of Education, the Department of Health and Hospitals, and the Department of Public Safety.

Special Services by the Governor

In 2005, Governor Kathleen Blanco took action to bring help to areas damaged by Hurricanes Katrina and Rita. She worked to help make Louisiana a good place to live again. Many citizens of Louisiana helped too.

REVIEW How does the executive branch of Louisiana's government provide so many services to citizens?

Vocabulary

governor the head of the state government

constitution written plan for government

▶ **Kathleen Blanco became governor of Louisiana in 2004.**

▶ **Louisiana Legislative Branch**

LA9

You read about ways the government provides services to the people of Louisiana. Did you know that the government also needs help from citizens? Good citizenship means caring for and helping people, especially when there is an **emergency**.

Good Citizenship in Ville Platte

What would you do if you found out that thousands of people suddenly needed your help? This is what happened to the people of Ville Platte. On August 29, 2005, Hurricane Katrina forced people near the Gulf Coast to leave their homes. Thousands traveled to Ville Platte. Several thousand more people came to Ville Platte because of Hurricane Rita.

▶ Some supplies were delivered to Ville Platte in a helicopter.

The people of Ville Platte were good citizens. They welcomed many of the newcomers into their homes as guests. Others stayed at the Civic Center. There, the newcomers had beds, blankets, and clean clothes. Doctors and nurses gave free care to the sick. They helped newcomers find jobs. They helped find family members. No one in Ville Platte was paid to help. The citizens felt they were just doing what was right.

Vocabulary

emergency sudden and terrible trouble

REVIEW How did the people of Ville Platte show good citizenship?

▶ The citizens of Ville Platte cooked and served meals each day at the Civic Center.

Economics

Louisiana farmers grow crops that are sold all over the United States. The farmers earn a living by selling their crops. Sugar cane is one of the most important crops grown by farmers in Louisiana.

How Sugar Cane Came to Louisiana

Louisiana is sometimes called the Sugar State. It is the oldest area in the United States for the production of sugar. In the 1700s, people brought sugar cane to New Orleans and planted it there. The sugar cane grew well in the hot climate of southern Louisiana. Others began to grow sugar cane.

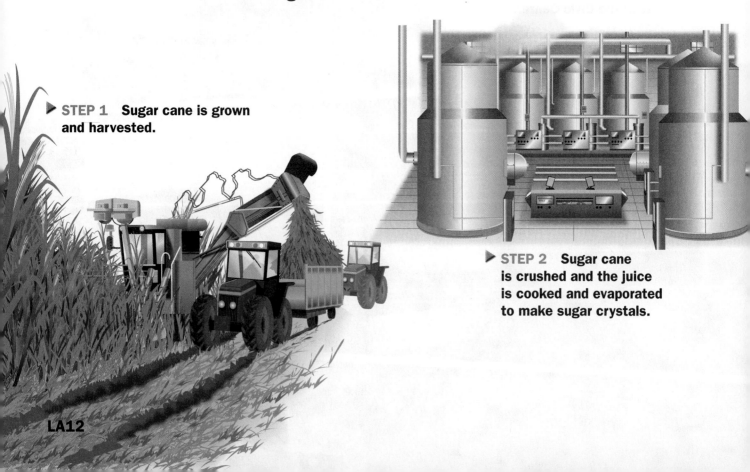

▶ STEP 1 Sugar cane is grown and harvested.

▶ STEP 2 Sugar cane is crushed and the juice is cooked and evaporated to make sugar crystals.

Making Sugar

Sugarcane is really a tall grass. Sugar is stored in the cane stalk. The first farmers did not have a way to **process** cane into sugar. Instead, they cut the stalks into little pieces for people to eat.

In the late 1700s, Etienne de Boré arrived in the Louisiana area. He knew a way to make the cane into grains that look like the sugar you see today. Sugar mills were started to process the cane. Later, machines called harvesters replaced workers in the fields. Today, many thousands of workers process sugar cane in Louisiana.

Vocabulary

process change or make something

REVIEW Describe the effects of the sugar industry to Louisiana's economy.

▶ STEP 3 **Sugar is packaged.**

▶ STEP 4 **Sugar is sent to stores, where we can buy it.**

LA13

Science and Technology

Vocabulary

construct make or build

Did you know that railroads helped the state of Louisiana develop and grow? In the late 1800s workers began to **construct** many miles of railroad tracks. Soon, railroads crossed the state from east to west and from north to south.

Railroads Helped Towns Grow

Many people came to our state to live along the new railroads. They opened stores and businesses. Louisiana farmers shipped their crops in railroad cars. The railroad cars also carried lumber from Louisiana forests.

▶ The railroad has been used to ship goods for many years.

Railroads helped start the towns of Ruston, DeQuincy, DeRidder, and Jennings. Today, people can learn about railroads at the DeQuincy Railroad Museum.

Since the 1800s, other methods of transportation have been used in Louisiana. Farmers ship their crops by boat. People travel in cars and on airplanes. However, the destruction from Hurricanes Katrina and Rita in 2005 reminded people about the importance of the railroad. Railroad cars brought the supplies needed to repair the damaged roads.

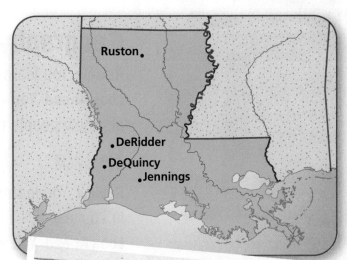

REVIEW How did railroads change life in Louisiana?

▶ **Jennings began as a railroad town.**

Review and Look Ahead

Geography

Review You learned what the land and water in Louisiana is like.
Look Ahead You will learn more about the land of Louisiana and how people protect its resources.

History

Review You learned about an important historical place in Louisiana.
Look Ahead You will read about events and important people from the past.

Culture

Review You learned about music in Louisiana.
Look Ahead You will read more about styles of music and the ways of life celebrated by Louisianians.

Civics

Review You learned about government in Louisiana. You also learned what good citizenship means.
Look Ahead You will learn about ways the government works. You will read about good citizens from all around the state.

Economics

Review You learned about processing sugar cane.
Look Ahead You will read about kinds of work, natural resources, and trade in Louisiana.

Science and Technology

Review You learned how railroads changed Louisiana.
Look Ahead You will learn more about inventions that helped people settle the land and use its resources.

SCOTT FORESMAN

SOCIAL STUDIES

LOUISIANA

SCOTT FORESMAN

SOCIAL STUDIES

LOUISIANA

PEARSON

Scott
Foresman

Editorial Offices: Glenview, Illinois • Parsippany, New Jersey • New York, New York
Sales Offices: Boston, Massachusetts • Duluth, Georgia • Glenview, Illinois •
Coppell, Texas • Sacramento, California • Mesa, Arizona

www.sfsocialstudies.com

CONTENT CONSULTANT

Dr. Lawrence N. Powell
Professor, Department of History
Tulane University
New Orleans, Louisiana

TEACHER REVIEWERS

Cherie Leger McIntyre
Walter L Abney Elementary
Slidell, Louisiana

Edris Lodge
Dalton Elementary School
Baton Rouge, Louisiana

Judy Roger
Live Oak Elementary School
Lafayette, Louisiana

Warrine Sam
Martin Luther King, Jr. Elementary School
New Orleans, Louisiana

Vickie H. Smith
Principal
L.S. Rugg Elementary School
Alexandria, Louisiana

Vicky Smith
Villa Del Rey Elementary School
Baton Rouge, Louisiana

ISBN: 0-328-24981-5

Copyright © 2008, Pearson Education, Inc.

All Rights Reserved. Printed in the United States of America. This publication is protected by Copyright, and permission should be obtained from the publisher prior to any prohibited reproduction, storage in a retrieval system, or transmission in any form by any means, electronic, mechanical, photocopying, recording, or likewise. For information regarding permission(s), write to: Permissions Department, Scott Foresman, 1900 East Lake Avenue, Glenview, Illinois 60025.

6 7 8 9 10 V042 15 14 13 12 11 10

Contents

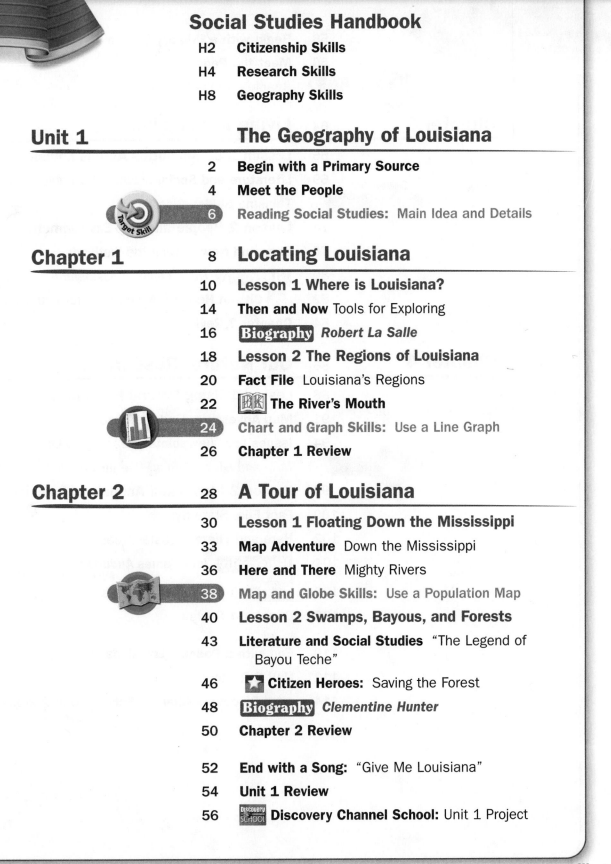

People and the Land

UNIT 5

Citizens and the Government

Reference Guide

★BIOGRAPHY★

Maps

Skills

Reading Social Studies

Map and Globe Skills

Thinking Skills

Research and Writing Skills

Chart and Graph Skills

Fact File

Citizen Heroes

Issues and Viewpoints

Then and Now

Here and There

Literature and Social Studies

Citizenship Skills

There are six ways to show good citizenship: respect, caring, responsibility, fairness, courage, and honesty. In your textbook, you will learn about people who used these ways to help their community, state, and country.

Respect
Treat others as you would want to be treated. Welcome differences among people.

Caring
Think about what someone else needs.

Responsibility
Do what you are supposed to do, and think before you act.

Fairness
Take turns and follow the rules. Listen to what others have to say.

Courage
Do what is right even when the task is hard.

Honesty
Tell the truth, and do what you say you will do.

★ Citizenship in Action ★

Good citizens make careful decisions. They learn to solve problems. How will these children act like good citizens? Here are the steps they will follow.

Problem Solving

The children need to have their classroom plants and animals taken care of during winter vacation.

1. **Identify the problem.**
2. **Gather information.**
3. **List and consider options.**
4. **Consider advantages and disadvantages.**
5. **Choose and try a solution.**
6. **Decide if the solution worked.**

Decision Making

The students are deciding what talent they want to show in the third grade talent show. Before making a decision, each student should follow these steps.

1. **Tell what decision you need to make.**
2. **Gather information.**
3. **List your options.**
4. **Tell what might happen with each choice.**
5. **Make a decision.**

When you need to find information for a report or a project, you can use three main reference resources: **Print Resources**, **Technology Resources**, and **Community Resources**. You can use many different reference sources to do research. A reference tool is any source of information.

Print Resources

Books are reference tools. Libraries often have reference shelves with books such as atlases, almanacs, and encyclopedias.

Encyclopedia An encyclopedia is a collection of articles, listed in alphabetical order, on many topics. When you need information quickly, an encyclopedia is a good choice.

Dictionary A dictionary is an alphabetical collection of words, their spellings, their meanings, and their pronunciations. You can use a dictionary to look up words you don't understand.

Atlas An atlas is a collection of maps. Some atlases have one kind of map. Others have many maps showing different things, such as elevation, crops, population, natural resources, languages spoken, and historical developments.

Almanac An almanac is a book that has lots of information about many different things. It has sections for different topics and often shows information in charts, tables, and lists. Almanacs are usually updated every year.

Nonfiction Books A nonfiction book is a book that was researched and written on a particular topic.

Technology Resources

There are many kinds of technology resources for you to use when you are looking for information. You can use the Internet, CD-ROMs, software, television programs, and radio programs.

The Internet is a system of computers that can store information so that people all over the world can find it. The World Wide Web, which is part of the Internet, has many different kinds of information.

Other technology resources can also help you find the information that you are looking for. There are CD-ROMs of maps, encyclopedias, and dictionaries. Television channels offer programs on history, science, the arts, and geography. Radio programs may give you information about a particular event that happened in history.

Use Community Resources

Besides technology and print resources, the people of your community are good sources of information. You can learn about the history and geography of your community by listening to a person who has lived there a long time.

Perhaps you've heard about a person in your community whose grandparent did something important for the community. You might want to meet with that person and learn more about those times. People who are doing important jobs in your community now are good sources of information too.

Interviews One way to find out what the people in your community know is to interview them. This means asking them questions about the topic you are studying.

Using a Survey Another way to gather information in your community is to do a survey. A survey is a list of questions that you ask people, recording everyone's answers. This gives you an idea of what the people in your community know, think, or feel about a subject. You can either use yes/no questions or short-answer questions. To record the things you find out, you will want to make a tally sheet with a column for each question.

Writing for Information Another way to get information from people or organizations is to e-mail or write a letter. Use the following steps:

- Plan what you want to say before you write.

- Be neat and careful about spelling and punctuation.

- Tell who you are and why you are writing.

- Thank the person you write to.

Write a Report

After you finish your research, you will need to share what you learned with others. One way to share is to write a report. Follow these five steps when you write.

1. **Prewrite** Decide on the topic for your report. Always organize your thoughts before you write. Take notes or make an outline to help you organize your information.

2. **Draft** Write what you learned in complete sentences and paragraphs. Use correct grammar, spelling, and punctuation.

3. **Revise** Read over your report. Does it make sense? Give it to a friend to read. Make changes that your friend suggests.

4. **Edit** Proofread your report. Correct any mistakes in spelling or punctuation that you found. Be sure you used correct grammar and capitalization.

5. **Publish** Write a final copy of your report. Make it as neat as you can.

Geography Skills

Five Themes of Geography

Geography is the study of Earth. People who study Earth sometimes look at it in five different ways. These ways are called the five themes of geography. Each theme is another way of thinking about a place on our planet. Look at the examples of Sabine National Wildlife Refuge below.

Location

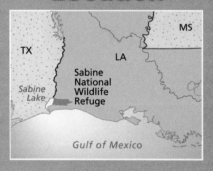

Sabine National Wildlife Refuge is located in southern Louisiana.

Place

The refuge has bayous, wetlands, meadows, and many kinds of animals.

Movement

Most of the refuge can only be explored by boat.

Places and People Change Each Other

People built walkways to allow visitors to get close to nature.

Region

The refuge is located on a long plain along the Gulf of Mexico.

Geography Skills

How Does Earth Look?

This is a photo of part of Earth as it looks from space. However, a complete view of Earth is best seen on a globe.

Which continent do you live on?

What Is a Globe?

This is a globe. A globe is a kind of map. It is a model, a small copy, of Earth in its actual round shape. You can turn a globe and see all of Earth's water and land.

Large areas of land are called continents.

Large bodies of salt water are called oceans.

Geography Skills

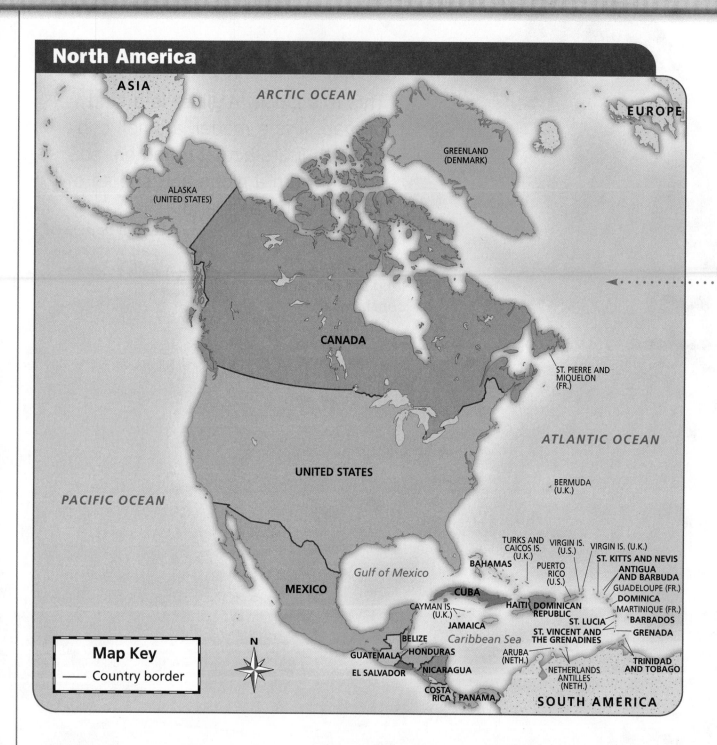

North America

ASIA

ARCTIC OCEAN

EUROPE

GREENLAND
(DENMARK)

ALASKA
(UNITED STATES)

CANADA

ST. PIERRE AND
MIQUELON
(FR.)

ATLANTIC OCEAN

UNITED STATES

BERMUDA
(U.K.)

PACIFIC OCEAN

TURKS AND
CAICOS IS.
(U.K.)

VIRGIN IS.
(U.S.)

VIRGIN IS. (U.K.)

ST. KITTS AND NEVIS

BAHAMAS

PUERTO
RICO
(U.S.)

ANTIGUA
AND BARBUDA

GUADELOUPE (FR.)

Gulf of Mexico

DOMINICA

MARTINIQUE (FR.)

MEXICO

CUBA

CAYMAN IS.
(U.K.)

HAITI

DOMINICAN
REPUBLIC

ST. LUCIA

BARBADOS

JAMAICA

ST. VINCENT AND
THE GRENADINES

GRENADA

BELIZE

Caribbean Sea

GUATEMALA

HONDURAS

ARUBA
(NETH.)

TRINIDAD
AND TOBAGO

EL SALVADOR

NICARAGUA

NETHERLANDS
ANTILLES
(NETH.)

COSTA
RICA

PANAMA

SOUTH AMERICA

N

Map Key

— Country border

What Is a Map?

A flat map is a drawing of a place. Maps show us where Earth's land and water are. A map can be a drawing of part of Earth.

This is a flat map of North America, one of Earth's seven continents. It also shows three of Earth's four oceans.

Vocabulary

border

title

symbol

key

compass rose

Map Features

Maps have many features that help us read and use them.

A border is a line that divides one state or country from another. How many states share a border with South Dakota?

Maps have titles. What is the title of this map? Many maps have symbols that stand for something else. A symbol could be a shape, a line, or a color. How many symbols are used on this map? A key, or legend, is the box in which all symbols on a map are explained. What does a circled black star mean on this map?

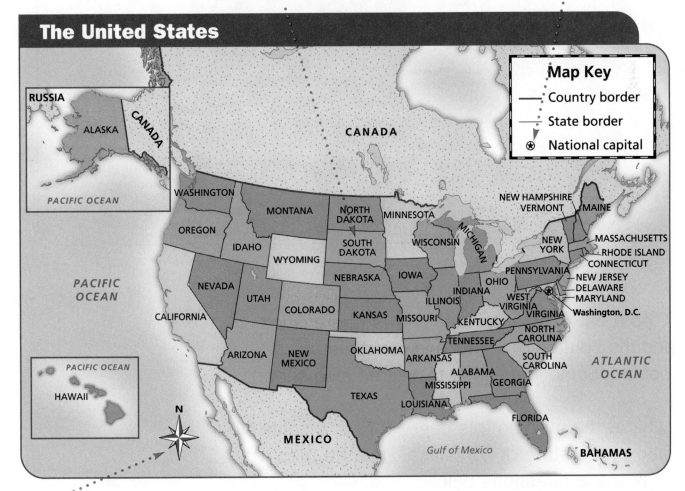

The United States

Map Key
— Country border
— State border
⊛ National capital

RUSSIA

ALASKA CANADA

PACIFIC OCEAN

CANADA

PACIFIC OCEAN

WASHINGTON
OREGON
MONTANA
IDAHO
WYOMING
NORTH DAKOTA
SOUTH DAKOTA
MINNESOTA
WISCONSIN
MICHIGAN
NEW HAMPSHIRE
VERMONT
MAINE
NEW YORK
MASSACHUSETTS
RHODE ISLAND
CONNECTICUT
NEVADA
UTAH
COLORADO
NEBRASKA
IOWA
ILLINOIS
INDIANA
OHIO
PENNSYLVANIA
NEW JERSEY
DELAWARE
MARYLAND
WEST VIRGINIA
VIRGINIA
Washington, D.C.
CALIFORNIA
KANSAS
MISSOURI
KENTUCKY
NORTH CAROLINA
TENNESSEE
ARIZONA
NEW MEXICO
OKLAHOMA
ARKANSAS
ALABAMA
MISSISSIPPI
GEORGIA
SOUTH CAROLINA
ATLANTIC OCEAN
PACIFIC OCEAN
HAWAII
TEXAS
LOUISIANA
FLORIDA
N
MEXICO
Gulf of Mexico
BAHAMAS

A compass rose is a decorative pointer that shows which direction on a map is north, south, east, or west. On the compass roses in this textbook, north is straight up and is marked with an "N." East is to the right, south is straight down, and west is to the left. In which direction would you travel to get from Louisiana to Iowa? In which direction is California from Utah?

Geography Skills

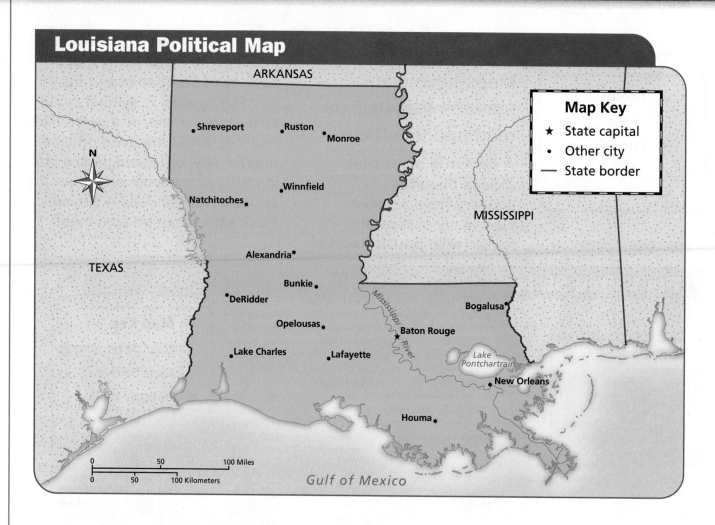

Louisiana Political Map

ARKANSAS

N

Shreveport

Ruston

Monroe

Map Key
★ State capital
• Other city
— State border

Winnfield

Natchitoches

MISSISSIPPI

TEXAS

Alexandria

Bunkie

DeRidder

Bogalusa

Opelousas

Baton Rouge

Lake Charles

Lafayette

Lake Pontchartrain

New Orleans

Houma

0   50   100 Miles
0   50   100 Kilometers

Gulf of Mexico

Read a Political Map

A **political map** of an area shows where cities and the borders of states and countries are located. Sometimes other things are also shown.

Look at the map on this page. This is a political map of the state of Louisiana. Use the map to answer the questions below.

1. What is the capital city of Louisiana?
2. How many states share a border with Louisiana? Name these states.

Louisiana Physical Map

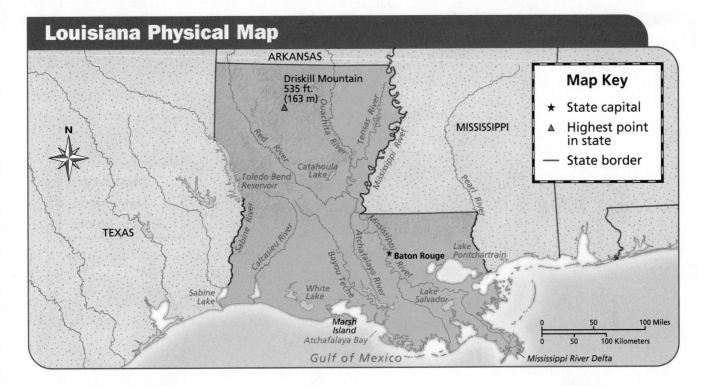

ARKANSAS

Driskill Mountain
535 ft.
(163 m)

Ouachita River

Red River

Tensas River

Mississippi River

MISSISSIPPI

Toledo Bend Reservoir

Catahoula Lake

Sabine River

Calcasieu River

Pearl River

TEXAS

Bayou Teche

Atchafalaya River

Mississippi River

★ Baton Rouge

Lake Pontchartrain

Sabine Lake

White Lake

Lake Salvador

Marsh Island
Atchafalaya Bay

Gulf of Mexico

Mississippi River Delta

Map Key

★ State capital

▲ Highest point in state

— State border

0   50   100 Miles

0   50   100 Kilometers

Read a Physical Map

A **physical map** of an area shows landforms and bodies of water. **Landforms** are different types of land on Earth's surface such as mountains, plains, and deserts. **Bodies of water** are oceans, gulfs, rivers, lakes, and so on. In addition, a physical map sometimes has political labels like cities, states, and countries.

Look at the map on this page. This is a physical map of the state of Louisiana. Use the map to answer the questions below.

1. What is the highest point in the state?
2. What river is located near Baton Rouge?
3. Into what body of water does the Mississippi River flow?

Vocabulary

political map

physical map

landforms

bodies of water

Geography Skills

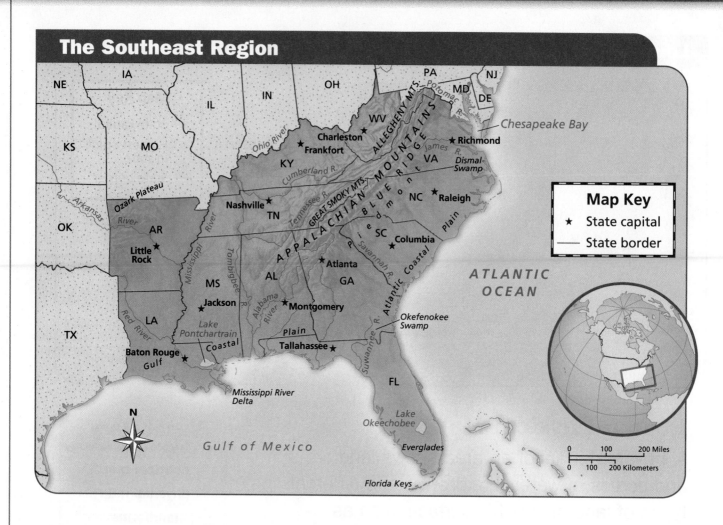

Different Kinds of Borders

This is a map of the southeastern United States. It shows state borders. On this map, you can see that some parts of state borders are formed by bodies of water such as rivers, gulfs, and oceans.

1. What forms a border between Mississippi and Arkansas?

2. What bodies of water form the borders of Florida?

Grid Map of New Orleans

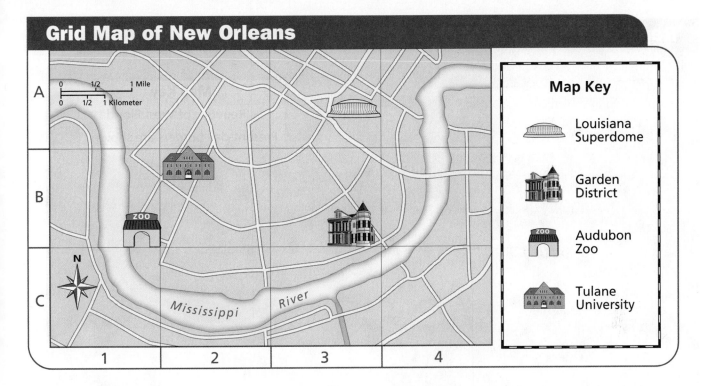

Vocabulary

natural features

grid

Read a Grid Map of a City

A city map shows the streets, buildings, and natural features of a city. **Natural features** are landforms or bodies of water that are not made by humans. What natural feature do you see on this map of New Orleans, Louisiana?

This map has a grid. A **grid** is a pattern of lines that form squares. The squares have numbers and letters. You can use a grid to find places on a map. Point to the Audubon Zoo. Name the square's letter and number. You can see that it is in square B1. What is found in square B3?

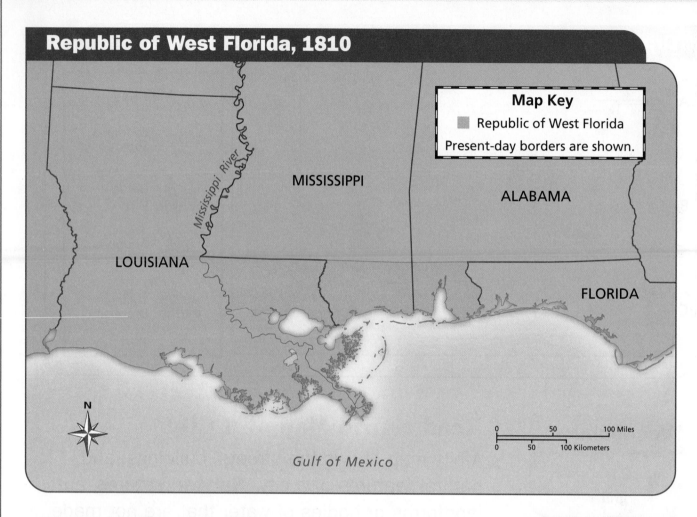

Republic of West Florida, 1810

Map Key

◼ Republic of West Florida

Present-day borders are shown.

MISSISSIPPI

ALABAMA

LOUISIANA

FLORIDA

Mississippi River

N

Gulf of Mexico

0   50   100 Miles

0   50   100 Kilometers

Read a History Map

The map on this page is a history map. A **history map** shows an area as it was at some time in the past. Studying a history map helps you understand how some things have changed.

This map shows the land that was once an independent country called the Republic of West Florida. In the early 1800s, Spain controlled this land. In 1810 settlers rebelled against Spain and declared West Florida to be an independent country. Two months later, the Republic of West Florida became part of the United States. Some of this land is now the part of Louisiana known as the Florida Parishes.

Vocabulary

history map

The Geography of Louisiana

What do you think makes Louisiana such a special place to live?

Begin with a Primary Source

"These bayous are sluggish [slow] streams that glide [move] sleepily along, sometimes running one way, and sometimes the very opposite...."
— from *Harper's Monthly* magazine, 1853

William Henry Buck painted *Bayou Scene* in the 1800s. Louisiana is well known for its bayous.

Meet the People

Robert La Salle

1643–1687
Birthplace: France
Explorer

- Explored the Mississippi River to the Gulf of Mexico
- Claimed the land around the Mississippi River for France
- Named what is now the state of Louisiana after King Louis XIV of France

Mark Twain

1835–1910
Birthplace: Florida, Missouri
Writer

- Was born Samuel Clemens but wrote under the name Mark Twain
- Steered steamboats on the Mississippi River
- Wrote many books, including *The Adventures of Tom Sawyer*

| 1650 | 1700 | 1750 | 1800 |

1643 • Robert La Salle 1687

Students can research the lives of significant people by clicking on *Meet the People* at **www.sfsocialstudies.com**.

Clementine Hunter

1886?–1988

Birthplace: Near Cloutierville, Louisiana

Artist

- Began painting when she was more than 50 years old
- Painted more than 4,000 paintings
- Showed her work in museums all across the United States

Caroline Dormon

1888–1971

Birthplace: Near Saline, Louisiana

Environmentalist

- Helped create the Kisatchie National Forest in 1930
- Became the first woman to work for the United States Forest Service
- Traveled the South giving speeches about protecting nature

1850   1900   1950   2000

1835 • Mark Twain   1910

1886? • Clementine Hunter   1988

1888 • Caroline Dormon   1971

Louisiana's State Parks

Target Skill

Main Idea and Details

- To find the **main idea** in a paragraph, ask "What one important idea do all the sentences tell about?"

- To find **supporting details**, ask "Which sentences give information that supports the main idea?"

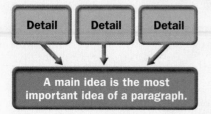

| Detail | Detail | Detail |

A main idea is the most important idea of a paragraph.

Read the following paragraph. The main idea is highlighted in blue. The supporting details are highlighted in yellow.

There are always exciting things to do in Louisiana's state parks. There are places for people to swim and fish. People can also ride bicycles, go picnicking, or go camping at state parks.

Word Exercise

Words with Multiple Meanings Many words have more than one meaning. For example, the word *kind* can have different meanings.

The brown pelican, the state bird of Louisiana, is one *kind* of bird that people like to watch.

- gentle
- type
- nice

Which meaning of the word *kind* makes sense in this sentence? Use each definition in the sentence to find out. For example, you can say: *The brown pelican, the state bird of Louisiana, is one type of bird that people like to watch.*

6

Visiting Grand Isle

Grand Isle is a very special place to visit. Here you will find Grand Isle State Park. Many people come to the park to fish or catch crabs. There are also many other activities. There is a beach for swimming and a picnic area. People can also watch birds such as the brown pelican, the state bird of Louisiana.

Many people living on Grand Isle work in jobs related to helping travelers. They work in restaurants, hotels, and the state park. Other people on Grand Isle work on fishing boats.

In 2005, Hurricane Katrina hit Grand Isle hard. Many people worked to fix Grand Isle State Park.

Use the reading skill of main idea and details to answer questions 1 and 2. Then answer the vocabulary question.

❶ Which sentence in the first paragraph expresses the main idea of all of the paragraphs?

❷ Name one detail from the first paragraph and one detail from the second paragraph that tell more about the main idea.

❸ Reread the first sentence of the second paragraph. The word *related* can mean "from the same family," "connected to," or "told." In this sentence, which meaning is correct?

Chapter 1

Locating Louisiana

Lesson 1

Louisiana

Louisiana is located in the southern United States.

1

Lesson 2

Bodcau Bayou

Bodcau Bayou is in the West Gulf Coastal Plain region of Louisiana.

2

CANADA

NORTH
AMERICA

UNITED STATES

2

1

PACIFIC OCEAN

ATLANTIC
OCEAN

Bodcau
Bayou

LOUISIANA

MEXICO

Gulf of Mexico

Why We Remember

Think about where you live. What does the land around you look like? Do you live near a forest, a river, or the coast? Do you live in a large, busy city or a small, quiet town? Did you know that you could find all of these in our state? Learning more about Louisiana helps us understand how special our state is.

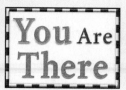

LOUISIANA

Focus on the Main Idea
Louisiana is a state in the United States.

PLACES
Louisiana
United States

PEOPLE
Robert La Salle

VOCABULARY
hemisphere
geography
explorer

▶ The space shuttle
Atlantis lifts off
into space!

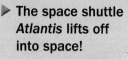

Where is Louisiana?

You Are There You are riding in a space shuttle high around Earth. You look out the window. Bright stars twinkle above you. "Take a look to your left," says the astronaut next to you in the space shuttle. "That's Earth!"

You can see our planet. Blue oceans cover most of Earth. You also see land. White clouds swirl above the land and water.

You decide to look for a special place on Earth. You want to find your home state, Louisiana.

"Do you think we can find where Louisiana is?" you ask. "Let's try," he says. How will you find it?

 Main Idea and Details As you read, look for details that tell about the location of Louisiana.

New Orleans

Gulf of Mexico

High Above Louisiana

How would you find Louisiana if you were up in space? You might look for shapes of land or bodies of water. Look at the photograph above. It is a photograph taken from space. The shape of our state is drawn on the picture.

Does the shape of Louisiana remind you of anything? People often say that Louisiana is shaped like a boot. The bottom of the boot lies along the southern coast. The "toe" of boot-shaped Louisiana sticks out into the Gulf of Mexico and points toward the east. The city of New Orleans is located in the "toe."

▶ This picture was taken from space. The lines for the states have been added.

▶ Daniel T. Barry is an astronaut from Louisiana.

REVIEW Describe Louisiana's shape.
Main Idea and Details

11

Louisiana

United States

North America

Western Hemisphere

▶ This diagram helps show Louisiana's location on Earth.

DIAGRAM SKILL Location
Describe Louisiana's location in the Western Hemisphere.

Finding Louisiana

You can use the diagram on this page to help you find Louisiana's location in the world. The top of the diagram shows Louisiana.

The next map in the diagram shows the **United States,** the country we live in. Louisiana is shown in red. The diagram shows the borders of Louisiana and the United States. Louisiana is one of the 50 states in the United States.

Based on the second map, what is Louisiana's location in the United States? You can see that Louisiana is located in the southern part of the United States.

The third map shows that the United States is on the continent of North America. A continent is one of Earth's large land areas.

The fourth map shows that North America is in the Western Hemisphere. *Hemi* means "half." A **hemisphere** is one half of Earth.

Now you can describe the location of Louisiana in the world. You can say that Louisiana is located in the United States, on the North American continent, and it is in the Western Hemisphere of Earth.

REVIEW Describe Louisiana's location in the world. ⟲ **Main Idea and Details**

Where Do You Live?

Nate lives in New Orleans. "I have lots of neighbors in the big city," he says. Josie lives in Haughton. It is east of Shreveport. "I like being close to nature in a small town," she says.

Maps can help you find where you live. The map below uses dots and labels to show where some of Louisiana's cities and towns are located. See if the name of the town or city where you live is on the map. If not, find the closest city that you know of.

REVIEW How can maps help you find where you live? 🔍 **Main Idea and Details**

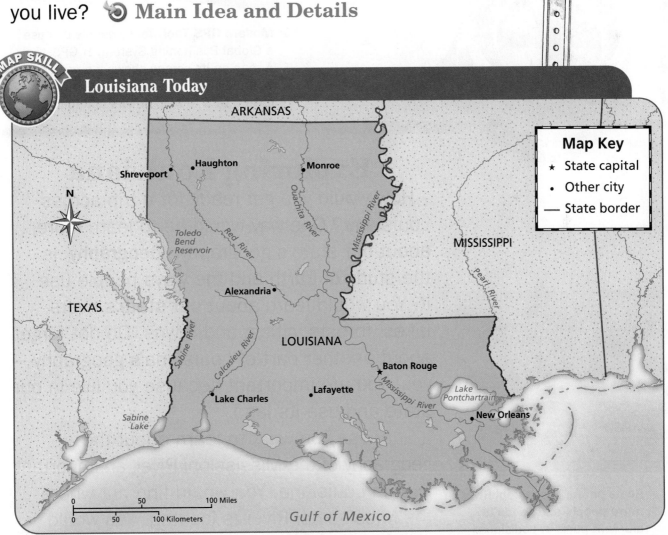

MAP SKILL Louisiana Today

Map Key
- ★ State capital
- • Other city
- — State border

ARKANSAS

Shreveport • Haughton · Monroe

Ouachita River

Toledo Bend Reservoir

Red River

Mississippi River

MISSISSIPPI

Pearl River

Alexandria •

TEXAS

Sabine River

Calcasieu River

LOUISIANA

Baton Rouge ★

Lafayette •

• Lake Charles

Lake Pontchartrain

New Orleans •

Mississippi River

Sabine Lake

0   50   100 Miles
0   50   100 Kilometers

Gulf of Mexico

▶ Louisiana is bordered by the states Texas, Arkansas, and Mississippi, and by the Gulf of Mexico.

MAP SKILL Use a Map Key *Name three rivers that form part of Louisiana's borders.*

Tools for Exploring

Then and Now

Suppose you were an explorer in Louisiana hundreds of years ago. There were few maps then. What tools might you have used to locate where you were? What tools might have helped you find where you wanted to go? Look at the tools below to compare how people found their way years ago and today.

▶ **Compass** A compass has an arrow that always points north. This helps you also figure out which way is south, west, or east. This compass is from the 1500s, about 500 years ago.

▶ **Modern GPS Tool** Today people can use a Global Positioning System, or GPS, tool. A map on its screen shows a person exactly where on Earth he or she is. Some cars have a GPS to help drivers find roads.

Exploring Louisiana

How would you get ready for a trip across Louisiana? One way would be to learn more about our state's geography. **Geography** is the study of Earth and the ways people use it. You would learn about our state's rivers, lakes, forests, cities, and towns. Do not forget about another part of Louisiana's geography— you! You are important because you live in our state and use its land.

Suppose you want to learn about the geography of the Mississippi River, an important river in Louisiana. You would find out where the Mississippi River is located. You would also learn about how people use the river for shipping goods and seeing parts of our state.

▶ Boats on the Mississippi River move people and goods to different parts of Louisiana.

Long ago people explored Louisiana without knowing much about its geography. An early explorer to our state was **Robert La Salle.** An `explorer` is a person who travels looking for new lands and discoveries. You will read more about Robert La Salle and the geography of Louisiana on the next two pages.

`REVIEW` What is geography?
⦿ **Main Idea and Details**

Summarize the Lesson

- Louisiana is a state located in the southern United States.

- Maps can help you learn the location of your town or city.

- Geography is the study of Earth and how people use it.

LESSON 1 REVIEW

Check Facts and Main Ideas

1. ⦿ **Main Idea and Details**
   On a separate sheet of paper, draw a diagram like the one shown below. Fill in some details about the location of Louisiana.

The location of Louisiana can be described in many ways.

2. In what state and country do you live?

3. What symbol is used on the map on page 13 to show the location of cities and towns?

4. How can knowing Louisiana's `geography` help you more easily explore the state?

5. **Critical Thinking:** *Interpret Maps* How would you describe the location of the place where you live in Louisiana? Use the map on page 13 to help you.

Link to ⊶ Geography

Draw a Mental Map Study the map of Louisiana on page 13. Close your book and try to draw a map of Louisiana from memory on a piece of paper. Then compare your map with the one in the book. What differences are there in the shapes?

Meet
Robert La Salle

1643–1687 • Explorer

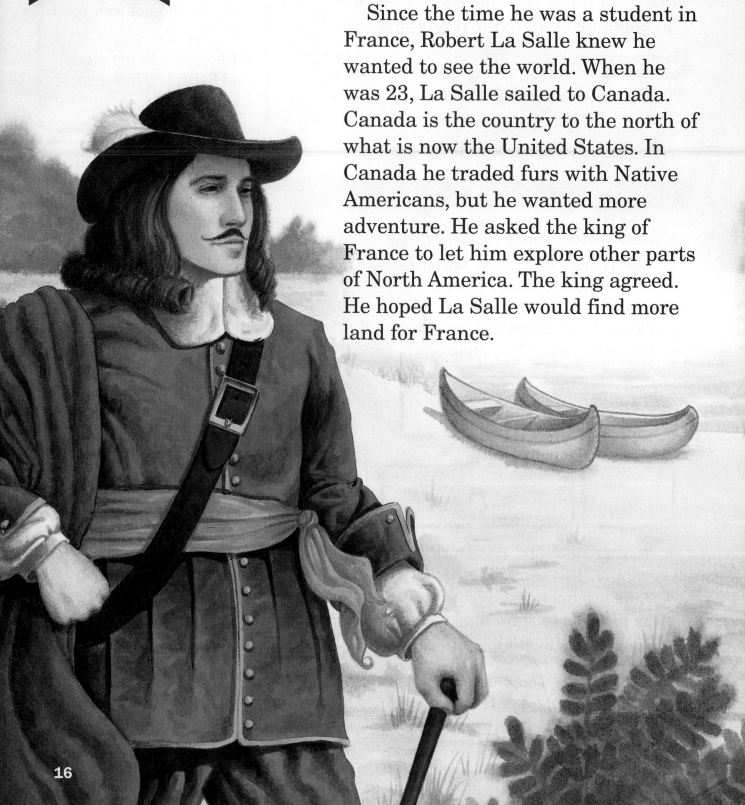

Since the time he was a student in France, Robert La Salle knew he wanted to see the world. When he was 23, La Salle sailed to Canada. Canada is the country to the north of what is now the United States. In Canada he traded furs with Native Americans, but he wanted more adventure. He asked the king of France to let him explore other parts of North America. The king agreed. He hoped La Salle would find more land for France.

Native Americans told La Salle about a river called the Mississippi. They believed this river led to the sea. La Salle wanted to see where the river ended. On February 13, 1682, La Salle and a group of travelers, including French and Native American people, began canoeing south on the Mississippi River. On April 9 the group reached the Gulf of Mexico. La Salle claimed the land he had found along the Mississippi River for France. He said,

"I . . . take, in the name of His Majesty, . . . possession of this country of Louisiana . . . ."

Robert La Salle brought a red coat with him on his journeys. He wore it on special occasions, such as when he claimed Louisiana for France.

BIOFACT

La Salle named this huge area of land Louisiana after Louis XIV, the king of France. France controlled the area for more than 100 years.

Learn from Biographies

How did Robert La Salle's decision to become an explorer affect the history of Louisiana?

 Students can research the lives of significant people by clicking on *Meet the People* at **www.sfsocialstudies.com**.

Lesson 2

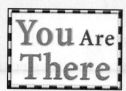

The Regions of Louisiana

Preview

Focus on the Main Idea
Each of Louisiana's three regions has special features.

PLACES

Mississippi River Plain
West Gulf Coastal Plain
East Gulf Coastal Plain
Bodcau Bayou
Mississippi River Delta

VOCABULARY

region
landform
bayou
delta

You Are There
Autumn is almost here. You and your family are planning a trip in Louisiana. How will you travel? Maybe you will travel by bike, boat, or car. You may see the most sights by car or boat. Biking might be more fun, though.

What places will you visit? You can go along the coast. Maybe you will follow the path of the Mississippi River. Perhaps you will most enjoy a trip to a forest. There are so many great places to see!

Main Idea and Details
As you read, look for details that describe Louisiana's regions.

18

What Are Regions?

Louisiana has three main land regions. A **region** is a large land area with special features that make it different from other areas. The **Mississippi River Plain** follows the path of the Mississippi River. The **West Gulf Coastal Plain** covers the land west of the Mississippi River Plain. The **East Gulf Coastal Plain** is the smallest region. It is made up of the land east of the Mississippi River and north of Lake Pontchartrain.

▶ These boys are fishing in a river in the West Gulf Coastal Plain.

REVIEW What regions make up Louisiana?

🎯 **Main Idea and Details**

MAP SKILL

Louisiana's Regions

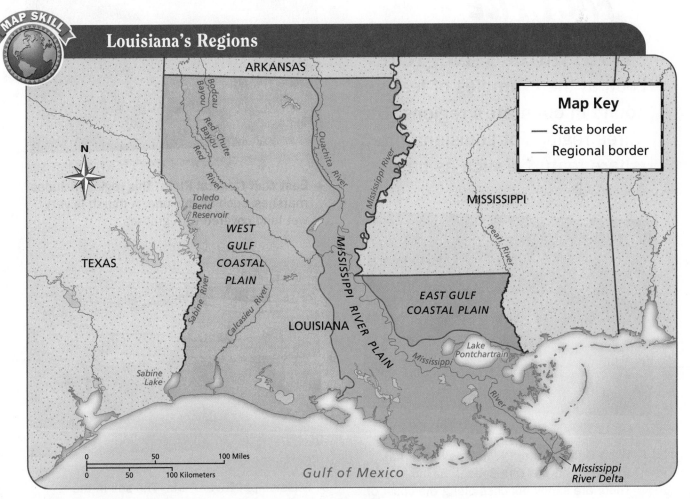

ARKANSAS

Bodcau Bayou

Red Chute Bayou

Red River

Ouachita River

Mississippi River

Map Key
— State border
— Regional border

MISSISSIPPI

N

Toledo Bend Reservoir

WEST GULF COASTAL PLAIN

TEXAS

Sabine River

Calcasieu River

LOUISIANA

MISSISSIPPI RIVER PLAIN

Pearl River

EAST GULF COASTAL PLAIN

Lake Pontchartrain

Mississippi River

Sabine Lake

0   50   100 Miles
0   50   100 Kilometers

Gulf of Mexico

Mississippi River Delta

▶ The West Gulf Coastal Plain is Louisiana's largest region.

MAP SKILL Use a Map *In what region is the Calcasieu River?*

Land and Water

▶ Driskill Mountain is a landform in Louisiana. It is in the West Gulf Coastal Plain.

Louisiana's regions include different landforms. A **landform** is a natural shape on Earth's surface, such as a plain. A plain is a flat area of land. Driskill Mountain, Louisiana's only mountain, is another example of a landform.

Our state also has many bodies of water. You can find rivers, lakes, bayous, and ponds in each region. A **bayou** is a slow-moving stream. The Fact File shows **Bodcau Bayou,** in the West Gulf Coastal Plain.

FACT FILE

Louisiana's Regions

Look at the examples of features found in our state's regions. The three regions of Louisiana often share features, such as bayous.

▶ **East Gulf Coastal Plain** This region includes marshes, such as this one. A marsh is very wet land covered with grasses.

▶ **West Gulf Coastal Plain** This region has tree-filled bayous like Bodcau Bayou, above. There are sandy beaches along the coast of the region. As you travel north, you will find forests growing on hilly land.

▶ **Mississippi River Plain** The soil in the plains along the Mississippi River is good for farming. Crops such as soybeans grow well in this region.

A special landform in Louisiana is the **Mississippi River Delta,** in the Mississippi River Plain. It is located at the mouth of the Mississippi River. The "mouth" of a river is where the river flows into a larger body of water. When the Mississippi River enters the Gulf of Mexico, it drops small pieces of sand and soil called silt that it has carried away from the land as it flows. The new land that builds up from the silt dropped by a river is called a **delta.** You will read more about the river's mouth on pages 22 and 23.

REVIEW How is the Mississippi River Delta formed? *Cause and Effect*

Summarize the Lesson

- Louisiana has three geographic regions: the Mississippi River Plain, the West Gulf Coastal Plain, and the East Gulf Coastal Plain.

- Louisiana's regions have different landforms and many bodies of water.

- The Mississippi River Delta is formed at the mouth of the Mississippi River.

LESSON 2 REVIEW

Check Facts and Main Ideas

1. Main Idea and Details

On a separate sheet of paper, draw a diagram like the one shown below. Write a main idea that fits the details.

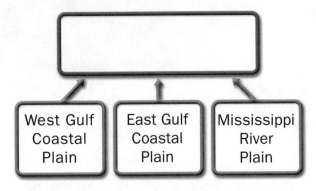

2. Describe the location of Louisiana's three **regions.**

3. Give an example of two **landforms** in Louisiana.

4. What is the "mouth" of a river?

5. Critical Thinking: *Analyze Pictures* Write a paragraph describing one photograph in this lesson to someone who has never seen it.

Link to 🔗 Geography

Make a Poster Use the map on page 19. Do research to find out which region of Louisiana your town or city is in. Create a travel poster to attract visitors to your region. Include drawings, facts about the region, and a fun title.

At the mouth of a river, its banks curl outward to become the seashore. The tide brings in salt water that affects plant and animal life. These plants and animals can be found at the mouth of a river.

Flocks of oystercatchers and other wading birds crowd onto the mud at low tide, searching for worms, shrimps, shellfish, and crabs.

Sea Spurge

The sea spurge's stem spreads through the sand dunes at the river's mouth. It has thick, fleshy leaves.

Gull

The rich animal life of the river's mouth attracts gulls of all kinds.

The calmer waters of the river's mouth are nature's dumping ground. You can find anything from dried-out seaweeds and eel grass to feathers, bits of weeds, and dead crabs.

Feathers

Crab

Eel grass

Pipefish

Oystercatcher chicks can take up to 26 weeks to learn how to feed from their parents.

The pipefish is a relative of the seahorse. It has hardened outer skin and moves using its back fin. It can live in salt water.

Oystercatcher and chick

Oyster shell

Tellina shell

Cockleshell

Hole pecked by bird

Cockleshell

These mollusk shells have been pecked through by birds that ate the animal inside.

Tellina shell

Young sheldrakes look like most other ducklings, but the adults look more like geese. This bird eats not only shellfish but also fish, worms, and other animals.

Sheldrake and chick

Lugworm

Squiggly marks on the mud mark the lugworm's U-shaped burrow.

Use a Line Graph

What? A line graph shows how something changes over time. Look at the line graph below. It shows how the normal monthly daytime temperature in Alexandria changes over six months. Alexandria is near the Red River in the West Gulf Coastal Plain region.

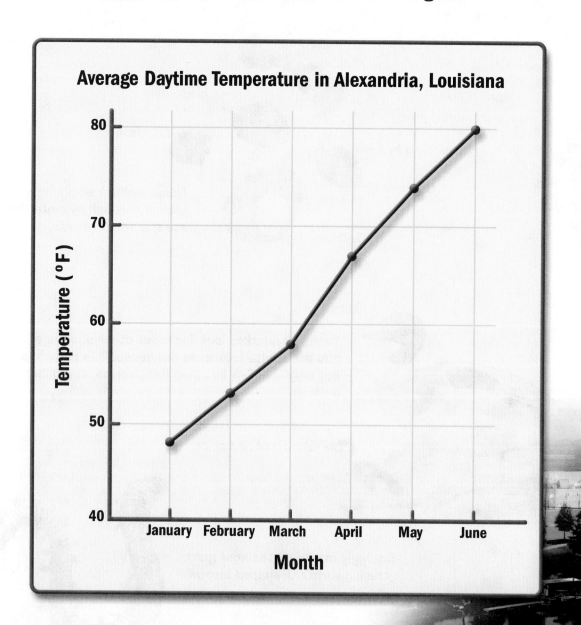

Average Daytime Temperature in Alexandria, Louisiana

Why? A line graph can help you understand how things change over time. Knowing about these changes can help you better understand events that have happened.

How? When you read a line graph, look first at the graph title. It tells you what the graph shows. Look at the words and numbers along the left side and the bottom. They explain what is measured and over what time period it is measured. Each dot on the graph shows an amount at a point in time. When you follow the line connecting the dots, you will see how the amount changes over time.

Think and Apply

1 What is the average temperature in January?

2 In which month is the average temperature almost 60°F?

3 What is the warmest month shown on the graph?

▶ Cities usually get cooler at night when the sun goes down.

Chapter Summary

Main Idea and Details

On a separate sheet of paper, fill in details about Louisiana's location.

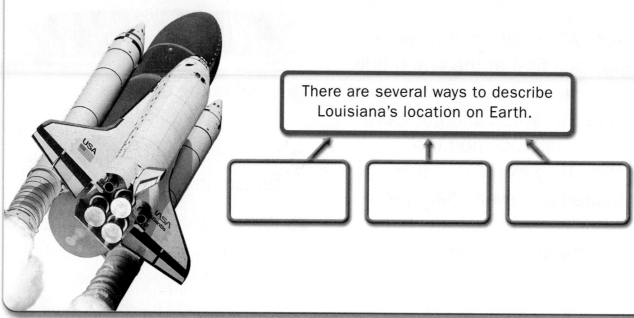

There are several ways to describe Louisiana's location on Earth.

Vocabulary

Match each word with the correct definition or description.

1. hemisphere (p. 12)

2. explorer (p. 15)

3. landform (p. 20)

4. bayou (p. 20)

5. delta (p. 21)

a. a natural shape on Earth's surface

b. land that builds up from silt dropped by a river

c. one half of Earth

d. a person who travels looking for new lands

e. a slow-moving stream

Facts and Main Ideas

1 How does studying geography help you learn more about Louisiana?

2 How does the Mississippi River Delta form?

3 **Main Idea** Describe Louisiana's location on Earth.

4 **Main Idea** Describe the locations of Louisiana's three regions.

5 **Critical Thinking: *Classify*** In which of Louisiana's regions is your city or town located?

Write About It

1 **Write three interview questions** that you would ask Robert La Salle about what he saw when he explored Louisiana.

2 **Write a description** of how you would tell an astronaut to locate Louisiana from space.

3 **Write an advertisement** encouraging people to move to your community. Include details such as the name of the community, the region in which it is located, and the kind of weather you usually have.

Apply Skills

Use a Line Graph Use the line graph on page 24 to answer the questions below.

1 In what month is the average daytime temperature in the 70s?

2 What is the coldest month shown on the graph?

3 Do any of the temperatures shown on the graph fall below freezing? Freezing is 32°F.

Internet Activity

To get help with vocabulary, people, and terms, select the dictionary or encyclopedia from *Social Studies Library* at **www.sfsocialstudies.com.**

A Tour of Louisiana

1

2

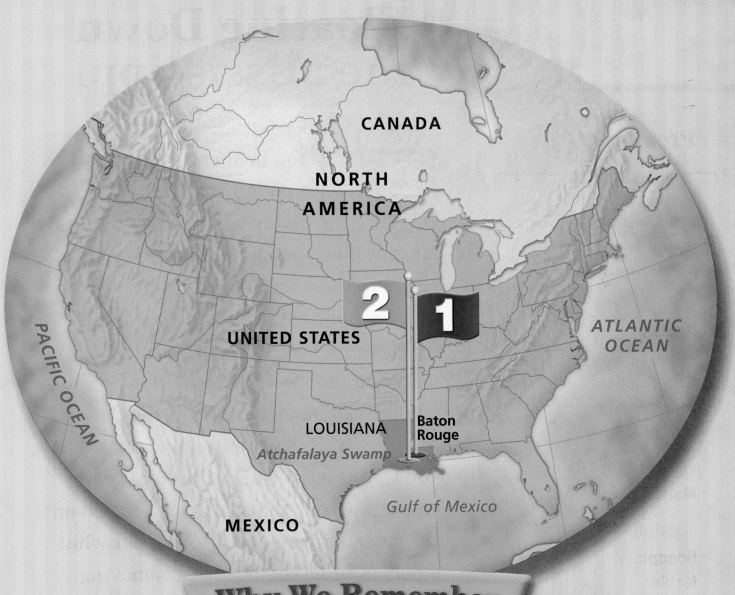

CANADA

NORTH AMERICA

UNITED STATES

PACIFIC OCEAN

ATLANTIC OCEAN

2

1

LOUISIANA

Baton Rouge

Atchafalaya Swamp

Gulf of Mexico

MEXICO

Why We Remember

What do you think is the most beautiful place in Louisiana? Maybe it is the top of Driskill Mountain. It might be the Mississippi River Delta or Bayou Teche. It could be your own town or city. Louisiana has too many beautiful places to choose just one. Take a tour of our state in this chapter and decide for yourself.

Baton Rouge

New Orleans ★

Gulf of Mexico

Mississippi River

Floating Down the Mississippi

Preview

Focus on the Main Idea
The Mississippi River is an important river in Louisiana.

PLACES
Mississippi River
New Orleans
Baton Rouge
Gulf of Mexico

PEOPLE
Mark Twain

VOCABULARY
floodplain
fertile
population
port

You Are There You hear the loud blast of a paddleboat's whistle. Today you will begin a journey down one of the most important rivers in the United States, the Mississippi River. You and your family will board a boat in Louisiana and travel on the river.

What's so important about the Mississippi River? Your older sister tells you that the river helps farmers grow crops. She says that ports are located on the river. You are about to ask her what a port is when the boat starts moving. Your adventure has just begun!

Main Idea and Details As you read, look for details about the importance of the Mississippi River.

▶ Mississippi River paddleboat

STEAMER NATCHEZ
PORT OF NEW ORLEANS

30

Farms and Plains

The Mississippi River is the largest and longest river in the United States. It flows more than 2,300 miles from the northern part of the country to the Gulf of Mexico. Writer and riverboat pilot Mark Twain described the Mississippi River as "a wonderful book . . . for it had a new story to tell every day."

As you travel by boat, you see farms on the land along the Mississippi River. Snow melting to the north or heavy rains can cause the waters of the river to flood, or spill over onto the land. This land is called the floodplain. The flood leaves behind some of the river's silt on the floodplain. When the floodplain dries out, the silt that is left behind is fertile soil. It is good for growing crops. Farmers grow crops such as cotton on the floodplain's fertile soil.

REVIEW Why is the floodplain along the Mississippi River good for growing crops?

🔄 **Main Idea and Details**

▶ Cotton is one of the main crops grown in Louisiana.

▶ Louisiana's capital, Baton Rouge, is located along the Mississippi River.

Two Big Cities

As you continue down the Mississippi River, you see Louisiana's largest cities, Baton Rouge and New Orleans. One way to tell about a city's size is by its population. **Population** (pahp yoo LAY shuhn) is the number of people living in an area. Both of these cities have large populations.

These cities, located along the Mississippi River, are ports. A **port** is a place where ships can load and unload goods from all over the world. **New Orleans** is one of the largest ports in the world. **Baton Rouge** is Louisiana's capital, where our state's government is located.

REVIEW Contrast New Orleans and Baton Rouge. **Compare and Contrast**

MAP ADVENTURE

Suppose you are a boat captain. You are traveling south on the Mississippi River from northern Louisiana to the Gulf of Mexico. Study the map and answer the questions.

ARKANSAS

BEGIN

Shreveport

Cotton Museum

Red River

Waterproof

TEXAS

LOUISIANA

Map Key
★ Capital City
● Other City
■ Place of Interest

MISSISSIPPI

Mississippi River

Baton Rouge

Lake Pontchartrain

Holly Beach

New Orleans

Gulf of Mexico

END

- You plan to visit the Cotton Museum and to visit your family near Waterproof. Which will you be able to do first?

- You then take a cousin to New Orleans. Will you pass the capital before you reach New Orleans?

- Can you reach Shreveport by traveling on the Mississippi River? Explain.

Breton Sound

Mississippi River

Mississippi River Delta

Gulf of Mexico

West Bay

East Bay

Gulf of Mexico

▶ Some people believe that the Mississippi River Delta looks like a fan or a bird's foot.

▶ Some herons live in the Mississippi River Delta.

The Delta and the Gulf

Now you are on the final part of your trip down the Mississippi River. After you leave New Orleans, you enter the Mississippi River Delta. You learned in Chapter 1 that a delta is an area of land at the mouth of a river, where it enters a larger body of water.

Look at the photograph of the Mississippi River Delta above. This photograph was taken from space in 1985. Notice how the Mississippi River starts to branch out into smaller rivers as it enters the **Gulf of Mexico.**

The land of the delta is always changing. New land forms at the delta as silt builds up at the mouth of the Mississippi River. The waters of the Gulf of Mexico wash away land from the delta at the same time.

Your adventure down the Mississippi River ends at the Gulf of Mexico. You notice a heron in the distance. It walks on its thin legs in the shallow waters of a marsh. Maybe you will see more wildlife on your next trip down the Mississippi River!

REVIEW How does new land form in the Mississippi River Delta?
Cause and Effect

Summarize the Lesson

- The Mississippi River flows through Louisiana to the Gulf of Mexico.
- The floodplain of the Mississippi River is covered with fertile soil.
- New Orleans and Baton Rouge are ports located on the Mississippi River.
- The Mississippi River Delta is always changing.

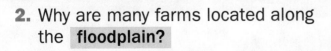

LESSON 1 REVIEW

Check Facts and Main Ideas

1. **Main Idea and Details** On a separate sheet of paper, draw a diagram like the one shown below. Fill in the missing details.

   The Mississippi River is important to Louisiana.

   Farmers grow crops on the floodplain.

2. Why are many farms located along the **floodplain?**

3. How are Baton Rouge and New Orleans similar?

4. Why is the Mississippi River Delta always changing?

5. **Critical Thinking:** *Express Ideas* Mark Twain described the Mississippi River as "a wonderful book." Do you agree? Explain.

Link to ⌖⌖ **Writing**

Write a Journal Write a journal entry with five to six sentences about a trip down the Mississippi River. Describe what you would see along the way.

Mighty Rivers
The Mississippi River and the Amazon River

What do the Mississippi River and the Amazon River have in common? They are the longest and largest rivers on their continents. The Mississippi River flows through the United States, on the North American continent. It travels through Louisiana and ends in the Gulf of Mexico.

The Amazon River is on the South American continent. It flows through several countries and ends in the Atlantic Ocean. Look at the pictures of the two rivers. How else are the Mississippi and Amazon rivers alike?

▶ Boats such as these travel on the Mississippi River to different ports every day.

▶ The Mississippi River is about 2,300 miles long. It is hard to measure exactly because the delta is always changing.

NORTH AMERICA
Mississippi River
LOUISIANA
UNITED STATES
ATLANTIC OCEAN
PACIFIC OCEAN
Amazon River
SOUTH AMERICA

▶ The Amazon River is about 4,000 miles long. It is almost twice as long as the Mississippi River. Parts of both rivers can get very muddy.

▶ People can travel by boat to many places along the Amazon River.

Map and Globe Skills

Use a Population Map

What? You have read that New Orleans and Baton Rouge are Louisiana's largest cities. What other parts of Louisiana have large populations? What kind of map could help you find this information? Look at the map of Louisiana below. It is a population map. A **population map** shows you the number of people living in different areas.

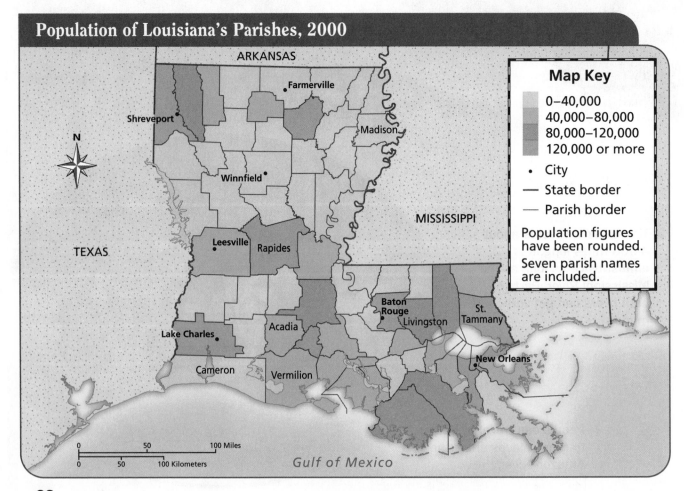

Population of Louisiana's Parishes, 2000

ARKANSAS

Farmerville

Shreveport

Madison

N

Winnfield

Leesville   Rapides

TEXAS

MISSISSIPPI

Baton
Rouge   St.
      Livingston Tammany

Acadia

Lake Charles

Cameron   Vermilion

New Orleans

Map Key

0–40,000
40,000–80,000
80,000–120,000
120,000 or more

• City
— State border
— Parish border

Population figures have been rounded.
Seven parish names are included.

0   50   100 Miles
0   50   100 Kilometers

Gulf of Mexico

▶ New Orleans has a large population.

Why? Population maps help you see places with large and small populations. This map shows the populations of Louisiana's 64 parishes. A parish is an area of local government within a state. In other states, a parish is called a county. Some of the parishes on the map are labeled.

How? First look at the key. You can see on this map that different colors are used to show different numbers of people. What does the color green stand for? On this map, green stands for 40,000 to 80,000 people. That shows you that between 40,000 and 80,000 people live in each parish that is shaded in green.

Find the parish of St. Tammany on the map. It is shaded in red. By looking at the map key, you can see that 120,000 people or more live in this parish.

Now find the parish of Cameron. It is shaded in yellow. About how many people live in Cameron?

Think and Apply

1. What is a **population map?** Why is it useful?

2. Look at the map. How many parishes have a population between 80,000 and 120,000 people?

3. How many people live in Rapides Parish? How many people live in Acadia Parish? Which parish has more people? How can you tell?

Internet Activity

For more information, go online to the *Atlas* at www.sfsocialstudies.com.

▲ Driskill Mountain

Atchafalaya Swamp

Bayou Teche

Swamps, Bayous, and Forests

Preview

Focus on the Main Idea
Swamps, bayous, and forests are located in all parts of Louisiana.

PLACES
Atchafalaya Swamp
Bayou Teche
Driskill Mountain
Kisatchie National Forest

PEOPLE
Caroline Dormon
Clementine Hunter

VOCABULARY
wetlands
elevation

You Are There

Hoot, hoot, hoot! As the sun sets, you hear the hoot of an owl. You and your family are on a boat in the Atchafalaya Swamp in southern Louisiana. Your boat gently drifts past hanging tree branches.

Plop! You see a frog jump into the water. You let the boat glide quietly as you listen for more sounds of the swamp. You may even see an alligator, but you hope it will be far away!

Main Idea and Details As you read, look for details about Louisiana's swamps, bayous, and forests.

▶ Louisiana is one of the few states where alligators live.

Wetlands

The **Atchafalaya Swamp** (uh chaf uh LY uh) surrounds much of the Atchafalaya River in southern Louisiana. This giant swamp is one of several kinds of wetlands found in Louisiana. **Wetlands** are marshes, swamps, or other kinds of land that are damp or covered with water. In Chapter 1, you learned that marshes are very wet land covered with grasses. Swamps are like marshes, but they have trees and very little grass.

Wetlands are important because they are home to many kinds of animals and plants. Louisiana has more wetlands than most other states in the United States. Snakes, frogs, owls, crabs, otters, and deer are just some of the animals that live in wetlands.

REVIEW How are swamps and marshes alike and different? **Compare and Contrast**

► Animals such as these owls live in the Atchafalaya Swamp, below.

Louisiana Bayous

Many of the animals that live in Louisiana's swamps and marshes also live in its bayous. Our state is known for its bayous. That is why Louisiana is often called the Bayou State.

Bayou Teche (TESH), in southern Louisiana, is a popular place for visitors to see Louisiana's natural beauty. The photograph below shows why Bayou Teche is a special place. The Literature and Social Studies on the next page tells one legend about how the bayou got its name.

▶ Lots of crawfish live in the waters of Louisiana. Breaux Bridge is a town alongside Bayou Teche. It is known for its crawfish festival.

Many people take boat tours on bayous to see the sights. On boat tours, guides tell the history of the people who live near the bayous. Guides also point out animals such as alligators and water snakes and teach visitors how these animals live.

REVIEW What can people learn on bayou boat tours? ⟳ **Main Idea and Details**

Literature and Social Studies

The Legend of Bayou Teche

This story tells how Chitimacha (chihd uh MAH shuh) Native Americans gave Bayou Teche its name. In the Chitimacha language, *teche* means "snake."

Years ago there was a huge snake that was many miles long. It was destroying the way of life of the Chitimacha. The Chitimacha warriors bravely fought the snake with bows and arrows and clubs. As the snake died, it twisted and turned. This twisting caused the ground where the snake lay to sink. Later the sunken land filled with water. Today it is called Bayou Teche.

43

Louisiana State Parks and National Forest

Lake D'Arbonne
Chemin-A-Haut
Lake Claiborne
Lake Bistineau
Poverty Point Reservoir
Jimmie Davis
MISSISSIPPI
Lake Bruin
North Toledo Bend
TEXAS
Chicot
Fairview-Riverside
Sam Houston Jones
Tickfaw
Fontainebleau
Lake Fausse Pointe
Bayou Segnette
St. Bernard
Cypremort Point
Gulf of Mexico
Grand Isle

Map Key
- State park
- Kisatchie National Forest

0 50 100 Miles
0 50 100 Kilometers

▶ Kisatchie National Forest is located in several different areas of Louisiana.

MAP SKILL Understand Map Symbols **How many state parks are pictured on this map?**

High and Low

New Orleans is the lowest point in our state. Parts of the city are below sea level! Special structures help keep the city from flooding. In 2005, some of these structures failed during a strong hurricane. The lowest parts of the city were flooded, and many people lost their homes.

Driskill Mountain, in northern Louisiana, has the highest elevation in our state. **Elevation** is the height of something above or below sea level. Driskill Mountain has an elevation of 535 feet. That is very low for a mountain.

Driskill Mountain is covered with forests. Forests cover almost half of our state's land. **Kisatchie National Forest** is Louisiana's only national forest. It was formed with the help of **Caroline Dormon**.

▶ People can explore Louisiana's forests on trails in our state parks.

You will also read about **Clementine Hunter** on pages 48 and 49. She is one of the many artists who have painted pictures of trees and other beautiful features of our state.

REVIEW What is elevation?
🎯 **Main Idea and Details**

▶ **Brown pelicans live at low elevations.**

Summarize the Lesson

- Marshes and swamps are wetlands with many plants and animals.
- Louisiana is known for its bayous.
- Driskill Mountain is the highest point in the state.

LESSON 2   REVIEW

Check Facts and Main Ideas

1. 🎯 **Main Idea and Details** On a separate sheet of paper, draw a diagram like the one shown. Fill in details about the land of Louisiana.

The geography of Louisiana is special for many reasons.

| Louisiana has many wetlands. | | Driskill Mountain and New Orleans are Louisiana's highest and lowest points. | |

2. Why are **wetlands** important places in Louisiana?

3. Why is Louisiana called the Bayou State?

4. What places have the highest and lowest elevations in our state?

5. **Critical Thinking: *Analyze Primary Sources*** Why did the Chitimacha give Bayou Teche this name?

Link to 〜 **Geography**

Draw a Route Draw a map of Louisiana state parks based on the map on page 44. Suppose you want to visit some of the state parks. Draw a route on your map from the first to the last state park you would like to visit on your trip.

Saving the Forest

When she was a young girl, Caroline Dormon enjoyed taking long walks with her father through a forest they owned called Briarwood. Caroline's father taught her about the trees, flowers, and animals of the forest.

▶ Caroline Dormon was the first woman to work for the United States Forest Service.

BUILDING CITIZENSHIP
★ Caring
Respect
Responsibility
Fairness
Honesty
Courage

When Dormon grew older she became a teacher. She continued to love the forest. Dormon spent a lot of time gathering her favorite Louisiana plants and flowers and growing them at Briarwood. She liked being surrounded by the trees and flowers that she loved. She also wanted to be sure that these special Louisiana plants would not disappear from the forest.

Dormon wanted other people in Louisiana to be able to enjoy nature as much as she did. She worked with the United States Forest Service to help form Kisatchie National Forest. Today the forest covers a large part of northern and central Louisiana. Kisatchie National Forest has 24 hiking trails and more than 130 miles of waterways. Visitors can see more than 100 kinds of flowers.

▶ In the early 1900s, many of the trees in the Kisatchie Forest were cut for their wood. After Kisatchie was made a national forest, workers planted thousands of new trees.

Caring in Action

Link to Current Events Caroline Dormon cared about protecting the beautiful forest for people to enjoy in the future. What could you do to help keep your community beautiful for the future? Could you plant flowers in the park? Could you clean up litter? As a class, make a list of ideas and then choose one project to do together.

Meet
Clementine Hunter

1886?–1988 • Artist

Clementine Hunter was born in central Louisiana. When she was young, African American women had few choices for the kind of work they could do. Yet Clementine Hunter became a famous artist. Her paintings often show people working or playing outdoors in Louisiana.

This painting by Clementine Hunter is called *Wash Day*. It shows people washing their clothes outside.

48

When she was growing up, Clementine and her family picked cotton for the owners of large farms. When she was older, she worked as a cook at a farm called Melrose. Once, Hunter found some paint left behind by an artist who had visited the house. Hunter was more than 50 years old and had never painted before. But she said, "You know . . . I could mark [paint] a picture if I set my mind to it."

Once Hunter started painting, she could not stop! Her paintings show things such as farm life, marriages, funerals, and the flowers of Louisiana. She painted on anything she could find, including bottles and a window shade.

Hunter liked to show her paintings to visitors. A sign outside her porch said,

**"Clementine Hunter, Artist,
50 cents to look."**

By the 1980s, Hunter was well known. She was the first African American artist to have a show in the New Orleans Museum of Art. Museums all over the country have also shown her work.

Clementine Hunter also painted boxes. She painted flowers and birds on this box that holds recipes.

BIOFACT

Learn from Biographies

How do you think Clementine Hunter's life and surroundings helped her decide what to paint?

Students can research the lives of significant people by clicking on *Meet the People* at **www.sfsocialstudies.com.**

Chapter Summary

Main Idea and Details

On a separate sheet of paper, fill in some details about the land and waterways of Louisiana.

> Louisiana has important rivers, forests, and a mountain.

Vocabulary

Fill in each blank with the letter of the vocabulary word that best completes the sentence.

1 The place where the waters of a river spill over onto the land is called a _____.

2 Ships can load and unload goods from all over the world at a _____.

3 _____ is the number of people living in an area.

4 _____ are marshes, swamps, or other kinds of land that are damp or covered with water.

a. floodplain (p. 31)
b. population (p. 32)
c. port (p. 32)
d. wetlands (p. 41)

Facts and Main Ideas

1 How does the floodplain along the Mississippi River become fertile?

2 Describe the highest and lowest elevation points in Louisiana.

3 **Main Idea** Name two ways that the Mississippi River is important to the people in our state.

4 **Main Idea** Why is it important to protect the swamps, bayous, and forests in Louisiana?

5 **Critical Thinking:** *Compare and Contrast* How are the Mississippi River Delta and the Atchafalaya Swamp different?

Write About It

1 **Write a letter** to a friend about a boat trip through the Mississippi River Delta. Tell about the kinds of land and animals you might see.

2 **Write an advertisement** for the United States Forest Service. Explain why it is important for Louisiana's forests to be used wisely.

3 **Write a fact sheet** about one of the natural features of Louisiana. Include at least three interesting facts about the feature.

Internet Activity

To get help with vocabulary, people, and terms, select the dictionary or encyclopedia from *Social Studies Library* at **www.sfsocialstudies.com.**

Apply Skills

Use a Population Map Use the population map on page 38 to answer the questions below.

1 About how many people live in Vermilion Parish?

2 Do more people live in Livingston Parish or Madison Parish? How can you tell?

3 Why do you need a key to read a population map?

End with a Song

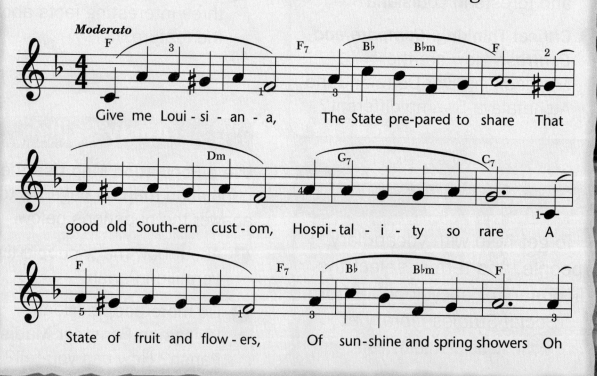

Give Me Louisiana

Words and music by Doralice Fontane

This is part of the official song of Louisiana. What does the writer of the song like about Louisiana? Make a list of things you like about our state that you would add to the song.

Moderato

Give me Loui - si - an - a, The State pre-pared to share That

good old South-ern cust - om, Hospi - tal - i - ty so rare A

State of fruit and flow - ers, Of sun-shine and spring showers Oh

Review

Main Idea and Vocabulary

TEST PREP

Read the passage. Then answer the questions.

Louisiana is located on the continent of North America. It is in the southern part of the United States.

When we study Louisiana's <u>geography</u>, we learn about its three regions. Each region has many features. One feature is the Mississippi River Delta, located at the mouth of the Mississippi River.

The Mississippi River flows through Louisiana to the Gulf of Mexico. This river helps make fertile land, which is good for growing crops. People in Louisiana's port cities rely on the river to ship goods in and out of the state.

Louisiana also has swamps, bayous, and forests. The Atchafalaya Swamp is an example of a wetland.

....

1 According to the passage, where is Louisiana located?
  A in the Mississippi River
  B in the western United States
  C in North America
  D in the Atchafalaya Swamp

2 According to the passage, which of the following is an important feature of Louisiana's geography?
  A the Mississippi River Delta
  B North America
  C the Gulf of Mexico
  D the United States

3 In the passage, what does the word *geography* mean?
  A a continent
  B the study of Earth's land and the ways people use it
  C a port city
  D the study of how people ship goods

Vocabulary

Write three sentences describing the geography of Louisiana. Use three or more of the vocabulary words below.

explorer (p. 15)   fertile (p. 31)

region (p. 19)   wetlands (p. 41)

landform (p. 20)   elevation (p. 44)

delta (p. 21)

Apply Skills

Create a Temperature Graph
Together with your class and your teacher, record the temperature at noon every day for a week. Then make a line graph that shows the date of each day recorded and the temperature. Use your graph to answer these questions: *What was the highest temperature? What was the lowest temperature?*

Read on Your Own

Look for books like these in the library.

Write and Share

Research a Mississippi River Town
Gather information about a town that is located on the Mississippi River in Louisiana. Make a poster about that town. Include information such as the town's location, population, and weather. Explain your poster to your classmates.

UNIT 1 Project

Eye on Our Region

Take visitors on a tour of your region of Louisiana. Show what is great about it.

1 **Form** a group. Choose a topic about your region of Louisiana.

2 **Make** a map of your region.

3 **Draw** pictures about your topic. Write a sentence or two to describe each picture.

4 **Put** your group's pictures together. This is your tour to share with the class.

Internet Activity

For more information and activities, go to www.sfsocialstudies.com.

People and the Land

How are people in Louisiana affected by their surroundings?

Begin with a Primary Source

"The Mississippi [River] has affected the nature of many... states and cities."
—Irish writer Sean O'Faolain, 1961

Simon Gunning painted *The Deep Blue Stern* in 2003. It shows a ship docked in a canal that leads to the Mississippi River.

Meet the People

John James Audubon

1785–1851

Birthplace: Saint-Domingue (now Haiti)

Nature artist

- Was one of the first artists to make lifelike drawings of birds
- Lived and worked in Louisiana to support himself while painting
- Published pictures of North American birds in the books *The Birds of America*

Henry Miller Shreve

1785–1851

Birthplace: Burlington County, New Jersey

River captain and steamboat builder

- Built a new kind of steamboat for shallow waters
- Built a steamboat that pulled up snags, or sunken tree trunks
- Was honored when the city of Shreveport was named for him

| 1775 | 1800 | 1825 | 1850 | 1875 |

1785 • John James Audubon 1851

1785 • Henry Miller Shreve 1851

Students can research the lives of significant people by clicking on *Meet the People* at **www.sfsocialstudies.com**.

Kimberly Willis Holt

b. 1960

Birthplace: Pensacola, Florida

Writer

- Gets her ideas for her books from her childhood memories
- Worked as a radio news director, a marketer for a water park, and an interior decorator
- Wrote the novel *My Louisiana Sky*, which was published in 1998

Rose Fisher-Blassingame

b. 1962

Birthplace: Pineville, Louisiana

Weaver and teacher

- Creates baskets in the traditional Choctaw way
- Decided to learn the tradition because it was no longer done by anyone in her Native American community
- Teaches other Choctaw members the art of split cane basketry

| 1900 | 1925 | 1950 | 1975 | 2000 |

1960 • Kimberly Willis Holt

1962 • Rose Fisher-Blassingame

Large and Small Cities

Compare and Contrast

To compare means to find things that are alike.
To contrast means to find things that are different.
Knowing how to compare and contrast information will
help you understand some kinds of writing.

Compare | **Contrast**
Alike | Different

- Clue words for likenesses include *like, alike,* and *both.*

- Clue words for differences include *yet, but,* and *however.*

Read this passage. Likenesses have been highlighted in yellow. Differences have been highlighted in blue.

> Each of Louisiana's regions is located in a different part of the state. All of the regions include bodies of water, such as rivers, lakes, bayous, and ponds.

Word Exercise

Context Clues Often you can use clues from the text and what you already know to figure out the meaning of a word you do not know. Figure out the meaning of *tourist.*

> Like visitors to other cities, these tourists come for the fun of the celebrations.

Context Clues
Tourists are like visitors to other cities.

What I Already Know
Visitors often travel to see interesting sights.

What I Think *tourist* Means
"someone traveling for fun"

▶ New Orleans   ▶ Natchitoches

Two Louisiana Cities

Louisiana has many kinds of cities. Natchitoches (NACK uh tish) is a small city. It has a population of about 18,000 people. New Orleans, however, is a large city. More than 100,000 people live there.

New Orleans is in southern Louisiana, yet Natchitoches is in northern Louisiana. New Orleans is near the coast, but Natchitoches is a long distance from the coast.

Both Natchitoches and New Orleans hold Mardi Gras (MAR dee grah) festivals each year. Mardi Gras has been celebrated for hundreds of years in Louisiana.

Many tourists come to New Orleans and Natchitoches during Mardi Gras. Like visitors to other cities, these tourists come for the fun of the celebrations. Tourists watch parades of people who wear colorful costumes.

Apply it!

Use the reading skill of compare and contrast to answer questions 1 and 2. Then answer the vocabulary question.

1 How are Natchitoches and New Orleans similar?

2 How are Natchitoches and New Orleans different?

3 Using the clues in the second paragraph, what do you think the word *distance* means in the passage?

Chapter 3 — Living in Louisiana

Lesson 1

Jefferson Parish

Many people live in suburban communities such as the ones in Jefferson Parish.

Lesson 2

Shreveport

People had to change their surroundings to build cities such as Shreveport.

CANADA

NORTH AMERICA

2

1

UNITED STATES

PACIFIC OCEAN

ATLANTIC OCEAN

Shreveport

Jefferson Parish

LOUISIANA

Gulf of Mexico

MEXICO

Why We Remember

Have you ever used an umbrella when it rains so you will not get wet? This is an example of nature affecting how people live. Have you ever helped an adult build something, such as a birdhouse, out of wood? This is an example of people changing nature. In Chapter 3, you will learn how people in Louisiana work with nature.

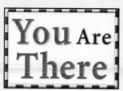

Communities Across Louisiana

Preview

Focus on the Main Idea
People have built different kinds of communities all over Louisiana.

PLACES
Lake Charles
Athens
Forest Hill
Jefferson Parish

PEOPLE
Kimberly Willis Holt

VOCABULARY
community
urban community
rural community
suburban community

You Are There

Dear Pen Pal,
I live in Lake Charles, in the southern part of the state. Our city was built next to a lake with white sandy beaches. There are some tall buildings next to the lake.

We have lots of parks, and all year long there are outdoor festivals with music and great food. Since we live so close to the lake, my family and I go there a lot! We walk and ride bikes on the path near it. We also go swimming and sailing a lot.

Please write back and tell me about where you live in Louisiana.

Compare and Contrast
As you read, look for what is alike and what is different about the places in this lesson.

Dear Pen Pal,

Danielle D'Andrea
123 Salem Lane
Harrisonburg, Louisiana
71340

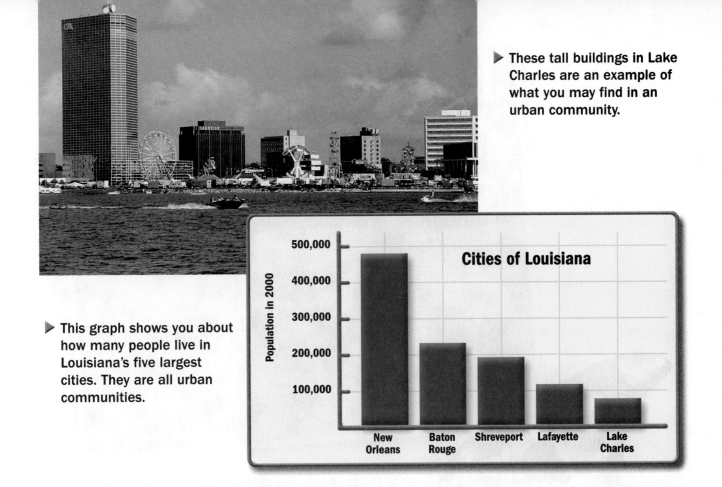

▶ These tall buildings in Lake Charles are an example of what you may find in an urban community.

▶ This graph shows you about how many people live in Louisiana's five largest cities. They are all urban communities.

Cities of Louisiana

Population in 2000

500,000
400,000
300,000
200,000
100,000

New Orleans | Baton Rouge | Shreveport | Lafayette | Lake Charles

Urban Communities

People have built many different kinds of communities around the state. A **community** is a place where people live, work, and have fun together.

Lake Charles is an urban community. An **urban community** is a community that is in a city. Urban communities usually have tall buildings and busy streets. They also have large populations. Do you know which city had the largest population in Louisiana in 2000? Look at the bar graph on this page to find the answer.

REVIEW Is the community of Lake Charles like or different from your own community? Explain. ◔ **Compare and Contrast**

▶ These people are celebrating a festival in the rural community of Homer, in Claiborne Parish.

▶ Butterflies are common in Haynesville, the "Butterfly Capital" of Louisiana.

Rural Communities

Have you ever heard of **Athens,** Louisiana? Athens is a small town located in Claiborne Parish, in northern Louisiana. Athens is an example of a rural community. A **rural community** is in the countryside, where towns are small and far apart. Rural communities have small populations.

Open fields, forests, or farmland usually surround rural communities. Rolling hills surround Athens and other small towns of Claiborne Parish. There are green forests and grassy fields. This is a perfect place for butterflies to live. In fact, the town of Haynesville in Claiborne Parish is known as the "Butterfly Capital" of Louisiana.

Growing up in a rural area of Louisiana can be a lot of fun. Just ask **Kimberly Willis Holt.** When she was a young girl, Holt lived with her family in the small town of **Forest Hill,** in central Louisiana. She remembers, "Forest Hill is the kind of town where neighbors care when you're sick and show up at your door with chicken and dumplings."

Today Kimberly Willis Holt is a writer of books for young readers. Many of her stories take place in rural communities in Louisiana.

REVIEW How are rural communities different from urban communities?

Compare and Contrast

Literature and Social Studies

My Louisiana Sky

by Kimberly Willis Holt

In this book, a girl named Tiger Ann Parker lives in a rural community. Here, Tiger talks about one of the ways to have fun in her part of Louisiana.

Momma, Jesse Wade, and I floated on inner tubes at Saitter Creek with our legs dangling over the rubber and our feet dipping in the cold water. It was mid-June, and the day was hotter than the Fourth of July. My hand shaded my eyes from the sun as I watched clouds dance around the tips of trees towering above us, and listened to the grasshoppers chirping loudly in the tall grass.

▶ You probably have lots of neighbors if you live in the suburbs! You may also live near many stores or shopping centers.

Suburban Communities

Some people reading this book may be thinking, *I don't live in a rural or an urban community. When is this book going to talk about suburbs?* A **suburban community** is a community that is located near a large city. Suburbs often surround large cities. Many people who live in the suburbs work in the city.

If you cross the Mississippi River and drive west out of New Orleans, it will only take you a short while to reach the suburban community of Marrero. Marrero is in **Jefferson Parish**, near New Orleans. In Marrero you will find streets lined with houses and trees. You will also find parks, movie theaters, shopping malls, and office buildings.

Another suburb of New Orleans is Metairie. Like many suburbs, Metairie used to be open farmland. In the early 1900s, an electric streetcar began driving back and forth from Metairie to New Orleans. Families began building homes in Metairie. Each day, people traveled from their home in Metairie to their work in New Orleans. People do the same thing today. Only now, most people drive cars on busy roads.

REVIEW How are suburban communities different from rural communities?

◎ **Compare and Contrast**

Summarize the Lesson

- People have built many different kinds of communities in Louisiana.
- Urban communities are in cities and have large populations.
- Rural communities are in the countryside, where towns are small and far apart.
- Suburban communities are located near large cities.

LESSON 1 REVIEW

Check Facts and Main Ideas

1. ◎ **Compare and Contrast**
   On a separate sheet of paper, fill in the diagram to compare and contrast the two communities of Lake Charles and Athens.

Compare/Alike	Contrast/Different

2. Describe **urban communities** and give one example of an urban community in Louisiana.

3. Describe **rural communities** and give one example of a rural community in Louisiana.

4. Describe **suburban communities** and give one example of a suburban community in Louisiana.

5. **Critical Thinking: *Express Ideas*** What kind of **community** do you live in? What are some things you like about this kind of community?

Link to ⚭ Geography

Draw a Communities Map Using the locator map on page 66 as a guide, draw your own map of communities in Louisiana. Include all the places talked about in this lesson. Include labels saying which type of community each place is. Also include your own community. Give your map a name.

Thinking Skills

Classify

What? When you **classify,** you place things that have similar features together in a group. You can classify, or group, objects, ideas, living things, and even communities. This chart shows how to classify some objects.

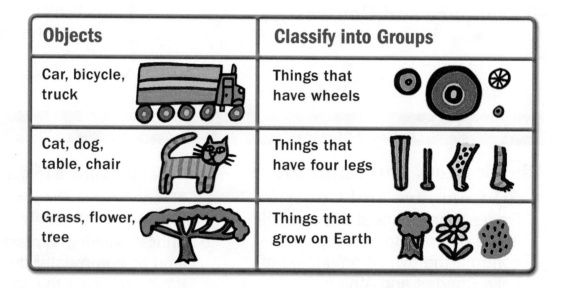

Objects		Classify into Groups	
Car, bicycle, truck		Things that have wheels	
Cat, dog, table, chair		Things that have four legs	
Grass, flower, tree		Things that grow on Earth	

Why? Classifying can help you better understand the things you put into groups. One reason people classify communities is so they can learn how communities that are alike solve problems.

How? To classify things, you find features of one group that make it different from other groups. For example, cities in Louisiana have larger populations than suburbs or rural communities in the state. This population feature helps you decide whether a community fits into the city group.

A feature of rural communities is that they are in the countryside. A feature of suburbs is that they are near cities. You can list communities and their features in a chart.

Features of a Community	Classify into Groups
• In the countryside • Small population	Rural community
• Near a city • Usually medium-sized population	Suburban community
• In a city • Large population	Urban community

Use the information in this paragraph to **classify** these communities in Louisiana.

In 2006 Baton Rouge had a population of more than 250,000 people. It is the largest community in Louisiana. About 11 miles north of Baton Rouge is Baker, a much smaller community. Many people who live in Baker work in Baton Rouge. In the countryside, about 50 miles from Baton Rouge, is the community of Napoleonville. Its population is fewer than 700.

1 Which community is a city? What feature helped you decide?

2 Which community is a suburb? What feature helped you decide?

3 Which community is a rural community? What feature helped you decide?

People and the Environment

Preview

Focus on the Main Idea
People change the environment to help them meet their needs. They also change the way they do things because of the environment.

PLACE
Shreveport

PEOPLE
Henry Miller Shreve
Rose Fisher-Blassingame

VOCABULARY
environment
levee
adapt

You Are There
Suppose that you have just arrived in Louisiana. Only this is not the Louisiana you know today. This is Louisiana ten thousand years ago! There are no cities, no stores, no roads, and no farms. All you see are forests, lakes, and lots of wild animals, such as birds and turtles.

What would you do first? You might collect wood to build a fire. Or maybe you would make tools for hunting and fishing. You might even try to figure out how to build some kind of home or shelter. You'd better do something soon—the sky is looking dark, rain is starting to fall, and you are getting very hungry!

Compare and Contrast As you read, contrast the effects nature has on people with the effects people have on nature.

Changing the Land

Our **environment** is made up of all the things that surround us, such as land, water, air, and trees. People sometimes change the environment to help them meet their needs. For example, people need places to live. To help meet this need, people have cleared land to build towns and cities.

In the 1830s, **Henry Miller Shreve** changed the environment in Louisiana. Thousands of fallen trees were floating in the Red River. Boats could not use the river. Shreve cleared the trees from the river. Once boats could use the Red River, more people could travel by water to other parts of northern Louisiana. In 1839 they began building the city of **Shreveport** on the Red River.

▶ To build the city of Shreveport, below, construction workers had to change much of the land.

REVIEW How was the Red River different after the work of Henry Miller Shreve?

⟳ **Compare and Contrast**

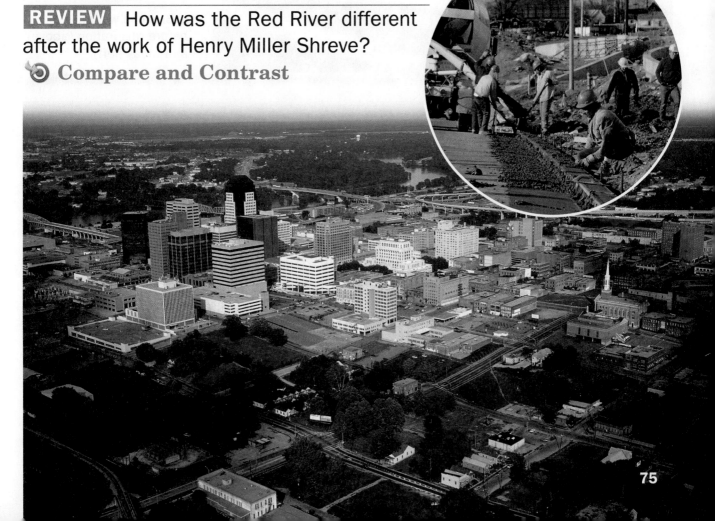

Saving the Wetlands

Louisiana's coastal wetlands and barrier islands are our state's first defense against hurricanes and other strong storms. However, they are being destroyed rapidly. Steps are being taken to rebuild our wetlands.

▶ Work on a railroad changed the flow of water through Bayou LaBranche, destroying much of the wetlands there over time. Scientists and engineers have piped soil from the bottom of Lake Pontchartrain to rebuild some of these wetlands.

▶ LaBranche wetlands before restoration (above) and today (left).

The Danger of Floods

"I remember mom and dad getting us children up bright and early, because you could just hear the roar of the waters from way far away." That was what a young boy named Ory Poret remembered about a huge flood on the Mississippi River in 1927.

Muddy river water spread out across much of Louisiana. The rushing water lifted houses right off the ground. People, dogs, and even cows climbed onto boats or the roofs of floating houses. There were no other dry spots in sight!

For as long as people have lived in Louisiana, they have seen flooding from the Mississippi River. So it makes sense that people have tried to change the environment to protect themselves from floods. For example, people have built up levees along the river. A **levee** is a high bank or wall, built along the sides of a river to keep it from overflowing. Louisiana's levees have been made higher and higher over the years.

To protect from flooding, levees must be very strong. When Hurricane Katrina hit the Gulf Coast in 2005, some of the levees that protected New Orleans failed. They did not stand up against such a powerful storm. Parts of the city flooded, and many people lost their homes, businesses, and schools. Some people lost their lives.

People also build dams to prevent flooding. A dam is a wall built across a river to hold back the water. Dams control how fast a river flows.

▶ Piling sandbags near a river is another way to keep it from overflowing.

REVIEW What is a levee?
Main Idea and Details

▶ Levees can be made of concrete or dirt. They help prevent floodwaters from damaging buildings and crops.

▶ Canoeing is a way of adapting to the environment in order to go places.

Adapting to the Land

People do not always change the environment. Sometimes people adapt to the environment. To **adapt** means to change the way you do something. Suppose you just moved here from a much colder state, such as Alaska. You cannot change the weather, can you? You would adapt to the weather in Louisiana by changing the way you dress.

You know that Louisiana has many rivers and bayous. People have adapted to this by building boats and traveling by water. Did you know that many of the ponds in Louisiana are perfect for crawfish? People have adapted to this fact by catching and selling millions of crawfish every year. Some companies even build new ponds to grow crawfish.

▶ Instead of catching crawfish in the wild, some people grow them on farms.

Rose Fisher-Blassingame shows people another way to adapt to the environment. She is an expert at weaving baskets from plants. She makes the baskets according to the traditions of the Choctaw Native Americans. You will read more about her in the Biography after this lesson.

Think of other ways that you adapt to your environment. For example, how is your day different when it rains or when it is dry outside?

REVIEW How have people adapted to the fact that Louisiana has many rivers and bayous? **Main Idea and Details**

Summarize the Lesson

Summarize the Lesson

- People have changed the environment of Louisiana to help meet their needs.
- People in Louisiana have had to find ways to control floods.
- People have adapted to the environment of Louisiana.

LESSON 2 REVIEW

Check Facts and Main Ideas

1. 🎯 **Compare and Contrast**
   On a separate sheet of paper, contrast ways people affect their environment and ways nature affects how people live.

People affect the environment:	Nature affects people:

2. Name two ways people have changed the **environment** to meet their needs.

3. How have river changes affected Louisiana?

4. Name two ways people have **adapted** to the environment of Louisiana.

5. **Critical Thinking: *Draw Conclusions***
   Think about your community in Louisiana. What is one way people in your area have changed the environment? What is one way they have adapted to the environment?

Link to ◑━━◑ Writing

Write a Story Look back at You Are There at the beginning of this lesson. Then write your own story about what it might be like to travel back in time to Louisiana ten thousand years ago. What are three things you would try to do right away?

Meet
Rose Fisher-Blassingame

b. 1962 • Weaver and Teacher

Rose Fisher-Blassingame keeps Choctaw traditions alive through the art of basket weaving.

Rose Fisher-Blassingame is a member of the Jena group of the Choctaw Native Americans. She remembers stories she heard about her relatives weaving baskets out of a plant called river cane.

▶ Fisher-Blassingame teaches her students to wash the river cane and weave it into a basket (below).

"My great-great aunt . . . was the last Jena band Choctaw [who made baskets] and I grew up hearing stories about her, how she helped to support her family . . . with her basket weaving."

Choctaw baskets are made of river cane. River cane has a strong, flexible stem, which makes it useful for weaving. It grows along rivers and swamps.

Fisher-Blassingame weaves baskets in the traditional Choctaw way. Her first step is to gather the river cane. Then she must wash it. She does this in the traditional way, using river water and sand to clean the river cane. Then she splits and peels the river cane. Now it is ready to be woven into a basket.

Today Fisher-Blassingame teaches basket weaving. She hopes that her students will teach others what they have learned. She wants the Choctaw tradition of cane basket weaving to continue into the future.

Learn from Biographies

Why do you think Rose Fisher-Blassingame thinks it is important to teach others to weave traditional Choctaw baskets?

To teach even more people about Choctaw cane basket weaving, Fisher-Blassingame allowed her class to be filmed.

BIOFACT

▶ The first step to weaving a basket is to find river cane!

Students can research the lives of significant people by clicking on *Meet the People* at **www.sfsocialstudies.com.**

A New Path for Louisiana

Henry Shreve was only 14 years old when he began working on riverboats. Shreve felt a responsibility to help others sail on rivers that had once seemed impossible to travel on.

Steamboats did not always have enough power to travel against a river's current. Henry Shreve designed a stronger steamboat. In 1815 one of Shreve's boats became the first steamboat to travel up the Mississippi River.

▶ Lloyd Hawthorne's painting *Clearing the Great Raft from the Red River, 1833-38,* shows Captain Henry M. Shreve opening the Red River to Riverboat travel.

BUILDING
CITIZENSHIP

Caring

Respect

Responsibility

Fairness

Honesty

Courage

Then in the late 1820s, the United States government asked Shreve to help with another problem. Fallen logs often blocked the rivers. Steamboats often had a hard time getting past the logs. Shreve designed a special kind of boat, called a snag boat, to carry the logs away.

His biggest challenge was the "Great Raft." This was a large area of fallen trees that blocked the Red River in northern Louisiana. The logs were so thick that they often smashed steamboats that tried to travel over them.

Shreve began clearing the "Great Raft" in 1833. By 1838 the logs had been removed. Now boats could more easily move on the Red River. This made it easier for people such as traders to reach northern Louisiana. The camp where Shreve and his workers had stayed became a town in 1839. It was named Shreveport in his honor.

▶ Because of Henry Shreve, boats can easily travel on the Red River.

Responsibility in Action

Link to Current Events Shreve felt a responsibility to help clear the Red River. As a class, find out about a problem with the environment in your community. What steps are being taken to help solve it? What can you do to help?

Chapter Summary

Compare and Contrast

On a separate sheet of paper, draw the diagram shown below. Fill in the boxes to compare and contrast rural and urban communities.

Compare/Alike	Contrast/Different

Vocabulary

Fill in the blank with the letter of the vocabulary word that best completes each sentence.

1 A _____ is in the countryside.

2 The _____ is made up of all the things that surround us, such as land, water, air, and trees.

3 A _____ is located near a large city.

4 A _____ is a high bank or wall, built to keep a river from overflowing.

a. rural community (p. 68)

b. suburban community (p. 70)

c. environment (p. 75)

d. levee (p. 77)

Facts and Main Ideas

1. What is a community?

2. Why have levees been built along the Mississippi River?

3. **Main Idea** What are three kinds of communities in Louisiana? In general, where is each kind of community located?

4. **Main Idea** Why do people sometimes need to change the environment in which they live?

5. **Critical Thinking:** *Evaluate* How could a suburban community become an urban community?

Internet Activity

To get help with vocabulary, people, and terms, select the dictionary or encyclopedia from *Social Studies Library* at **www.sfsocialstudies.com.**

Write About It

1. **Write a magazine article** about the community in which you live. Tell whether it is rural, urban, or suburban. Include details about where people work and what they do for fun.

2. **Write a journal entry** about your first day living in either an urban, rural, or suburban community. Include details of how you must adapt to your new community.

3. **Write five interview questions** that you would like to ask Henry Shreve about how he cleared the "Great Raft" on the Red River.

Apply Skills

Classify Use the chart on page 73 to answer the questions below.

1. According to the chart, which kind of community has a large population?

2. How would you classify a community in the countryside with a small population?

3. How would you classify your own community?

Chapter 4

Our Natural Resources

Lesson 1

Avery Island

The salt domes of Avery Island contain solid salt for thousands of feet beneath the ground.

1

Lesson 2

Tensas River National Wildlife Refuge

The Tensas River National Wildlife Refuge protects plants and animals.

2

CANADA

NORTH AMERICA

UNITED STATES

1 **2**

PACIFIC OCEAN

ATLANTIC OCEAN

Tensas River National Wildlife Refuge

LOUISIANA
Avery Island

Gulf of Mexico

MEXICO

Why We Remember

What do you see in nature when you are outside? Louisiana has many different kinds of resources and animals. Many things in the environment can be used to help us live a better life. For example, trees can be cut down to make wood for building homes. But we must take care of Louisiana's plants and animals to protect them for the future.

87

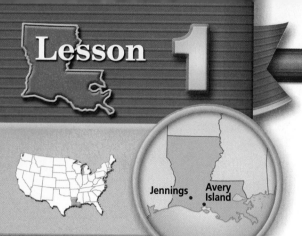

Using Natural Resources

Preview

Focus on the Main Idea
Louisiana is rich in many kinds of natural resources.

PLACES
Avery Island
Jennings

PEOPLE
Edmund McIlhenny

VOCABULARY
natural resource
scarcity
abundance
conserve

You Are There
Your class is taking a tour of Avery Island in southern Louisiana. There is grass all around you but no water.

"Why is this place called Avery Island?" you ask. "It doesn't look like an island."

"It's not really an island," your teacher explains. "It's actually a salt dome."

"So I'm standing on salt?" you ask.

"That's right," she says. "Salt domes are like mountains of salt. Most of the salt is underground, but the top of this salt dome rises about 150 feet above the land around it. That is what we are standing on. Beneath these plants and soil, there is solid salt for thousands of feet straight down!"

Main Idea and Details As you read, identify the natural resources found in Louisiana.

▶ Underground Avery Island salt mine

Natural Resources

Louisiana has many natural resources. Natural resources are materials found in nature that people can use. Water, soil, and trees are examples of natural resources. Natural resources have many important uses. People need natural resources such as water and soil to grow food. We use natural resources such as trees to build homes.

In the 1860s, Edmund McIlhenny (MAK il hen nee) found a way to use two of Louisiana's natural resources together. He used the rich soil of Avery Island to grow spicy red peppers. Then he mixed the peppers with Avery Island salt to make a hot pepper sauce. Today, pepper sauce from Avery Island is sold all over the world!

REVIEW Why are natural resources important? **Summarize**

▶ Edmund McIlhenny used peppers like these to make his pepper sauce.

▶ McIlhenny also created Jungle Gardens on Avery Island. Visitors can see many kinds of plants and animals there.

Energy Resources

In 1901 a rice farmer near the town of **Jennings** made an amazing discovery. There was oil deep beneath his land in southern Louisiana! In the years since, large supplies of oil and natural gas have been found all over the state.

What makes oil and natural gas so special? They are very important natural resources. Oil and natural gas can be burned to produce heat, light, and other forms of energy. We burn oil and natural gas to heat homes, cook food, and run car engines.

Louisiana is one of the country's top producers of oil and natural gas. Today, much of Louisiana's oil and gas is found offshore. In other words, most of it is found off the coast of Louisiana. Offshore rigs drill down into the rocks beneath the Gulf of Mexico.

REVIEW What is one way that your family uses oil or natural gas? **Draw Conclusions**

▶ Oil was first drilled in Louisiana near Jennings in the early 1900s.

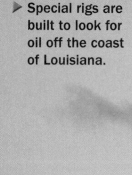

▶ Special rigs are built to look for oil off the coast of Louisiana.

MAP ADVENTURE

Take a tour of our state to find Louisiana's natural resources. The map below will help you in your search. Study the map and answer the questions.

- Near what cities is natural gas found?

- Sulfur is used in thousands of products, including matches, paper, and paint. Where is this resource found?

- Which resource on this map would you use to build a house? Where in the state is this resource found?

91

▶ As wood is being used to make new homes, new trees are being planted to protect this resource.

Conserving Resources

You know that Louisiana has many useful natural resources. However, there are still not enough resources to make everything that people want. There is a scarcity of most natural resources. **Scarcity** means there is not enough of something to meet all of people's wants and needs. There is a shortage.

Wood, oil, and natural gas are examples of scarce natural resources. Louisiana has a lot of these resources, but not enough to make everything that people want.

There is an abundance of some natural resources in Louisiana. **Abundance** means there is more than enough of something. There is a large supply. Salt is an example of an abundant natural resource. The salt domes in southern Louisiana have huge amounts of salt.

Since most resources are scarce, people try to conserve them. To **conserve** resources means to use them carefully. We want to make sure they will last! Have you ever seen people planting trees? This is a way of conserving wood. We plant new trees to replace the trees we cut down.

REVIEW Name an abundant resource in Louisiana. **Main Idea and Details**

Summarize the Lesson

- Natural resources are materials found in nature that people can use.
- Louisiana has many natural resources, including oil, natural gas, and wood.
- Most resources are scarce, so people try to conserve them.

LESSON 1   REVIEW

Check Facts and Main Ideas

1. **Main Idea and Details** On a separate sheet of paper, fill in details for the main idea.

```
Louisiana has many
natural resources.
```

2. Where are some of Louisiana's most important resources found?

3. Describe the importance of the **natural resources** oil and natural gas.

4. Define **scarcity** and **abundance**.

5. **Critical Thinking:** *Apply Information* Why do people try to **conserve** natural resources?

Link to ⚭ **Science**

Explore Resources Find out more about one of the natural resources of Louisiana. Describe this resource. Tell where it is found and how it is gathered. Explain how people use this resource.

Cleaning up Litter

Children and adults in St. Landry Parish are working together to stop littering. They have tried to find ways to get everyone to help keep their community clean.

One way is to have customers at fast food restaurants ask for a trash bag for their food wrappers. A note on each bag tells people not to litter.

Parish workers Velton Stelly and Celeste Gomez had another idea. They helped to post signs that ask people to call a phone number when they see someone littering. People who are caught littering have to pay a fine and help clean up trash.

The city of Opelousas (ah peh LOO sehs) had a "Trash Bash" in 2004. The people of Opelousas collected 70 bags of litter. Some of the students who took part decided to start a litter patrol in their schools.

▶ You can help clean up litter at beaches, parks, and schools.

DON'T LITTER

LITTER HOTLINE
1-888-LITRBUG
"SAINTS" TEAM WORKING TOGETHER

"We cleaned by the school and there were all kinds of candy paper."

Nicholas, age 12

"We are not trying to punish people. We are trying to prevent litter."

Velton Stelly

"It was looking bad and then we cleaned across the street too."

Rondell, age 12

"We would never litter because then we're just going to have to come back and pick it up."

Zaccheus, age 12

Issues and You

As a class, make a list of ways that you could help to clean up litter in your school and neighborhood. What could you do to help stop people from littering in the first place?

Map and Globe Skills

Use Intermediate Directions

What? A **compass rose** shows you the **cardinal directions** on a map—north, south, east, and west. You use these directions to tell someone where you are going or to tell them where you have been. Sometimes you are going somewhere in between one of these cardinal directions. Then you use an **intermediate direction,** or a direction that is in the middle of two cardinal directions. Then you can say, for example, that you are going **northeast** or **southwest.**

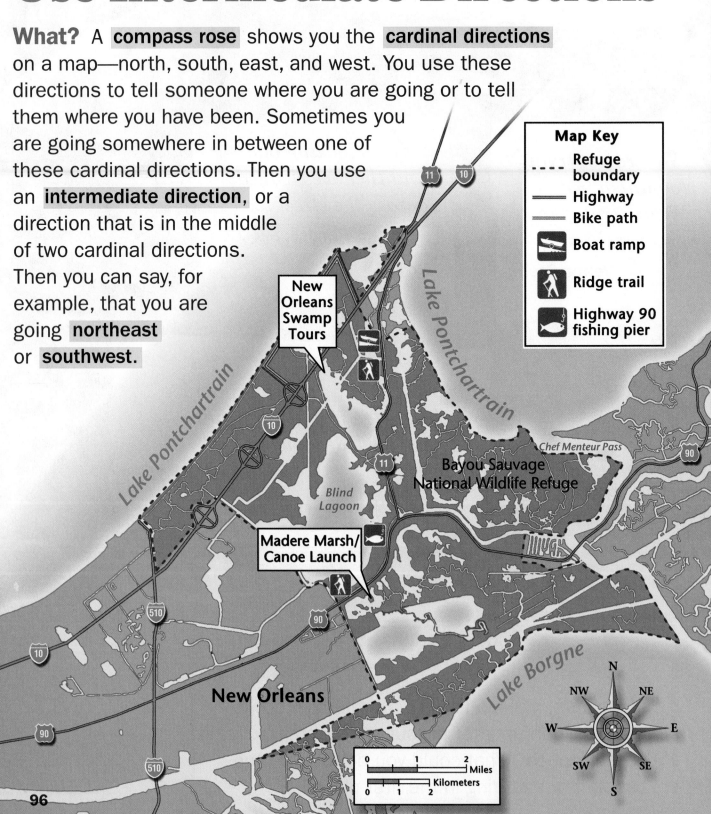

Map Key

- - - - Refuge boundary

——— Highway

═══ Bike path

Boat ramp

Ridge trail

Highway 90 fishing pier

New Orleans Swamp Tours

Lake Pontchartrain

Lake Pontchartrain

Chef Menteur Pass

Bayou Sauvage National Wildlife Refuge

Blind Lagoon

Madere Marsh/ Canoe Launch

New Orleans

Lake Borgne

N
NW   NE
W   E
SW   SE
S

0   1   2 Miles

0   1   2 Kilometers

Why? Intermediate directions help you better explain where a place is located or how to get somewhere. Look at the map of Bayou Sauvage National Wildlife Refuge in New Orleans. A wildlife refuge is land set aside to protect plants and animals.

How would you describe the location of Lake Borgne (born)? To be exact, you can use intermediate directions. Lake Borgne is **southeast** of Madere Marsh/Canoe Launch.

How? To use intermediate directions, pick a place on a map. Suppose that the compass rose is directly over that place. Then trace along the arrows of the compass rose between that place and a second place.

Point to the Highway 90 fishing pier on this map. If you travel from this pier to the New Orleans Swamp Tours, which way will you go? Trace along the compass rose in the direction that you will go. You will go **northwest.**

1 Name the four **cardinal directions.**

2 Name the four **intermediate directions.**

3 Find the symbol on the map for the Highway 90 fishing pier. In what direction will you go from there to reach Chef Menteur Pass where it meets Lake Pontchartrain?

4 There is a bike path that starts near the New Orleans Swamp Tours. Use the map key to find the bike path on the map. The bike path follows three intermediate directions before it ends. Which three directions does the bike path follow?

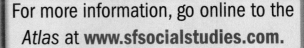

Internet Activity

For more information, go online to the *Atlas* at **www.sfsocialstudies.com.**

Tensas River National Wildlife Refuge

Preview

Focus on the Main Idea
People in Louisiana work to protect the state's wildlife and land.

PLACE
Tensas River National Wildlife Refuge

PEOPLE
John James Audubon

VOCABULARY
wildlife
erosion

Plants and Animals of Louisiana

You Are There
"Do you think we'll really see a bear?" your brother Alex asks.

"I don't know," you say. "I read that black bears are pretty hard to spot. They usually try to hide from people."

"That's fine with me," Alex says.

Your family is hiking in the Tensas River National Wildlife Refuge in northeastern Louisiana. This refuge is home to wild turkeys, bobcats, opossums, and about 100 Louisiana black bears. Each bear can grow to more than 400 pounds!

This is going to be an exciting hike!

Draw Conclusions As you read, think about why people protect Louisiana's wildlife and land.

▶ Opossums

Protecting Wildlife

Animals and plants that live in the wild are known as **wildlife.** Some wildlife populations are not as large as they used to be. They are becoming scarce. This is mostly because people have built communities where wildlife live. To help protect wildlife, Louisiana has many parks and wildlife refuges. The **Tensas River National Wildlife Refuge** is one of the only places to see Louisiana black bears in the wild.

Louisiana zoos also protect wildlife. The Audubon Zoo in New Orleans provides a home for rare Louisiana animals. This zoo is named for **John James Audubon** (AW duh bahn). You will read his story in the Biography after this lesson.

REVIEW Why does some wildlife need to be protected? **Draw Conclusions**

▶ Animals such as **blue herons** are protected in **Louisiana** parks, wildlife **refuges,** and **zoos.**

▶ Many deer live in the forests of the Tensas River National Wildlife Refuge.

FACT FILE

State Symbols

Here are some of Louisiana's state symbols. A symbol is an object that represents something else. These animals and plants represent Louisiana.

▶ Brown pelican, state bird

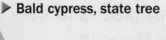
▶ Bald cypress, state tree

▶ Louisiana black bear, state mammal

▶ Alligator, state reptile

▶ Magnolia, state flower

Protecting the Coast

Louisiana's nickname is the Pelican State. Pelicans live along the coast of Louisiana. This coastal region faces a serious danger. Erosion is causing wetlands along the coast to slowly disappear. **Erosion** is the slow wearing away of land by water, wind, and other natural forces. The waters of the Gulf of Mexico are washing away, or eroding, the soil of the coastal wetlands.

Thousands of people live in this coastal region. Millions of birds and fish also rely on these coastal wetlands. That is why people in Louisiana are looking for ways to slow down coastal erosion.

REVIEW Why is coastal erosion a serious problem? **Summarize**

Summarize the Lesson

- Louisiana's parks, wildlife refuges, and zoos help protect wildlife.
- Louisiana has named some of its animals and plants as state symbols.
- Erosion is a danger to Louisiana's coast.

LESSON 2   REVIEW

Check Facts and Main Ideas

1. Draw Conclusions Copy this diagram. Fill in a conclusion you could draw from the facts.

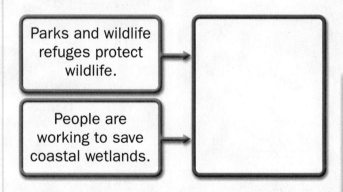

Parks and wildlife refuges protect wildlife.

People are working to save coastal wetlands.

2. How does Louisiana protect its **wildlife?**

3. Identify two animals or plants that are symbols of Louisiana.

4. How is **erosion** affecting Louisiana's coast?

5. Critical Thinking: *Express Opinions* Explain why it is important to protect Louisiana's wildlife.

> **Link to** ──◦◦── **Art**
>
> **Draw a Poster** Draw a poster showing some of the symbols of Louisiana. You can include the symbols shown on page 100. Find out what other animals and plants are symbols of our state.

Coastal Areas

Louisiana and Maine

Planting grasses on the beach helps protect the Maine coast.

You know that Louisiana's coast is in danger. This is also a problem in the state of Maine, in the northeastern part of the United States. Erosion, litter, and too much building are destroying the areas where people and wildlife live on the coasts.

Many people are taking responsibility to help protect the coasts. You can help too! One way to help is by picking up litter on the beach. Learn more about coastal areas in the pictures on these pages.

▶ Part of Maine's rocky coast is protected at Acadia National Park, below.

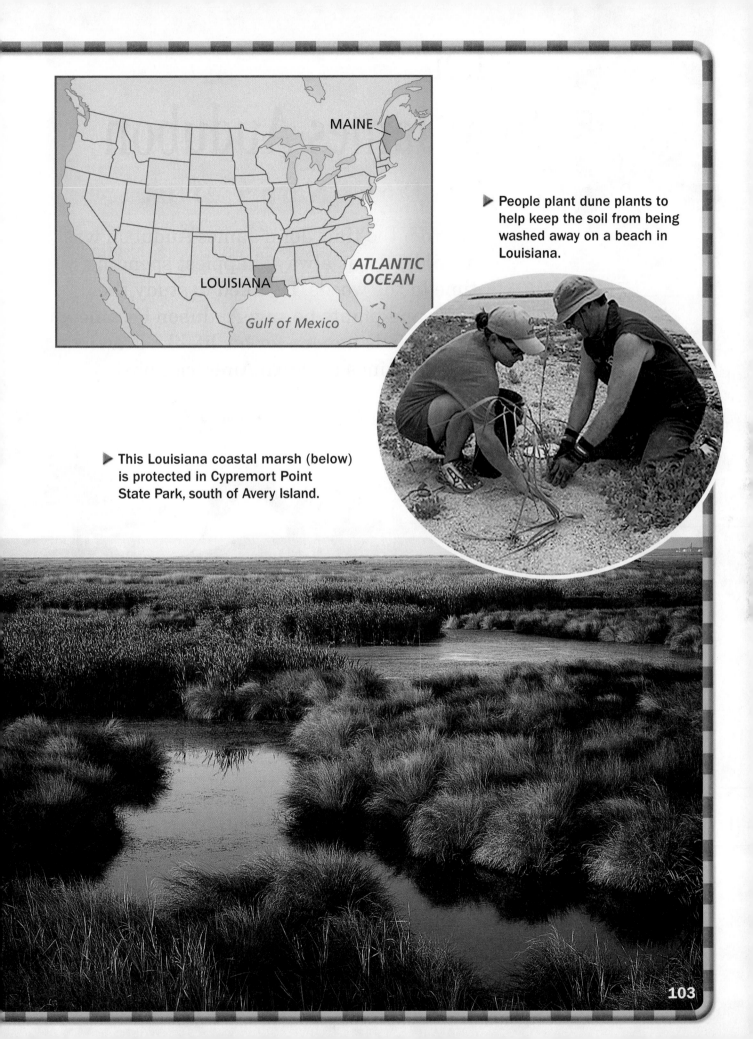

MAINE

ATLANTIC OCEAN

LOUISIANA

Gulf of Mexico

▶ People plant dune plants to help keep the soil from being washed away on a beach in Louisiana.

▶ This Louisiana coastal marsh (below) is protected in Cypremort Point State Park, south of Avery Island.

Meet
John James Audubon

1785–1851 • Nature Artist

From the time John James Audubon was a child, he was always happiest spending time in the woods. He liked to study the birds and plants he saw. Audubon became an artist. He is famous for his lifelike drawings and paintings of North America's birds.

John James Audubon was born in the country now called Haiti and spent part of his childhood in France. He came to the United States when he was 18 years old. In 1821 he arrived at a house called Oakley Plantation, about 100 miles from New Orleans. He taught drawing to a young girl whose family lived there.

Audubon was happy to come to Oakley Plantation because it had a large forest filled with birds that he could study and draw. He described Oakley Plantation in his journal,

Audubon was the first person in the United States to use "bird banding." By tying silver threads to the legs of birds, he could see which birds returned to their nests in the spring after leaving for the winter.

BIOFACT

> **"Surrounded once more by numberless warblers and thrushes [two kinds of birds], I enjoyed the scene."**

Before leaving Oakley Plantation, Audubon worked on 32 of his bird paintings. He then spent almost 20 years traveling all over the United States. He made more than 1,000 paintings of birds. These pictures were made into a series of books called *The Birds of America*.

Learn from Biographies

How did Audubon's years in Louisiana affect his work?

Audubon painted these tanagers (above) and the Louisiana heron (opposite page).

Students can research the lives of significant people by clicking on *Meet the People* at **www.sfsocialstudies.com**.

Today's main offshore oil fields are in the North Sea, Gulf of Mexico, Persian Gulf, and off the coasts of South America and Asia. Many people work on offshore oil platforms to drill for oil and natural gas.

Dead plants and bacteria from ancient seas fell to the seafloor and were covered by mud layers. Heat and pressure turned them into oil, and then into gas.

Oil platforms called rigs are built in sections on shore. The largest section is towed out to sea and tipped upright onto the seabed, then living quarters are added. A tall steel tower called a derrick holds drilling equipment.

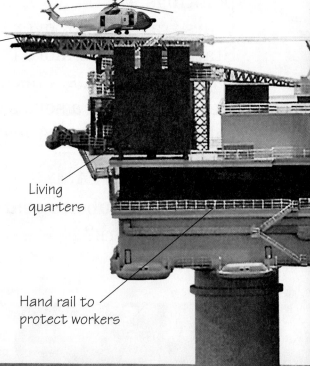

A helicopter brings fresh food to the platform.

Helicopter pad

Living quarters

Hand rail to protect workers

Helicopters deliver supplies to oil platforms far out at sea. Up to 400 people can live and work on an oil platform. Workers fly by helicopter for breaks onshore every few weeks.

The tallest structure on this platform is the flare stack, which is used for safety reasons.

A flare stack burns off any gas that rises with the oil and cannot be used.

Derrick

Oxygen is carried in cylinders on the back.

Divers who explore the deep sea for oil wear special thick-walled "hardsuits." In a suit such as this, divers can explore the ocean floor more than a thousand feet deep. Joints in the arms and legs allow the diver to move.

The crane raises supplies up to the platform from ships

On an oil platform, some people work on deck operating the drill. Others work inside with computers. Geologists (earth scientists) examine rock, oil, and gas samples. Mechanics keep the machines going. Cooks and cleaners look after the crew.

Fireproof lifeboats give people a better chance of survival in case of an emergency.

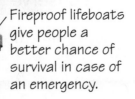

A strong structure protects the oil platform from wind and waves.

Chapter Summary

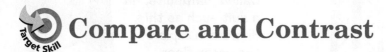 Compare and Contrast

On a separate sheet of paper, copy the diagram below. Fill in the boxes to compare and contrast Louisiana's natural resources and wildlife.

Natural Resources and Wildlife

Alike	Different

Vocabulary

Write a paragraph using each vocabulary word below. Include details you learned from this chapter in each sentence.

scarcity (p. 92)   conserve (p. 93)

abundance (p. 92)   wildlife (p. 99)

Facts and Main Ideas

1 Which of Louisiana's resources did Edmund McIlhenny use to make his sauce?

2 How does the Audubon Zoo help protect Louisiana's wildlife?

3 **Main Idea** What are natural resources? Name two natural resources found in Louisiana.

4 **Main Idea** How does coastal erosion affect Louisiana's wildlife?

5 **Critical Thinking: *Draw Conclusions*** You have read that trees are an important natural resource in Louisiana. What do you think might happen if people do not conserve trees?

Internet Activity

To get help with vocabulary, people, and terms, select the dictionary or encyclopedia from *Social Studies Library* at **www.sfsocialstudies.com.**

Write About It

1 **Write a postcard** to a friend from the Tensas River National Wildlife Refuge. Talk about the animals you have seen.

2 **Write a paragraph** about one state symbol. Tell why you think it represents Louisiana well.

3 **Write a newspaper article** for a 1901 newspaper about the discovery of oil near Jennings. Explain how people living there felt about this discovery.

Apply Skills

Use Intermediate Directions Use the map on page 96 to answer the questions below.

1 In what direction is Highway 510 from the New Orleans Swamp Tours?

2 In which two intermediate directions is Lake Pontchartrain from the Bayou Sauvage National Wildlife Refuge?

3 In what direction is the boat ramp from Chef Menteur Pass?

Louisiana

By Jean McGivney Boese

This poem describes the beauty of nature in Louisiana. How many different kinds of animals can you count in the poem? Why do you think the writer loves our state?

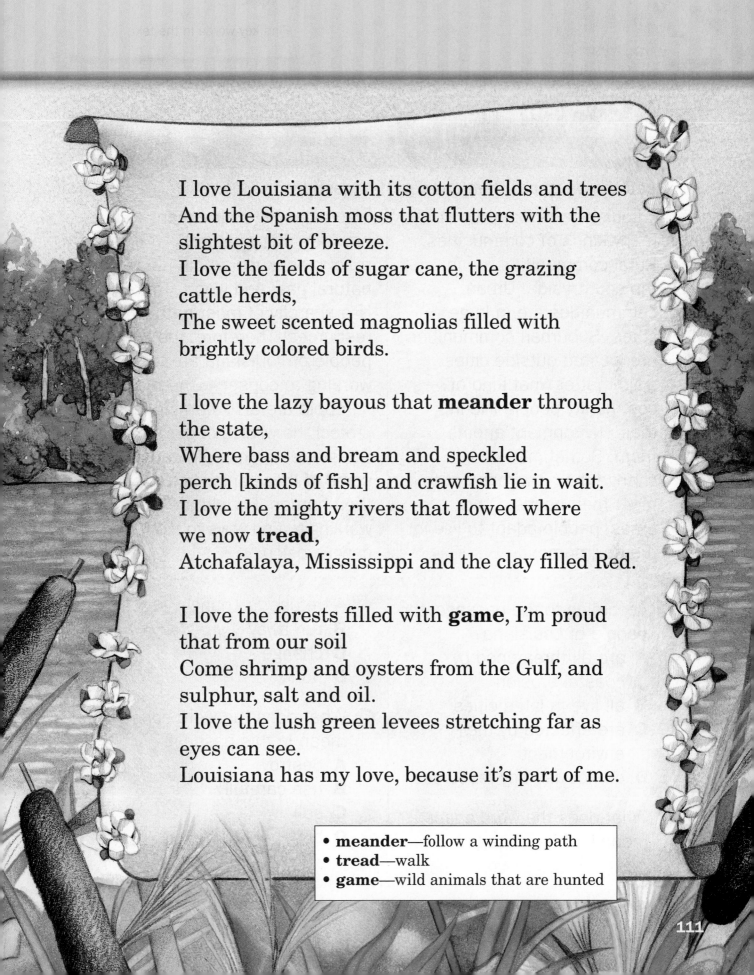

I love Louisiana with its cotton fields and trees
And the Spanish moss that flutters with the
slightest bit of breeze.
I love the fields of sugar cane, the grazing
cattle herds,
The sweet scented magnolias filled with
brightly colored birds.

I love the lazy bayous that **meander** through
the state,
Where bass and bream and speckled
perch [kinds of fish] and crawfish lie in wait.
I love the mighty rivers that flowed where
we now **tread**,
Atchafalaya, Mississippi and the clay filled Red.

I love the forests filled with **game**, I'm proud
that from our soil
Come shrimp and oysters from the Gulf, and
sulphur, salt and oil.
I love the lush green levees stretching far as
eyes can see.
Louisiana has my love, because it's part of me.

- **meander**—follow a winding path
- **tread**—walk
- **game**—wild animals that are hunted

Review

Main Ideas and Vocabulary

TEST PREP

Read the passage. Then answer the questions.

Louisiana is made up of many kinds of communities. Rural communities are in the countryside. Urban communities are in large cities. Suburban communities are located outside cities.

No matter what kind of community people live in, their environment affects them. Sometimes people change their environment to meet their needs. Other times, people <u>adapt</u> to live in the environment.

Louisiana's environment provides many natural resources, such as oil, natural gas, and wood. There is a scarcity of most natural resources. Therefore, the people of Louisiana are working to <u>conserve</u> them.

People are also working to protect the wildlife of our state. Coastal erosion could cause some of these animals to lose their homes. People are working to find ways to slow down erosion.

1 According to the passage, the people of Louisiana
   A are all threatened by coastal erosion
   B all live in large cities
   C are affected by their environment
   D do not use any resources

2 What does the word *adapt* mean in this passage?

   A refuse to change
   B run away
   C change
   D hurry

3 What does the word *conserve* mean in this passage?
   A destroy
   B use carefully
   C sell
   D buy

Vocabulary

Copy the sentences. Fill in each space with the correct letter.

   a. community (p. 67)
   b. urban community (p. 67)
   c. natural resource (p. 89)
   d. erosion (p. 101)

1 _____ is slowly wearing away the coastal wetlands.

2 A _____ is a place where people live and work.

3 Oil is one _____ that can be used to make energy.

4 Lake Charles is an _____ with a large population.

Write and Share

Create a Communities Chart As a group, write "urban," "suburban," and "rural" in different columns on a large piece of paper. In each column list at least two good things about living in each community. Then draw a picture to represent each community. Finally, write a sentence explaining which kind of community you would most like to live in and why. Share your Communities Chart with your class.

Apply Skills

Use Intermediate Directions Look at this map of a carnival. Use intermediate directions to answer the questions.

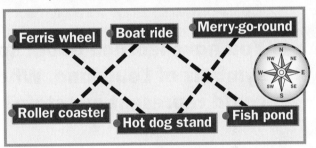

1 In what direction would you walk to get from the roller coaster to the boat ride?

2 In what direction would you walk to get from the merry-go-round to the hot dog stand?

3 In what direction would you walk to get from the fish pond to the boat ride?

Read on Your Own

Look for books like these in the library.

UNIT 2 Project

Louisiana Symbols

You have learned about some of the state symbols of Louisiana. What other things could represent our state?

1 **Form** a group.

2 **Make** a list of people, places, plants, animals, or other things that you think would make good symbols for Louisiana.

3 **Draw** pictures of the symbols on your list.

4 **Write** a sentence for each symbol telling why you think it represents Louisiana well.

5 **Show** your list of symbols to the class.

Internet Activity

For more information and activities, go to www.sfsocialstudies.com.

The Story of Louisiana

What was Louisiana like long ago?

Begin with
a Primary Source

1700

1720

1740

1760

1780

1699
Louisiana
becomes a
French colony.

1716
Enslaved Africans
are brought to
Louisiana.

1762
Spain takes
control of
Louisiana.

"Very near the village is a settlement of Indians [Native Americans] .... The women make very pretty reed cane baskets ...."

— Louisiana teacher and writer, Alcée Fortier, 1894

This painting shows a Chitimacha village from long ago. The Chitimacha are Native Americans from Louisiana.

1800

1820

1840

1860

1880

1803
The Louisiana Purchase doubles the size of the United States.

1812
Louisiana becomes a state.

1849
Louisiana's capital moves to Baton Rouge.

1861
The Civil War begins.

1865
The Civil War ends and Reconstruction begins.

Meet the People

Hernando de Soto

1496?–1542
Birthplace: Spain
Explorer
- Left Spain and sailed across the Atlantic Ocean when he was a teenager
- Led a journey across the southeastern United States to search for gold
- Led a group of the first Europeans to reach the Mississippi River

Bernardo de Gálvez

1746–1786
Birthplace: Spain
Army officer, governor
- Was an officer in the Spanish army in Louisiana
- Became governor of the Spanish colony of Louisiana in 1777
- Helped the Americans during the American Revolution

P. G. T. Beauregard

1818–1893
Birthplace: St. Bernard Parish, Louisiana
Army officer
- Graduated from the United States Military Academy at West Point
- Left the United States army to become a general in the Confederate army
- Fought in major battles during the Civil War

1500　　　　　1550　　　　1700　　　　　1750

1496? • Hernando de Soto 1542

1746 • Bernardo de Gálvez

Students can research the lives of significant people by clicking on *Meet the People* at **www.sfsocialstudies.com.**

Louis C. Roudanez

1823–1890

Birthplace: St. James Parish, Louisiana

Doctor, newspaper publisher

- As a doctor, treated black and white patients
- Started the first daily newspaper published by African Americans in the United States
- Printed the *New Orleans Tribune* in both English and French

Sarah Morgan

1842–1909

Birthplace: New Orleans, Louisiana

Writer

- Kept a diary about her experiences during the Civil War
- Wrote articles for the Charleston *Daily News*
- Had her diary published by her son under the title *A Confederate Girl's Diary*

1800	1850	1900	1950

1786

1818 • P. G. T. Beauregard   1893

1823 • Louis C. Roudanez   1890

1842 • Sarah Morgan   1909

119

Reading Social Studies

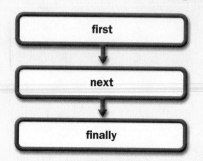

In What Order?

Sequence

- Sequence is the order in which events take place.
- One way to find sequence is to put dates in order.
- Words such as *first, after, next, finally, then,* and *later* can also help you find the sequence of events.

first

↓

next

↓

finally

Read the following paragraph. Words that help show sequence are highlighted in blue. Dates are highlighted in yellow.

First, Native Americans came to the land of Louisiana. Next, in 1682, La Salle claimed it for France. Then Louisiana belonged to several different countries. The United States bought Louisiana in 1803, and made it a state in 1812. Later, Louisiana joined the Confederate states in the Civil War. After the war, Louisiana became part of the United States again.

Word Exercise

Irregular verbs do not follow a regular pattern. Regular verbs—such as *decide*—have *-ed* added to create the past tense form of *decided*. Irregular verbs have a different past tense form. One example is shown below.

Present	Past
become	became

The path *becomes* very steep here.

We *became* very tired after walking for an hour.

Flags of Louisiana

Many flags have flown over Louisiana. Our state has been a part of several nations.

First, Native Americans came to the land that is now Louisiana. In 1682 the French explorer Robert La Salle claimed the land for France.

Later, France, Britain, and Spain ruled parts of Louisiana at different times.

In 1803 the United States bought Louisiana from France. Louisiana became the 18th state in 1812.

The Civil War began in 1861. A few months before that, Louisiana was briefly an independent country. Then it joined the Confederate states.

A few years after the Civil War, Louisiana joined the United States again. In 1912 Louisiana chose the state flag that it uses today.

Apply it!

Use the reading skill of sequence to answer questions 1 and 2. Then answer the vocabulary question.

❶ Did Louisiana join the Confederate states in the Civil War before or after it was purchased by the United States?

❷ Name three words in the passage, other than dates, that show sequence.

❸ List three words from the passage that are irregular verbs.

Lesson 1

Poverty Point

Poverty Point was built by Native Americans thousands of years ago.

1

Lesson 2

Natchitoches

Natchitoches is the oldest permanent settlement in Louisiana.

2

CANADA

NORTH AMERICA

UNITED STATES

ATLANTIC OCEAN

PACIFIC OCEAN

2   1

Poverty Point

Natchitoches

LOUISIANA

Gulf of Mexico

MEXICO

Why We Remember

Did you ever wonder how our state and cities got their names? Some cities, such as Opelousas, were named after Native Americans. They were the first people to live in this land. Louisiana was named by people who came here from France. You will learn more about the history of Louisiana in this chapter.

Poverty Point

The First People of Louisiana

Preview

Focus on the Main Idea
Native Americans were the first people to live in the land that is now Louisiana.

PLACE
Poverty Point

PEOPLE
Lovelin Poncho

VOCABULARY
settlement

You Are There It is hundreds of years ago and you are living in what is now Louisiana. You watch the adults get ready for a deer hunt. Soon you will be old enough to hunt too. You are allowed to help make arrow-shaped spear tips from stones.

Your sister helps by looking for food in the forest. She joins the other girls and women to look for berries, nuts, seeds, and plants. You and your sister help to feed your family and other members of your group.

Sequence As you read, look for details about how the way of life of Native Americans changed over time.

▶ Early Native Americans used arrow-shaped spear tips like these to hunt for food.

Early Native Americans

Many scientists believe that people first arrived in Louisiana about 15,000 years ago. Scientists have studied artifacts left by the first people. Artifacts are objects made by people in the past, such as spear points.

Early Native Americans moved from place to place in search of food. They used spears to hunt animals such as deer. They also caught fish and gathered plants.

Later, groups of Native Americans began to settle down. One group started a settlement at **Poverty Point.** A **settlement** is a place where people live. Today ridges, or raised hills, that people built from the land remain at Poverty Point.

REVIEW When did people first come to Louisiana? ⟳ **Sequence**

▶ Scientists found artifacts like these cooking stones at Poverty Point. The stones were heated and packed around food to cook it.

▶ This diagram shows the different parts of Poverty Point. Scientists are not sure why the people of Poverty Point built ridges and mounds, but the scientists have some ideas.

DIAGRAM SKILL *How many rows of ridges are at Poverty Point?*

The mounds may have been used as burial places.

Rows of ridges were built in a half circle. Homes may have been built on the ridges.

Mounds

Games, dances, or other activities may have taken place in the center plaza.

Bayou Macon

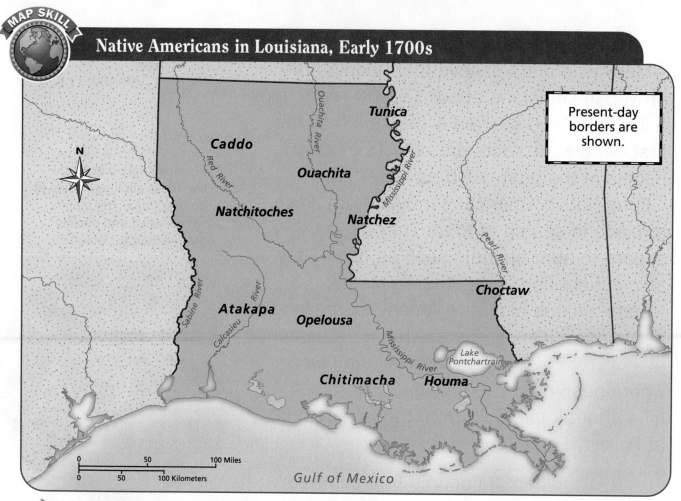

Native Americans in Louisiana, Early 1700s

Tunica

Caddo

Ouachita River

Red River

Mississippi River

Present-day borders are shown.

N

Ouachita

Natchitoches

Natchez

Pearl River

Sabine River

Calcasieu River

Atakapa

Opelousa

Mississippi River

Choctaw

Lake Pontchartrain

Chitimacha

Houma

0   50   100 Miles

0   50   100 Kilometers

Gulf of Mexico

▶ This map shows where major Native American groups were located in Louisiana in the early 1700s.

MAP SKILL **Human-Environment Interaction** *Near which river did the Ouachita live?*

New People Arrive

By the year 1500, several Native American groups lived in what is now Louisiana. The groups included the Natchez, Caddo, Choctaw, and the Chitimacha.

Native Americans used the environment to meet all of their needs. For example, the Caddo used grass and wood to build homes that looked like beehives. Native Americans still hunted, fished, and gathered plants for food like earlier people. They also grew crops such as corn, squash, and beans.

▶ Several Caddo families could live in one of the cone-shaped homes.

By the early 1700s, Europeans began to settle in Louisiana. Native Americans and Europeans traded goods. They shared ideas about how to grow crops. They also fought over land. Many Native Americans were killed in wars or forced to leave Louisiana.

Today about 25,000 Native Americans live in Louisiana. One group is the Coushatta (koo SHAH tuh). **Lovelin Poncho** is one of the group's leaders. He writes, "We have a colorful history that must be remembered for all our children."

REVIEW When did Europeans begin to settle in Louisiana? ↻ **Sequence**

Summarize the Lesson

- Scientists believe that the earliest Native Americans came to Louisiana about 15,000 years ago.
- Native Americans used the environment to meet their needs.
- Europeans began to settle in Louisiana in the early 1700s.

LESSON 1 REVIEW

Check Facts and Main Ideas

1. ↻ **Sequence** Copy the chart on a piece of paper. Fill in the missing events about Louisiana's history.

```
┌─────────────────────────────────────┐
│      About 15,000 years ago          │
│ Native Americans first came to Louisiana. │
└─────────────────────────────────────┘
                   │
                   ▼
┌─────────────────────────────────────┐
│               1500                   │
└─────────────────────────────────────┘
                   │
                   ▼
┌─────────────────────────────────────┐
│            Early 1700s               │
└─────────────────────────────────────┘
```

2. How did the earliest Native Americans in Louisiana adapt to the environment?

3. What can you see at the Poverty Point **settlement** today?

4. What Native American groups lived in Louisiana by 1500? How did they use the environment to meet their needs?

5. **Critical Thinking:** *Cause and Effect* How did the arrival of Europeans affect Native Americans?

Link to ∞ **Science**

Study a Diagram Suppose you are a scientist studying the ridges at Poverty Point. Study the diagram on page 125. Then write a letter to a friend describing the ridges at the early settlement.

Use a Time Line

What? A time line shows when events occurred. The time line can be divided into sections of single years, decades, or even centuries. A **decade** is 10 years. A **century** is 100 years. The events are placed on the time line in the sequence, or order, that they happened. Look at the time line showing important events in Louisiana between 1700 and 1800.

Why? Time lines can help you find out when something happened in history. They can also help you compare when events happened. Time lines can be very helpful as you read a social studies book.

1716
Fort St. Jean Baptiste is built.

1722
New Orleans becomes the capital of Louisiana.

1736
St. John's Hospital is founded in New Orleans. It is now Charity Hospital.

| 1700 | 1710 | 1720 | 1730 | 1740 | 1750 |

1716
The first enslaved Africans are brought to Louisiana.

1751
Sugarcane is first planted in Louisiana.

How? Start a time line in your notebook based on this chapter. Write in the date 1500. That is when many Native American groups were already living in the land that is now Louisiana. As you read through the chapter, keep a list of dates and events. At the end of the chapter, put all your dates together in order. Use the time line you started. Make sure to write what happened next to each date.

Look at the time line on these pages and answer the questions.

1 In what **decade** was St. John's Hospital founded?

2 When was sugarcane first planted in Louisiana?

3 Did the Acadians arrive before or after France gave control of Louisiana to Spain?

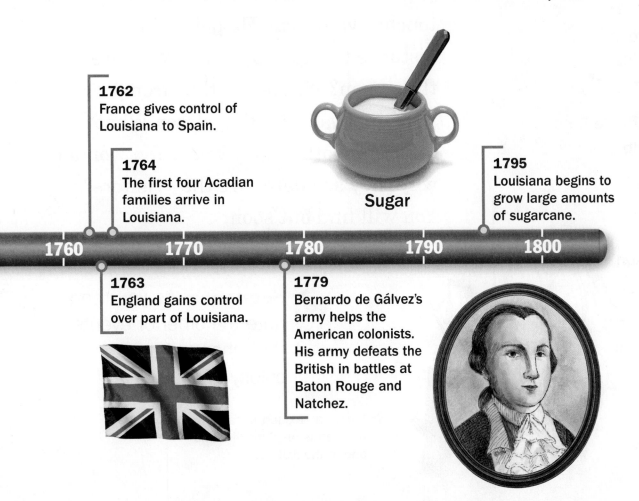

1762
France gives control of Louisiana to Spain.

1764
The first four Acadian families arrive in Louisiana.

Sugar

1795
Louisiana begins to grow large amounts of sugarcane.

1760   1770   1780   1790   1800

1763
England gains control over part of Louisiana.

1779
Bernardo de Gálvez's army helps the American colonists. His army defeats the British in battles at Baton Rouge and Natchez.

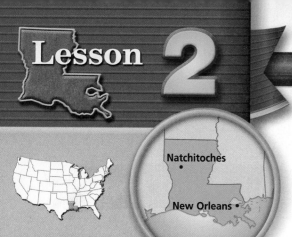

Natchitoches

New Orleans •

1700   1730   1760

1699 Louisiana becomes a colony of France.

1716 Enslaved Africans are first brought to Louisiana.

1762 Spain gains control of Louisiana.

The Colony of Louisiana

Preview

Focus on the Main Idea
Early explorers and settlers helped to build communities in the land of Louisiana.

PLACES
Natchitoches
New Orleans

PEOPLE
Hernando de Soto
Bernardo de Gálvez

VOCABULARY
colony
slavery
plantation

You Are There What a beautiful spring day! You are a Native American living in what is now Louisiana hundreds of years ago. You are walking near the river with your father. Suddenly your father touches your arm. He points in the distance to a group of men. Who are those men? Where are they from?

Now they are getting closer. What different clothes they wear! You wonder why they are here. Are they visitors? You will find out soon.

 Sequence As you read, note the order of events that changed the colony of Louisiana.

▶ European explorers sailed to new lands on ships like this one in the 1500s.

Europeans Arrive

In 1541 **Hernando de Soto** led a group of the first Europeans to reach the Mississippi River and arrive in what is now Louisiana. De Soto was from Spain. He came to look for gold, but he never found it. More than 100 years later, Robert La Salle came here. He claimed the land for France and called it Louisiana in 1682.

England and Spain already had colonies in the area. A **colony** is a place that is ruled by another country. The French king did not want England and Spain to get control of Louisiana. He sent other explorers to the area to start settlements. Louisiana became a colony of France in 1699.

▶ When Europeans and Native Americans met, they began to trade goods and to share ideas.

REVIEW Why did the French king make Louisiana a colony? **Cause and Effect**

New Colonists

Many Europeans moved to Louisiana to settle in the colony. Many of these early colonists came by France and Germany. Colonists are people who live in a colony.

The early colonists of Louisiana often lived in forts, or small villages built near a wall. Forts protected colonists from possible attacks by Native Americans and other Europeans. Settlers traded goods with Native Americans and other colonists at trading posts. Trading posts were often located in forts. One trading post was set up in 1716 at **Natchitoches** (NAK uh tish) on the Red River. Natchitoches, founded in 1714, is the oldest permanent settlement in Louisiana.

REVIEW How did forts protect colonists?
Draw Conclusions

▶ This woman is showing what cooking was like at Fort St. Jean Baptiste hundreds of years ago.

Then and Now

Natchitoches: A Historic Place

Colonists built Fort St. Jean Baptiste in Natchitoches in 1716. They traded goods such as cotton and gold there. Today, Natchitoches is a busy city with shops, restaurants, and a university.

▶ Visitors today can learn about life in Natchitoches many years ago. Actors show how people lived and dressed in earlier times.

▶ People still buy and sell goods in Natchitoches, but today many more people live there!

132

Slavery and Plantations

Some people who lived in the colony of Louisiana came from Africa. They were taken from their homes and forced to come here as slaves. **Slavery** is a system in which people are owned by other people and forced to work.

The first enslaved Africans were brought to Louisiana in 1716. Many brought special skills with them from Africa. For example, some enslaved people were skilled in rice growing and shipbuilding.

Most enslaved people were forced to work on plantations. A **plantation** is a large farm where crops such as sugarcane or cotton are grown. Many plantation owners became rich by selling these crops. However, the growth of plantations caused owners to want more enslaved people.

▶ Enslaved people worked on plantations cutting sugarcane, above. They lived in very simple houses.

REVIEW Why were Africans first brought to Louisiana? **Summarize**

"Evangeline"
by Henry Wadsworth Longfellow

"Evangeline" is a poem about Acadians who came to Louisiana. Acadians were French settlers in Canada. They were forced to leave when the British took control of French Canada in 1755. Like many Acadians, the characters in the poem came to Louisiana. Acadians in Louisiana were later called Cajuns. This part of the poem tells about the beauty of the land along Bayou Teche.

▶ Henry Wadsworth Longfellow

Beautiful is the land, with its prairies [fields of grass]
and forests of fruit trees;
Under the feet a garden of flowers, and the bluest of heavens [skies]
Bending above, and resting its dome on the walls of the forest.
They who dwell [live] there have named it the
Eden [garden] of Louisiana!

▶ The Cabildo, in New Orleans, was a government building when Spain ruled Louisiana. Today it is a museum.

A Growing Colony

The colonists in Louisiana earned money by selling crops to people in other colonies and in France. With the money they earned, Louisiana colonists bought goods such as furniture. The French wanted to build a port on the Mississippi River to make shipping goods easier. As a result, colonists founded the city of **New Orleans** in 1718. It was named after the Duke of Orleans, a ruler in France.

New Orleans grew, and more colonists came to Louisiana. Some colonists were from Acadia, in Canada. The poem in the Literature and Social Studies above is about Acadians.

In 1754 Europeans went to war for control of the land in North America. France lost the war and had to give control of Louisiana to Spain in 1762. One of the leaders of Spanish Louisiana was **Bernardo de Gálvez.**

During the American Revolution, Gálvez helped the American colonies win their freedom from Britain. You will learn more about Gálvez in the Biography on pages 138 and 139.

REVIEW Why did the French build New Orleans? **Main Idea and Details**

Summarize the Lesson

- **1699** Louisiana became a colony of France.
- **1716** Slavery began in Louisiana.
- **1762** Spain gained control of the Louisiana colony.

LESSON 2 REVIEW

Check Facts and Main Ideas

1. **Sequence** Complete this chart on a separate sheet of paper. List five major events from this lesson in the order they happened. Include a date for each event.

2. How did early explorers affect Louisiana?

3. How is Natchitoches today alike and different than it was in 1716?

4. Describe the types of communities colonists lived in, such as forts and **plantations.**

5. **Critical Thinking:** *Summarize* Describe three major events that happened in the Louisiana **colony** in the 1700s.

Link to — **Art**

Draw a Picture Reread part of the poem "Evangeline" on page 134. On a separate piece of paper, draw a picture that describes a scene in the poem.

Cajun Beginnings
Louisiana and Nova Scotia

You learned that the French Acadians were forced to leave their homes in Acadia in the 1700s. Present-day Nova Scotia is part of what was once Acadia. Thousands of Acadians settled in southern Louisiana. Many became farmers or caught fish. Louisianans whose relatives came here from Acadia long ago are still called Cajuns.

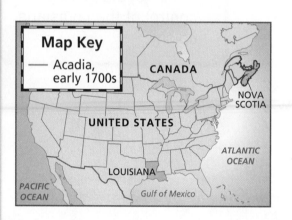

Map Key
— Acadia, early 1700s

CANADA
NOVA SCOTIA
UNITED STATES
ATLANTIC OCEAN
LOUISIANA
PACIFIC OCEAN
Gulf of Mexico

▶ **These men play Cajun music on the triangle and the accordion. Many Cajuns live near the wetlands of southern Louisiana, right, or the prairies of South Central Louisiana.**

Cajuns mixed their customs with those of other Louisiana settlers. They created their own style of cooking, music, and language. Some Cajuns still speak a form of the French language in their daily lives. Look at the photographs. What is one example of the Cajun way of life today?

▶ The mural *The Arrival of the Acadians in Louisiana* by Robert Dafford is at the Acadian Memorial in St. Martinville. It honors the first Acadians who came to Louisiana.

▶ Fishing towns like this one are common in Nova Scotia today. Some Cajuns still make a living catching fish in Louisiana.

Meet
Bernardo de Gálvez

1746–1786
Spanish Governor of Louisiana

Bernardo de Gálvez grew up in Spain. He joined the army at the age of 16. Gálvez fought in many battles in Europe and North America. He is best known for helping the colonists defeat the British in the American Revolution.

As you have read, Spain gained control of Louisiana in 1762. Gálvez came to Louisiana in 1776 as a member of the Spanish army. The next year, he became the governor, or leader, of the Spanish colony of Louisiana.

During the American Revolution, Gálvez helped the colonists in many ways. He controlled the port of New Orleans because he was governor of the Louisiana colony. He would not allow British ships to deliver supplies to British soldiers along the Mississippi River. He only let American, Spanish, and French ships sail on the Mississippi River. These ships brought the American troops weapons, money, food, and medicine.

Gálvez's troops defeated the British at Baton Rouge and Natchez. This forced the British to leave Louisiana. Gálvez and his troops also defeated the British at Pensacola in western Florida. His victories over the British were a great help to the American colonies.

The city of Galveston in Texas is named after Bernardo de Gálvez.

BIOFACT

Learn from Biographies

What is one way Bernardo de Gálvez helped the colonists defeat the British during the American Revolution?

 Students can research the lives of significant people by clicking on *Meet the People* at **www.sfsocialstudies.com.**

1650	1675	1700

1699
Louisiana becomes a
colony of France.

Chapter Summary

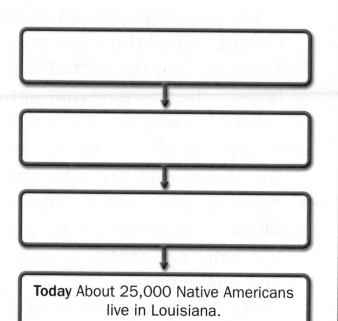

Sequence

Target Skill

Make a chart like this one on a
sheet of paper. Put the events
below in the order they happened.
Include the correct date.

- About 25,000 Native Americans
  live in Louisiana.

- Hernando de Soto's group arrives
  in what is now Louisiana.

- New Orleans is founded.

- Europeans begin to settle in
  Louisiana.

Today About 25,000 Native Americans
live in Louisiana.

Vocabulary

Match each word with the correct definition or description.

1 settlement (p. 125)

2 colony (p. 131)

3 slavery (p. 133)

4 plantation (p. 133)

a. a large farm where crops such as
sugarcane or cotton are grown

b. a place where people live

c. a system in which people are
forced to work for other people

d. a place that is ruled by another
country

1716
Enslaved Africans
are first brought
to Louisiana.

1762
Spain gains control
of Louisiana.

Facts and Main Ideas

1 How did early Native American groups adapt to Louisiana's environment?

2 How did slavery begin in Louisiana?

3 **Time Line** According to the time line above, which country ruled Louisiana first, France or Spain?

4 **Main Idea** Who were the first people to come to Louisiana?

5 **Main Idea** Why did early colonists build forts?

6 **Critical Thinking:** *Draw Conclusions* Why would people have to settle in one place before they can grow crops as a way of getting food?

Internet Activity

To get help with vocabulary, people, and terms, select the dictionary or encyclopedia from *Social Studies Library* at **www.sfsocialstudies.com.**

Write About It

1 **Write a list** of three things you would build first if you were an explorer starting a settlement in Louisiana.

2 **Write a paragraph** explaining what you think life was like for Native Americans before Europeans arrived.

3 **Write a letter** as a colonist in Natchitoches in the early 1700s. Describe daily life in the colony for a friend back in France.

Apply Skills

Use a Time Line Look at the Louisiana cities below and the dates they were founded. Make a time line. Put the cities on your time line in the correct order.

a. 1718 New Orleans

b. 1714 Natchitoches

c. 1720 Opelousas

d. 1719 Baton Rouge

Lesson 1

1815
New Orleans

Andrew Jackson defeated the British in the Battle of New Orleans.

1

Lesson 2

1863
Port Hudson

Confederate soldiers fought for 48 days to defend Port Hudson during the Civil War.

2

Why We Remember

The 1800s was an exciting and difficult time for the people of Louisiana. It became a state in the United States in 1812. However, people in Northern and Southern states had strong disagreements. In 1861 the North and the South went to war. The war ended in 1865. The results changed Louisiana forever.

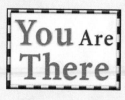

1800   1825   1850

1803
President Thomas Jefferson buys Louisiana from France.

1812
Louisiana becomes a state.

1849
Baton Rouge becomes Louisiana's capital.

New Orleans

A New State

Preview

Focus on the Main Idea
Louisiana went through many changes after it became a state in the United States.

PLACE
New Orleans

PEOPLE
Thomas Jefferson

VOCABULARY
Louisiana Purchase

▶ Beignets

You Are There The year is 1800. You and your family left Pennsylvania for the colony of Louisiana. You have been on a long boat ride down the Mississippi River.

Finally, you arrive in New Orleans. You hear people speaking different languages. Some people speak French. Others speak Spanish or English.

Your family walks into a small bakery. It smells wonderful. The owner hands you a French doughnut called a *beignet* (bin YAY). It tastes delicious. You are going to love living in New Orleans!

Sequence As you read, note the order that events occurred.

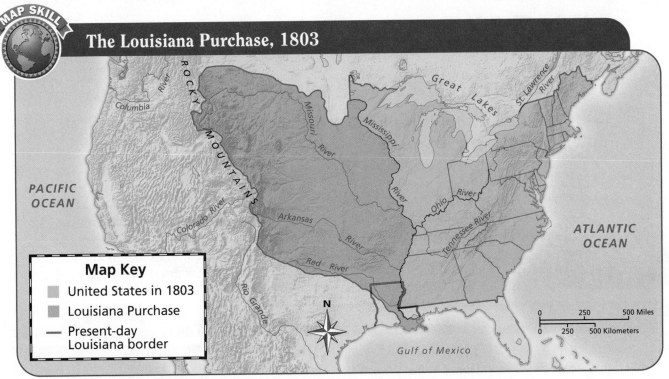

ROCKY MOUNTAINS

Columbia River

Missouri River

Mississippi River

Great Lakes

St. Lawrence River

Ohio River

Tennessee River

Colorado River

Arkansas River

Red River

Rio Grande

PACIFIC OCEAN

ATLANTIC OCEAN

N

Gulf of Mexico

Map Key

United States in 1803

Louisiana Purchase

— Present-day Louisiana border

0   250   500 Miles

0   250   500 Kilometers

▶ The United States paid France 15 million dollars for the Louisiana Purchase.

MAP SKILL Understand Borders *Did the Louisiana Purchase include part of present-day Louisiana? How can you tell?*

The Louisiana Purchase

By 1800 Spain had given Louisiana back to France. The President of the United States, **Thomas Jefferson,** offered to buy the port of **New Orleans** and some nearby land from France. The port would give the United States control of trade along the Mississippi River.

In 1803 France sold New Orleans. France also sold a huge amount of land west of the Mississippi River. The sale was called the **Louisiana Purchase.** It doubled the amount of land of the United States.

In 1812 Louisiana became the 18th state of the United States. Its population grew. Many Americans moved here to own their own land.

▶ Artist Rembrandt Peale painted this picture of Thomas Jefferson.

REVIEW Why did Thomas Jefferson want to buy New Orleans? **Main Idea and Details**

145

Louisiana Time Line: 1810–1850

Many things changed for the people of Louisiana in the first half of the 1800s. Read about some of the events below.

1815
The United States fought against Great Britain again in the War of 1812. General Andrew Jackson defeated the British in the Battle of New Orleans in 1815.

1849
Louisiana's capital moved from New Orleans to Baton Rouge in 1849. A new government building was built there (below).

1810	1820	1830	1840	1850

1812
Louisiana became a state in 1812. William Claiborne was our state's first governor, or state leader.

1816
Henry Miller Shreve first traveled in his steamboat *Washington* on the Mississippi River in 1816. Steamboats helped Louisiana ports become important shipping centers.

▶ William Claiborne

A Divided Country

By the middle 1800s, the United States had become a divided country. People in Northern and Southern states disagreed over several issues. Many Southerners believed in states' rights. They believed each state could refuse to obey a law passed by the United States government. Many Northerners believed that no state could refuse to obey a law passed by the United States government.

Slavery was one of the issues related to states' rights. By the early 1800s, most Northern states had outlawed slavery. Some people from the North wanted to end slavery in all states.

However, many Southerners thought of slavery as part of their way of life. Some wealthy Southern farmers believed they could not grow enough crops without the work of enslaved people.

Many people in the South feared that the United States government would pass a law ending slavery in all states. They believed Southern states should form their own government. Some people worried that war would break out between Northern and Southern states if that happened.

REVIEW Over what issues did Northerners and Southerners disagree?
Summarize

Summarize the Lesson

- **1803** The United States bought Louisiana from France.
- **1812** Louisiana became a state in the United States.
- **1849** Louisiana's state capital moved from New Orleans to Baton Rouge.

LESSON 1   REVIEW

Check Facts and Main Ideas

1. **Sequence** Copy the chart on a separate sheet of paper. Choose three events you learned in the lesson and put them in the correct sequence. Include the date of each event.

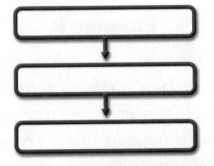

2. How did the Louisiana Purchase affect Louisiana's population?

3. Name two events that happened in Louisiana in the first half of the 1800s. Why were they important to Louisiana's history?

4. What was one issue that divided the United States in the middle 1800s?

5. **Critical Thinking: *Interpret Maps*** Look at the map on page 145. List the major bodies of water that were near or part of the Louisiana Purchase.

Link to Writing

Write About an Event Choose one of the events from the time line on page 146. Do research in your library to find out more information about it. Write a paragraph explaining what you learned.

Compare Primary and Secondary Sources

What? **Primary sources** are descriptions of events written by people who were there. A primary source could be a diary or an interview. Passage A is a primary source. It is a story about an enslaved person written in his own words.

Secondary sources are descriptions of events written by people who were not there. The author finds facts about an event and then writes them down. An example is a history textbook or an encyclopedia. Passage B is a secondary source about slavery.

Why? Both primary and secondary sources can teach you about events in history. Primary sources give you an idea of what it was like for one person to live through an event. Secondary sources can give facts about many different sides of an event.

Passage A

"My thoughts, as usual, wandered back to my wife and children. . .my heart was at home in Saratoga."

▶ *Twelve Years a Slave*, by Solomon Northrup, was published in 1853.

Passage B

Husbands and wives could be parted without warning. . . Children over the age of ten could be sold away from their mothers.

▶ This secondary source comes from a recent book about the history of Louisiana.

How? To find out if a text is a primary source, look for clue words that describe what the author thinks or feels. These can be words such as "I," or "we," or words that show emotions such as sadness or excitement.

Secondary sources usually include more general information about an event. Look for facts and details such as numbers or dates.

Think and Apply

1. What kind of source would tell you about someone's personal experiences as a slave?

2. What kind of source would tell you about the history of slavery in Louisiana over many years?

3. What clues tell you that Passage A is a **primary source?**

$100 REWARD! RANAWAY

TO BE SOLD & LET BY PUBLIC AUCTION, On MONDAY the 18th of MAY, 1829, UNDER THE TREES. FOR SALE, THE THREE FOLLOWING SLAVES,

▶ During slavery times, posters were used to announce when enslaved people would be sold or when a reward was offered for an enslaved person who had escaped.

1860   1865   1870

1861
The Civil
War begins.

1863
Union troops
gain control of
Port Hudson.

1865
The Civil War ends
and Reconstruction
begins.

Port Hudson

The Civil War

Preview

Focus on the Main Idea
The people of Louisiana faced many challenges during the Civil War and Reconstruction.

PLACE
Port Hudson

PEOPLE
P. G. T. Beauregard
Sarah Morgan
Louis C. Roudanez

VOCABULARY
Confederate States of America
Union
Civil War
Reconstruction

You Are There
It is November 1860. The newspaper headlines say that Abraham Lincoln has been elected President of the United States. Recently the North and South have become more divided over the issue of slavery. Now that Lincoln has been elected, you hear some adults talk about a possible war between the Northern and Southern states.

You wonder what will happen in Louisiana if there is a war. Will slavery end? Will the North and the South become two different countries?

Sequence As you read, note the order in which events took place during the Civil War.

▶ Abraham Lincoln

The War Begins

Many Southerners believed Lincoln would weaken states' rights and try to end slavery. So, Southern states began to leave the United States in 1860. They formed a new government called the **Confederate States of America,** or the Confederacy. A confederacy is a group of states joined together. Louisiana joined the Confederacy in March 1861.

The Northern states, or the **Union,** did not want the Southern states to leave. Fighting broke out between Union and Confederate soldiers on April 12, 1861. The soldiers fought at Fort Sumter, in South Carolina. The **Civil War** had begun.

▶ Louisianan P. G. T. Beauregard led Confederate troops at Fort Sumter.

REVIEW What two sides fought in the Civil War? **Main Idea and Details**

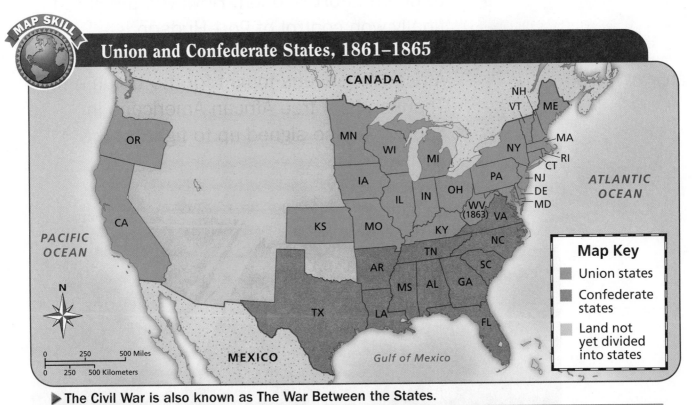

Union and Confederate States, 1861–1865

Map Key
- Union states
- Confederate states
- Land not yet divided into states

▶ The Civil War is also known as The War Between the States.

MAP SKILL Use a Historical Map *Were the states bordering the Gulf of Mexico Union or Confederate?*

Louisiana in the War

After the war began, some people had to choose sides. **P. G. T. Beauregard** left the United States army to become a general in the Confederate army. He led the Confederate soldiers who captured Fort Sumter.

Many young men from Louisiana joined the Confederate army after the war started. Life in the army was hard. Many soldiers died in battle. Others died from lack of food and from diseases.

Many Civil War battles were fought in Louisiana. In 1863 the Union army attacked **Port Hudson,** north of Baton Rouge. The Union hoped to gain control of the Mississippi River. There were many more Union soldiers than Confederate soldiers. The Confederate soldiers fought for 48 days to defend Port Hudson. However, the North finally won control of Port Hudson.

The battle at Port Hudson was the first time African Americans fought for the Union army. Thousands of free African Americans in Louisiana also signed up to fight for the Confederacy.

▶ The photograph below shows Confederate soldiers from Louisiana. This weekly newspaper from 1863 includes a drawing of the fighting at Port Hudson.

Women also worked hard to support the Confederacy. Some women whose husbands were fighting ran family farms or plantations. Other women sewed clothing for Confederate soldiers. **Sarah Morgan** kept a diary describing what life was like for her and her family during the war. You will read more about her in the Biography on pages 156 and 157.

REVIEW In what ways did women support the Confederacy? **Summarize**

MAP ADVENTURE

Louisiana Battles

This map shows where some of the major Civil War battles in Louisiana took place. Study the map and answer the questions below.

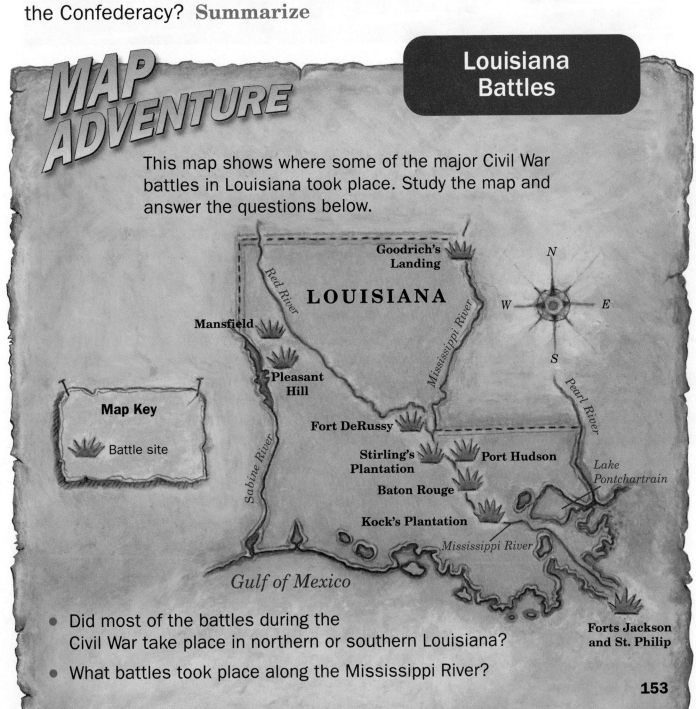

Map Key

🔥 Battle site

Goodrich's Landing

LOUISIANA

Red River

Mansfield

Pleasant Hill

Mississippi River

Fort DeRussy

Stirling's Plantation

Port Hudson

Baton Rouge

Kock's Plantation

Mississippi River

Lake Pontchartrain

Pearl River

Sabine River

Gulf of Mexico

Forts Jackson and St. Philip

- Did most of the battles during the Civil War take place in northern or southern Louisiana?

- What battles took place along the Mississippi River?

▶ A family stands near their home after it was destroyed in the Battle of Baton Rouge, in 1862.

After the War

The Union won the Civil War in 1865. More than 600,000 Union and Confederate soldiers lost their lives. Slavery ended in all states.

The fighting had caused much damage in the South. Plantations were burned, and buildings and railroad tracks were destroyed. Many people had no money or land.

After the war, the Union began to reunite with the former Confederate states. This period, from 1865 to 1877, is called **Reconstruction.** Southern states rebuilt their cities during Reconstruction. Many legal changes took place in Louisiana during this time because of the end of slavery.

Southern states also had to change some of their laws. African American men were able to vote and participate in government for the first time. **Louis C. Roudanez** published a newspaper in Louisiana that supported equal rights for African Americans.

▶ Modern reenactments, where events are acted out again, honor the Confederate soldiers who fought at Port Hudson.

154

Also for a few years during Reconstruction, some men who had been Confederate soldiers or leaders were not allowed to vote or serve in the government. All the Southern states became part of the Union again during Reconstruction.

REVIEW What happened to slavery after the end of the Civil War? **Summarize**

Summarize the Lesson

- **1861** Louisiana joined the Confederacy just before the Civil War began.
- **1863** Confederate troops defended Port Hudson for 48 days.
- **1865** After the Civil War, slavery ended in all states and Reconstruction began.

▶ Union and Confederate soldiers wore hats like these during the Civil War.

LESSON 2 ⧫ REVIEW

Check Facts and Main Ideas

1. 🎯 **Sequence** Copy the chart on a separate sheet of paper. Give the event that matches each date.

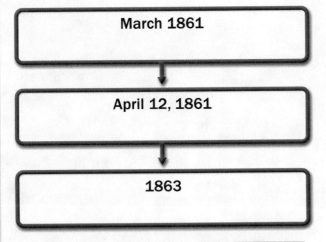

March 1861

↓

April 12, 1861

↓

1863

2. How did the start of the Civil War affect people in Louisiana?

3. Look at the map on page 151. How many states were part of the **Confederate States of America?**

4. Summarize the events at Port Hudson.

5. **Critical Thinking:** *Compare and Contrast* What changes occurred in Louisiana after the war?

Link to ⚭ Geography

Draw a Map Draw a map of Louisiana and label the Civil War battle sites from the map on page 153. Do research to find out what other battles took place in Louisiana. Add these battle sites to your map.

Meet
Sarah Morgan

1842–1909 • Writer

Have you ever kept a diary or journal? What would someone learn if they read your diary 100 years from now? Sarah Morgan started to keep a diary when she was nineteen years old. She did not know that her diaries would help people in the future learn about life during the Civil War.

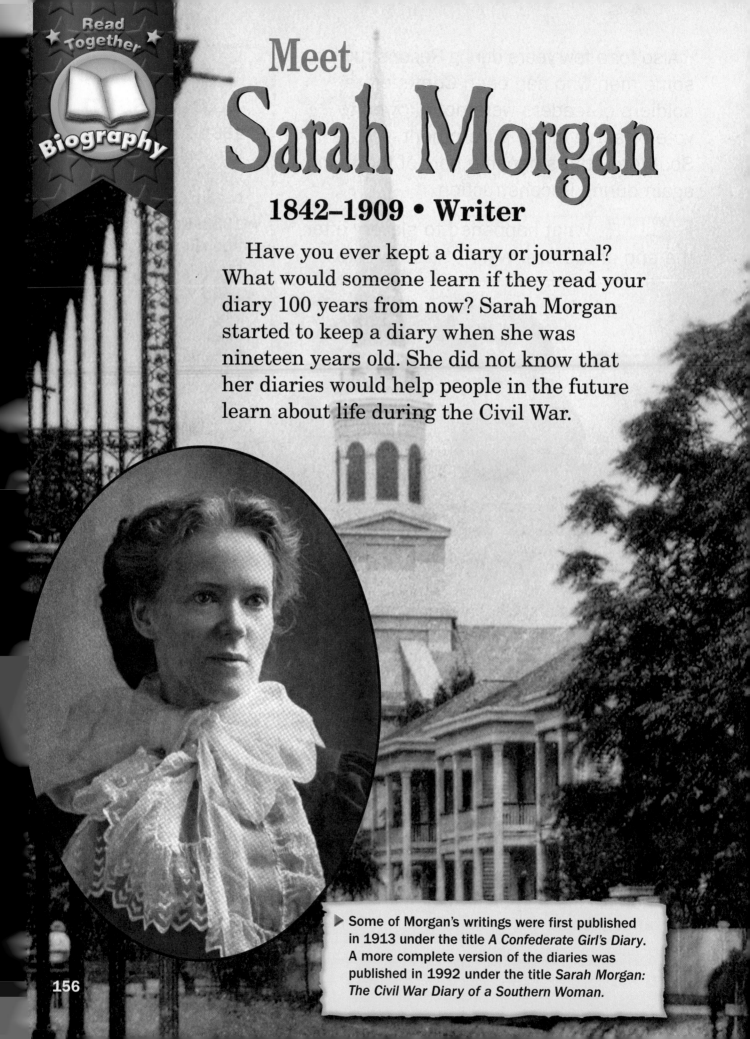

▶ Some of Morgan's writings were first published in 1913 under the title *A Confederate Girl's Diary*. A more complete version of the diaries was published in 1992 under the title *Sarah Morgan: The Civil War Diary of a Southern Woman*.

Morgan grew up in Baton Rouge as part of a large family. In 1861 her father and one of her brothers died. Soon after, Morgan started writing in her diary.

Many of the men in Morgan's family went off to fight during the Civil War. The women in the Morgan family had to leave Baton Rouge several times when fighting reached the city. After one battle, Morgan's sister Miriam returned to their house. Miriam's description of what she found made Morgan very sad. She wrote in her diary,

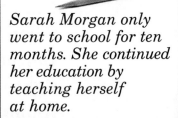

Sarah Morgan only went to school for ten months. She continued her education by teaching herself at home.

BIOFACT

> *"It was one scene of ruin. Libraries emptied, china [dishes] smashed... Mother's portrait half cut from its frame stood on the floor."*

Two of Morgan's brothers died fighting in the Civil War. After the war, Morgan lived in South Carolina. She got married and had children. Her son published her diaries after her death.

Learn from Biographies

How does the quote from Sarah Morgan's diary help you "see" what it might have been like to live in Louisiana during the Civil War?

Students can research the lives of significant people by clicking on *Meet the People* at **www.sfsocialstudies.com**.

Supporting Equal Rights

During the Civil War, African Americans hoped for a time when they would have the same rights as others in the United States. Yet even after the war, they still had to fight for fair treatment. In New Orleans, Dr. Louis Charles Roudanez published the first daily newspaper owned by African Americans. In his newspaper, Roudanez argued for fair treatment of all African Americans.

Roudanez was born in St. James Parish in 1823. His father was a French businessman, and his mother was a free African American. Roudanez was a black Creole. A black Creole is usually a Louisiana-born person who is of mixed French, African, and Spanish background.

Roudanez went to school in France and became a doctor. He came back to New Orleans and opened an office where he treated both black and white patients.

▶ Louis C. Roudanez published the *New Orleans Tribune* in both English and French.

BUILDING
CITIZENSHIP
Caring
Respect
Responsibility
Fairness
Honesty
Courage

In 1864, during the Civil War, Roudanez started a daily newspaper called the *New Orleans Tribune*. The *Tribune* called for equal rights for African Americans. It reported the stories of African Americans who had been treated unfairly when they tried to get jobs, go to school, or vote. One issue of the *Tribune* reported that free African Americans were "threatened in their lives, robbed of their liberties and deprived of the fruits of their... labor." Roudanez continued publishing the *Tribune* until 1870.

▶ The *New Orleans Tribune* was published from 1864 to 1870.

Fairness in Action

Fair treatment for African Americans was important to Louis C. Roudanez. Write a speech explaining in your own words why fairness is important.

Civil War soldiers spent almost all their time outdoors. When traveling to battle, most men simply slept on the ground, covering themselves with blankets. When they lived in camps, the troops slept in large tents. Soldiers spent their days practicing drills, doing chores, and repairing worn equipment.

Both Union and Confederate troops ate from tin plates and drank from tin cups.

During the Civil War, soldiers started a practice that continues to this day: carrying photographs of their wives and children.

Tin plate

Combination fork, spoon, knife

Spout

Hardtack (hard biscuit or bread)

Water was more important to the Civil War soldier than food and gunpowder. Many soldiers used tin canteens similar to this one.

This is the coat of Confederate General D. W. Adams. It was made of denim, not gray wool. In the war's last days, it was hard for the Confederacy to get wool and other supplies.

In the winter, troops built crude huts and cabins to protect themselves from the cold. A Confederate soldier painted this scene of his army in "winter quarters."

Wood slats covered with cloth

Paper

A letter was the quickest way for a soldier to get a message home. To write, a soldier might use a rolled-up lap desk made from small slats of wood. When unrolled, it became a smooth writing surface.

Postmark

Envelope

Pen tips

161

1800   **1805**   **1810**

1803
President Thomas Jefferson
buys Louisiana from France.

1812
Louisiana
becomes a state.

Chapter Summary

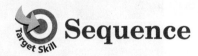 **Sequence**

On a separate sheet of paper, put these events in the correct order. Include the date of each event.

- Louisiana joins the Confederate States of America.

- Reconstruction begins.

- The Battle of New Orleans is fought.

- Louisiana becomes a state.

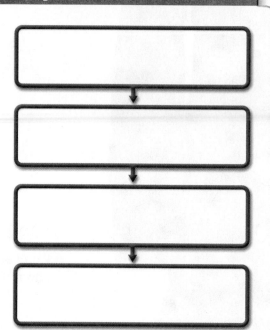

Vocabulary

Fill in the blank with the correct letter.

1 The Northern states fought the Southern states in the _____.

2 The _____ is the name for the new government formed by the Southern states.

3 The United States bought New Orleans and a huge amount of land west of the Mississippi River in the _____.

4 During the Civil War, the Northern states were called the _____.

   a. Louisiana Purchase (p. 145)

   b. Confederate States of America (p. 151)

   c. Union (p. 151)

   d. Civil War (p. 151)

1850	1855	1860	1865

1849
Baton Rouge becomes
Louisiana's capital.

1861
The Civil War
begins.

1863
Union troops
gain control
of Port
Hudson.

1865
The Civil War ends **and
Reconstruction begins.**

Facts and Main Ideas

❶ By the middle 1800s, what was one issue that was dividing the country?

❷ How was life difficult for Louisiana soldiers during the Civil War?

❸ **Main Idea** How did the Louisiana Purchase change the land of the United States?

❹ **Main Idea** How did the Civil War begin?

❺ **Critical Thinking:** *Compare and Contrast* How was Louisiana different after the Civil War than before the war?

Write About It

❶ **Write an article** for a newspaper in 1812. Tell how you think life may change after Louisiana becomes a state.

❷ **Write a paragraph** explaining how the Civil War affected Louisiana.

❸ **Write a speech** as a government leader during Reconstruction about your hopes for the country.

Apply Skills

Compare Primary and Secondary Sources Read the passage below. Then answer the questions.

> By 1865…homes, barns, roads, and railroads had been destroyed in Louisiana. Many residents had no food, work, or shelter.

❶ What kind of source is the passage?

❷ What clues tell you what kind of source it is?

Internet Activity

To get help with vocabulary, people, and terms, select the dictionary or encyclopedia from *Social Studies Library* at **www.sfsocialstudies.com.**

End with a Tale

MOON'S
Cloud Blanket

By Rose Anne St. Romain

This Native American story tells how Spanish moss began to grow on trees. According to the story, a woman and her two children in southern Louisiana had to climb a tree when rain flooded the land. When the rain finally stopped, the wind was very cold. The woman asked Moon to help keep them warm in the tree before she fell asleep. Moon asked Stars and Clouds for help, and for Wind to stop. Moon began to weave a blanket of clouds. Read on for the rest of the story.

In the morning, the little boy was the first one to awaken. He cried out to his mother: What was this covering them? When the woman opened her eyes she saw why her child was frightened.

They were covered by a strange blanket woven from grayish grass all wispy and tattered like the last clouds of a storm. The woman understood. She understood that Moon had woven a blanket for them from Clouds.

The woman told her children that it was Moon's Cloud Blanket that had kept them warm and safe. She and her children thanked Moon for the gift. They stayed nestled under Moon's Cloud Blanket for many days and nights.

Finally, when the floodwaters **receded**, the woman and her children could leave the tree. The woman tried to take the Cloud Blanket with her. But anything woven from Clouds is very fragile, and Moon's Cloud Blanket tore.

The woman was gifted with only a handful. She did not take more than the tree gave her. She thanked the tree for its protection and went on her way with her children.

But the Cloud Blanket? It was alive. It was alive! It grew and spread all through that first tree. Other trees whose branches **entwined** with that first one soon had Cloud Blanket growing along their limbs.

Little birds came from far away and took wisps of Cloud Blanket to keep their own babies' beds warm. And in this way, they say, Moon's Cloud Blanket was spread to many, many trees in Louisiana and the South.

And to this day, as we travel the highways and byways and bayous of Louisiana, we can see Moon's Cloud Blanket trailing elegantly from trees. But we no longer call it Moon's Cloud Blanket.

We call it Spanish moss.

- **receded**—went down, pulled back
- **entwined**—twisted together

Review

Test Talk

Narrow the answer choices. Rule out answers you know are wrong.

Main Ideas and Vocabulary

TEST PREP

Read the passage below. Then answer the questions.

Native Americans arrived first in the land that is now Louisiana long ago. By the early 1700s, Europeans began to settle in Louisiana.

Louisiana became a French <u>colony</u> in 1699. It then became a Spanish colony in 1762.

By 1800 Spain had given Louisiana back to France. The United States bought New Orleans and a large amount of land west of the Mississippi River from France in the Louisiana Purchase of 1803. In 1812 Louisiana became a state.

In 1861 the North and South began to fight in the Civil War. The war ended in 1865 and Reconstruction began. African Americans gained many rights during Reconstruction.

⓵ According to the passage, how did Louisiana become part of the United States?
  A Spain gave it away.
  B The United States bought it from France.
  C Europeans moved out.
  D The North and South fought the Civil War for it.

⓶ What does the word *colony* mean in this passage?
  A a country west of the Mississippi River
  B a place that is at war
  C a place where Native Americans live
  D a place that is ruled by another country

⓷ According to the passage, when did African Americans gain many rights?
  A during Reconstruction
  B in 1762
  C during the Louisiana Purchase
  D in 1812

Write and Share

Write a Biography Form a group and choose one of the key people you have read about in this unit. Do research to find more facts about his or her life. Write a short biography of the person you have chosen. Share your biography with your class. Combine all the biographies into a book called "Famous People in Louisiana's History."

Read on Your Own

Look for books like these in the library.

Apply Skills

Make a Time Line Create a time line of your life. Include the important events in the correct sequence on the time line. You may want to include events such as when you were born or when you started school. Draw a picture for each event on your time line.

Vocabulary

Write a paragraph about important events in Louisiana's history. Make sure to write about the events you choose in sequence. Use four or more of the vocabulary words below.

settlement (p. 125)

colony (p. 131)

slavery (p. 133)

Louisiana Purchase (p. 145)

Confederate States of America (p. 151)

Union (p. 151)

Civil War (p. 151)

Reconstruction (p. 154)

Discovery CHANNEL SCHOOL

UNIT 3 Project

This Just In

Report breaking news in Louisiana's history.

1 **Choose** an event from Louisiana's history.

2 **Choose** roles to play for a press conference to announce the event, such as news reporters and eyewitnesses.

3 **Research** the event. Write questions and answers about the event.

Louisiana Purchase!

4 **Create** a poster that a television news station might use to announce breaking news about an event.

5 **Hold** your press conference as a class activity.

Internet Activity

For more information and activities, go to www.sfsocialstudies.com.

The Economy of Louisiana

UNIT 4

What kinds of jobs do people in Louisiana have?

ALICE D.

FRANCE

> "I've done it all, and hard work is just getting the job done."
>
> — Louisiana restaurant owner, Todd Graves, 2002

France M. Folse painted *Golden Meadow* in 1960. Fishing and oil drilling are important to Louisiana's economy.

Meet the People

Madam C. J. Walker

1867–1919

Birthplace: Near Delta, Louisiana

Business owner

- Made hair products for African American women
- Founded and owned the Madam C. J. Walker Manufacturing Company
- Was one of the first African American women millionaires in the United States

Paul Prudhomme

b. 1940

Birthplace: Near Opelousas, Louisiana

Chef and restaurant owner

- Learned how to cook from his mother
- Owned his first restaurant when he was 17 years old
- Made his own mix of herbs and spices that is sold around the world

1860	1880	1900	1920

1867 • Madam C. J. Walker   1919

Students can research the lives of significant people by clicking on *Meet the People* at **www.sfsocialstudies.com.**

Madhu Beriwal

b. 1956

Birthplace: India
Business owner
- Went to school in India and Kansas
- Founded a company that helps prepare communities for possible disasters
- Received a Special Merit Award from the Louisiana Emergency Preparedness Association

Todd Graves

b. 1972

Birthplace: New Orleans, Louisiana
Restaurant owner
- Worked as a salmon fisherman in Alaska to earn money to start his own business
- Opened his first restaurant in Baton Rouge in 1996
- Owns restaurants in many states.

1940   1960   1980   2000

1940 • Paul Prudhomme

1956 • Madhu Beriwal

1972 • Todd Graves

173

What Caused Ruston to Grow?

Cause and Effect

- Sometimes writers use the words *cause* and *effect*.

A cause makes something happen. → An effect is the outcome or the result of the cause.

- Other times, words such as *because, then, now, result,* and *since* might be used to talk about cause and effect.

Read the following paragraph. Cause and effect have been highlighted for you.

Many new railroads were built after the Civil War. Railroads brought more people and more business to Louisiana. As a result, new towns and cities were built along the railroad lines.

Word Exercise

Compound Words Compound words are created when two words are joined together to form a new word. Below is a chart that shows some compound words from the passage.

Compound Words		
rail	road	railroad
through	out	throughout

Ruston, Louisiana

Railroads helped create the town of Ruston. A new railroad was built between Vicksburg, Mississippi, and Shreveport, Louisiana, in the late 1800s. Railroad workers needed a place to stay and get supplies. They built a village about halfway between Vicksburg and Shreveport.

Local landowner Robert E. Russ gave much of his land to the new community. The town was soon called Ruston, named after Russ.

The railroad shipped cotton from Ruston to other areas. The people of Ruston also built stores to sell products that the railroad brought.

Two state universities were founded in the area. As a result, Ruston continued to grow throughout the 1900s. Today, more than 20,000 people live there.

Use the reading skill of cause and effect to answer questions 1 and 2. Then answer the vocabulary question.

1. What caused people to build the town of Ruston?

2. What effect do you think the founding of two universities had on Ruston?

3. Ruston is a *town* named after *Russ*. How might this name have started out as a compound word if the spelling had changed?

Lesson 1

Monroe

The city of Monroe offers people entertainment such as the Fourth of July parade.

1

Lesson 2

Avondale

People work together to build ships in Avondale.

2

CANADA

NORTH
AMERICA

UNITED STATES

PACIFIC OCEAN

ATLANTIC
OCEAN

Monroe

LOUISIANA

Avondale

Gulf of Mexico

MEXICO

Why We Remember

What do you want to be when you grow up?
Maybe you will be a farmer and grow crops. Or
maybe you will be a teacher and help children.
There are many types of jobs you can do! In this
chapter, you will read about the different kinds of
jobs that Louisianans do. You will learn how
people work together in Louisiana.

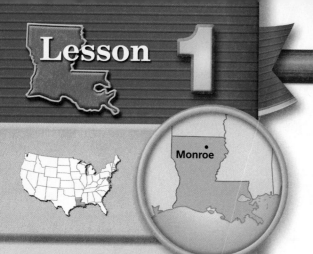

Monroe

Making Goods

Preview

Focus on the Main Idea
Selling goods and services keeps Louisiana's economy strong.

PLACE
Monroe

VOCABULARY
economy
goods
services
trade
import
export

GOOD WITH CORRESPONDING COUPON
4
ONE THROUGH FARE

▶ Railroad ticket

You Are There

Toot, toot! Listen to the train's whistle. Look at the puffs of smoke from the train's engine. Railroad tracks have just been built near your home in Covington. It is 1888, and you are riding on a train for the first time.

You look out the window. You see mile after mile of forest. Then you see loggers standing next to the pine trees they have cut down. Soon the trees will be taken to a mill and turned into lumber. The lumber will be loaded onto a train. It will be taken to a city and sold. Much of the lumber will be used to make furniture and new houses.

Cause and Effect As you read, look for the causes and effects of the growth of Louisiana's economy.

A Growing Economy

After Reconstruction, Louisiana's economy grew quickly. An **economy** is a system for making, managing, and delivering goods and services. Before the Civil War, Louisiana's economy had been based on sugarcane and cotton. Steamboats carried these products to other places for sale.

Railroads began to replace steamboats in the middle 1800s. Trains could go to areas where there were no rivers. Many products for sale could be sent by train to these areas. For instance, loggers cut down trees and sent the wood to other parts of the country.

Trains also brought more people to our state. New towns were built near train stations. Stores in these towns sold products to railroad companies and travelers.

▶ The sale of lumber is still important to the economy of Louisiana.

▶ This train carried logs in Claiborne Parish in the early 1900s.

REVIEW How did railroads affect Louisiana's economy?

◎ **Cause and Effect**

Goods and Services

Today many people in Louisiana have jobs making and selling goods. **Goods** are things made or grown by people to sell to others. Louisiana's farmers grow and sell goods such as cotton, sugarcane, soybeans, and rice.

Oil is an important part of Louisiana's economy. Many people in our state make a living by drilling, refining, and selling oil and natural gas. Refining oil means making the oil more pure and useable. Refining oil helps change it into other products.

Some workers in our state do not make goods. Instead, they sell services. **Services** are jobs that one person or group does for another. A teacher is an example of a person who provides a service.

The town of **Monroe** provides many services to tourists. Monroe has a ballet company, a symphony, theaters, a zoo, and many other places to visit. The people who work at these places offer goods and services to tourists.

REVIEW How do oil and natural gas affect Louisiana's economy? **Cause and Effect**

► The Pioneer Heritage Center in Shreveport shows visitors how people lived in the 1800s.

► The city of Monroe provides entertainment, such as parades and outdoor music, to tourists. This man shows visitors to the Folklife Festival how to make objects out of wood (below right).

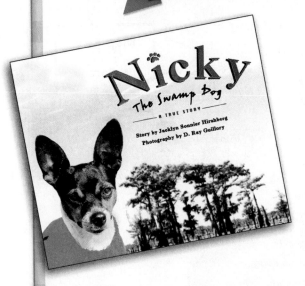

Nicky
the Swamp Dog

by Jacklyn Sonnier Hirshberg

This is a true story about a man named Half Pint Guillory and his dog, Nicky. Half Pint provides services to tourists. He and Nicky take people on boat tours to teach them about the swamps near the Atchafalaya River. Read about how Nicky entertains the tourists.

The visitors love to watch Nicky swimming with the beavers and baby alligators, especially when she brings a baby in her mouth over to the boat for people to see up close.

Nicky seems to enjoy having her picture taken and pleasing the visitors. She knows when they want to photograph her. She actually poses for the cameras!

▶ Actors at the Strauss Theatre Center in Monroe perform plays for audiences.

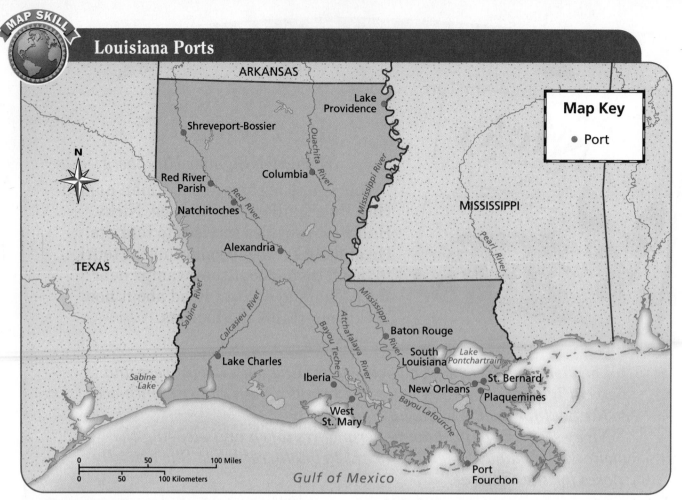

Map Key

● Port

ARKANSAS

Lake Providence

Shreveport-Bossier

Ouachita River

Columbia

Red River Parish

Red River

Natchitoches

Mississippi River

MISSISSIPPI

Alexandria

Pearl River

TEXAS

Sabine River

Calcasieu River

Bayou Teche

Atchafalaya River

Baton Rouge

South Louisiana

Lake Pontchartrain

Lake Charles

Iberia

Mississippi River

St. Bernard

New Orleans

Plaquemines

Sabine Lake

West St. Mary

Bayou Lafourche

0   50   100 Miles

0   50   100 Kilometers

Gulf of Mexico

Port Fourchon

▶ This map shows several Louisiana ports.

MAP SKILL Use a Compass Rose *What is the most northern port on the Mississippi River that is shown on the map?*

▶ Cotton is one of the goods that Louisiana exports to other countries.

Trading Goods

People in Louisiana trade with each other. **Trade** happens when goods and services are bought and sold.

People in Louisiana also trade with people in other countries. For example, many people in Louisiana drink coffee. It is not grown in Louisiana. Therefore, Louisiana imports coffee. **Import** means to bring goods from one country into another for sale.

People in other countries need goods from Louisiana. Goods such as oil products, cotton, plastics, and paper are exported from our state. **Export** means to send goods from one country to another for sale.

Trade is a major part of Louisiana's economy. Many people work in Louisiana's ports. They help to ship goods in and out of our state. Find the Port of South Louisiana on the map on page 182. More goods pass through this port than any other port in the United States.

REVIEW Why does Louisiana import coffee?
🎯 **Cause and Effect**

Summarize the Lesson

- Railroads helped Louisiana's economy grow after Reconstruction.
- Louisianans sell many goods and services.
- People in Louisiana trade goods with people in other communities and countries.

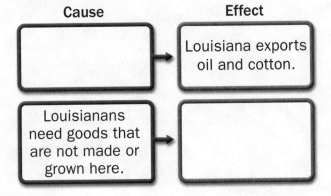

▶ Huge ships carry imported and exported goods in and out of Louisiana's ports.

LESSON 1   REVIEW

Check Facts and Main Ideas

1. 🎯 **Cause and Effect** On a separate sheet of paper, fill in the missing cause and effect.

Cause	Effect
	Louisiana exports oil and cotton.
Louisianans need goods that are not made or grown here.	

2. Compare Louisiana's **economy** before the Civil War and after Reconstruction.

3. What are some **goods** and **services** that are sold in our state?

4. Give examples of goods that Louisianans **import** and **export.**

5. **Critical Thinking:** *Evaluate* How does **trade** benefit Louisiana?

Link to ⬤⬤ Geography

Make a List Look at the map on page 182. On a separate piece of paper, write down the names of the ports shown on the map. Next to the names, write the name of a river or bayou that each port is near.

Sister Ports
New Orleans and Shanghai

The Port of New Orleans and the Port of Shanghai in China are on opposite sides of the world. So what do these ports have in common? Huge ships carry goods back and forth between New Orleans and Shanghai. This helps bring the two cities closer together. In fact, these two busy ports are sister ports, or ports that share a special relationship. As you look at the pictures, think about how these sister ports are alike.

▶ The Port of New Orleans exports vegetables, grains, meat, and other farm products to China.

▶ The ports of New Orleans and Shanghai are several thousand miles apart!

UNITED STATES · CHINA
Port of New Orleans · Port of Shanghai

▶ The Port of Shanghai exports goods such as steel and rubber to the Port of New Orleans.

▶ These people are working together to dock a ship at the Port of Shanghai.

Use a Cutaway Diagram

What? Have you ever wondered what is inside a building or an object? A **cutaway diagram** shows you what is inside and outside of a building or an object. Parts of the diagram are often labeled.

Why? This diagram shows many of the steps that take place inside a paper mill. Paper is one of the important goods made in Louisiana. A paper mill is a factory where paper is made. At each step inside the paper mill, a worker or machine has one job.

1 Logs are cut into smaller pieces, bark is removed, and logs are chopped into wood chips.

2 The chips are heated so they become very soft. The wood fiber is separated from the rest of the material.

3 Wood fiber is brown, so it is bleached white and washed. The fiber, or pulp, is beaten and mixed with chemicals and minerals.

How? To use the cutaway diagram below, find the number 1 on the diagram. It shows the first step in the sequence of making paper. Then find the label with the matching number and read about the picture. Continue following the numbers in order until you read all the steps showing how paper is made.

Think and Apply

1 What happens during the first step in the sequence of making paper?

2 What happens in the step before the paper is collected in large rolls?

3 How does a cutaway diagram help you to understand how paper is made?

4 The pulp is pressed to remove moisture.

5 The pressed paper is passed through a dryer.

6 The paper is collected in large rolls.

7 "Sheeters" cut the rolls of paper into different sizes.

Opelousas •
Avondale •

Preview

Focus on the Main Idea
Louisiana workers depend on each other to perform their jobs well.

PLACES
Opelousas
Avondale

PEOPLE
Paul Prudhomme
Madhu Beriwal

VOCABULARY
human resource
capital resource
specialize
interdependence
technology

Going to Work

 You hear a low rumble. It's your stomach growling. You're hungry!

You are visiting the busy kitchen of the restaurant where your father works. You hear pots and pans clanging together. Cooks are filling them with ingredients.

Hopefully, they will make you a muffuletta (muh fuh LAHT uh) sandwich. Louisiana is famous for this special sandwich. You can almost taste the muffuletta bread and lunchmeats and cheese. You especially like the toppings, like olives, oil, vinegar, and garlic. A sandwich like that will quiet your stomach!

 Cause and Effect As you read, notice how resources affect how people do their jobs.

▶ Muffuletta sandwiches

188

Jobs Today

Think about the adults in your community. What jobs do they have? There are all kinds of jobs in our state. Some Louisianans are airplane pilots or dentists. Others are farmers or teachers. Others catch fish or repair cars.

Whatever work they do, people in Louisiana try to do their jobs well. They take pride in their work and show up for work on time. They do a full day of work. Also, they are kind to the people they work with. These are some parts of a job performed well.

Paul Prudhomme is one Louisianan who does his job well. He was born on a farm near **Opelousas.** Prudhomme opened his own restaurant. He also wrote books about cooking. His hard work helped make the food of Louisiana even more famous. You can learn more about Paul Prudhomme on pages 194 and 195.

REVIEW List some of the jobs people have in your community. **Main Idea and Details**

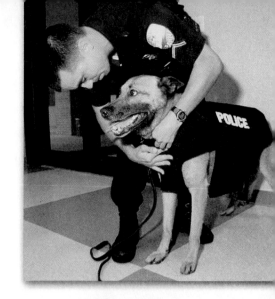

Police Officer

Bee Keeper

Teachers

Using Resources

People need resources to perform their jobs. Natural resources are useful materials found in nature. **Human resources** are the people who make goods or provide services. The machines, tools, and buildings that are used to make goods and provide services are called **capital resources.**

Resources help run your school. Oil and natural gas are natural resources used to make electricity. Teachers are human resources. Your school building is a capital resource.

REVIEW How are human and capital resources alike? **Compare and Contrast**

FACT FILE

Three Resources

People use resources to make goods and provide services. Read about the different kinds of resources below.

▶ **Human Resources**
Examples of human resources include teachers, doctors, bus drivers, and office workers like the one shown here.

▶ **Capital Resources**
Fishing boats, computers, and tractors like this one are capital resources.

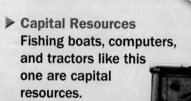

▶ **Natural Resources**
Trees are natural resources. Other natural resources include oil, fish, and water.

Working Together

Most jobs require people to work together. Here is an example of how workers rely on each other at the shipyards in Avondale. Avondale is a town on the Mississippi River near New Orleans. More than 6,000 people work to build ships in Avondale.

It would take too long if one person performed every task that is needed to make a ship. Instead, workers specialize in one job. To **specialize** means to do one job or make one part of a product. One worker specializes in using a crane to lift heavy parts. Another worker specializes in putting some of the parts together.

The shipyard workers depend on each other. The crane worker has to move the parts before other workers can put them together. Depending on each other is called **interdependence.** Trade is also an example of interdependence. People in Louisiana are interdependent when they trade goods with people in other states and countries.

REVIEW How do specialization and interdependence help people do their jobs?
🎯 **Cause and Effect**

▶ The shipbuilders in Avondale are interdependent. They each specialize in a job to build a ship.

Going to School in Louisiana

Compare the photographs of students. The one on the left shows a student in the middle 1900s. The photograph on the right shows students today. You can see that the tools students use have changed a lot.

▶ Many students today look up information with the help of computers.

▶ This photograph from the 1950s shows a student using a card catalog to look up information in the library.

▶ Madhu Beriwal uses technology to succeed in her business.

Technology at Work

Workers also rely on technology to do their jobs. **Technology** is the use of tools and ideas to solve problems. Technology often helps us complete tasks faster and more easily. Examples of technology are all around us. Cell phones help people talk to each other no matter where they are. Airplanes fly people and goods to other parts of the world. You use technology when you type your ideas on a computer.

Business leader **Madhu Beriwal** believes that the future of Louisiana's economy depends on new technology. Beriwal owns a company in Baton Rouge that relies on computers to help people in emergencies. She says, "New ideas come from people who love to read." Beriwal believes that people who gain knowledge from reading will never run out of ideas to make better technology. She was given the Technology Leader of the Year Award by Louisiana.

REVIEW Give two examples of how technology affects our lives.

⦿ Cause and Effect

▶ Farmers use technology to harvest their crops.

Summarize the Lesson

- Louisianans perform many different jobs. People do their best to do their jobs well.

- Louisianans use natural, human, and capital resources to make goods and provide services.

- Most workers are interdependent with other workers to do their jobs.

- The use of technology affects how people live and do their jobs.

LESSON 2 ⟩ REVIEW

Check Facts and Main Ideas

1. ⦿ **Cause and Effect** On a separate sheet of paper, fill in the missing effect.

Cause	Effect
Using technology →	

2. Name three jobs that people do in Louisiana. What are some qualities of a job performed well?

3. Give one example each of a natural resource, **human resource,** and **capital resource.**

4. What is **interdependence?**

5. **Critical Thinking:** *Point of View* Why do you think that Madhu Beriwal believes that the future of Louisiana's economy depends on new **technology?**

Link to ⎯∞⎯ **Writing**

Write a Paragraph Look at the Then and Now on page 192. Suppose you are a third grade student living 100 years in the future. Write a paragraph describing new types of technology you think people might be using.

Meet
Paul Prudhomme
b. 1940 • Chef

From the time that he was seven years old, Paul Prudhomme loved to cook. Today he is one of the most famous chefs in the United States. A chef is an excellent cook.

▶ Paul Prudhomme thinks it is good for family members to eat together. "When we'd sit down to dinner together as a family with my brothers and sisters we'd learn about each other....I wish more people would do this and recall the joy of life."

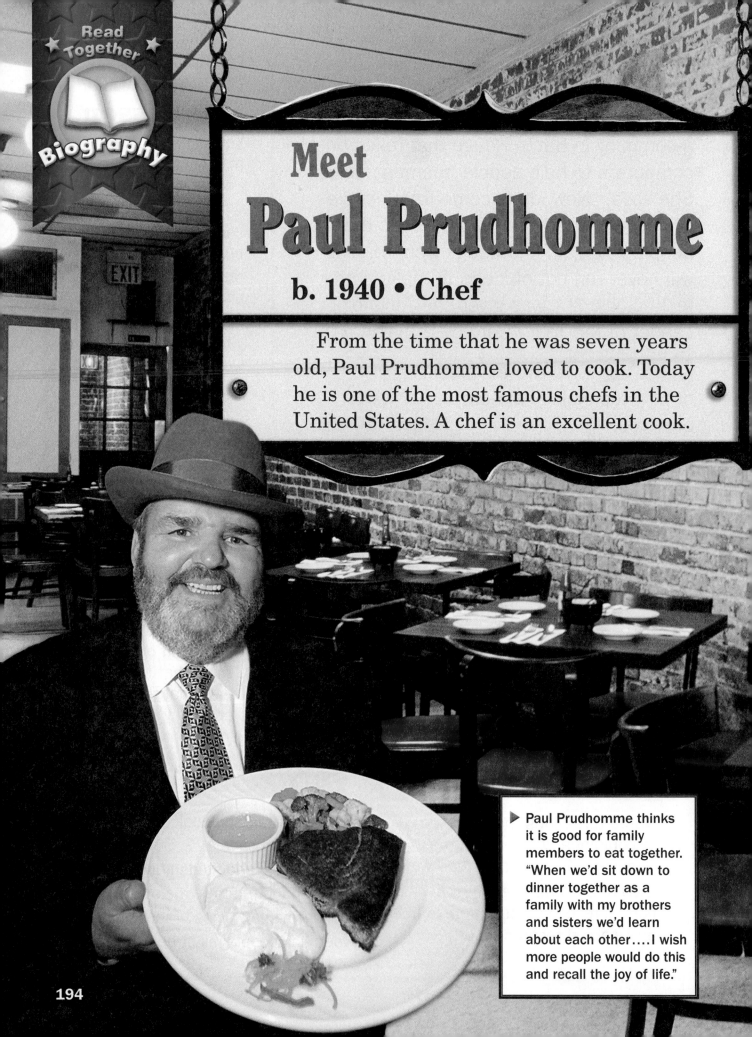

Paul was the youngest of thirteen children. He helped his mother in the kitchen when the older children grew up and moved away. His mother taught him to cook using only fresh ingredients, since they had no electricity or refrigerator. He later wrote,

". . . my mother's natural talent as a cook, our whole family's love of cooking and eating, and the joy we shared at meals, all influenced me as a chef."

Paul Prudhomme still uses fresh local ingredients in his recipes. He creates many of his dishes with seafood from the Mississippi River Delta. Prudhomme uses many traditional Louisiana recipes. He has also worked with chefs from different backgrounds and has added things from their recipes to his own.

Paul Prudhomme spent twelve years traveling around the United States. He learned different cooking styles from people all over the country. He believes that this experience has helped him succeed.

BIOFACT

Prudhomme's special recipes are very popular. Diners from all over the world come to his restaurant in New Orleans. He also started a company to sell the unique spice mixtures that add flavor to his dishes. He has written several cookbooks and won many awards for his cooking.

Learn from Biographies

How did the way Paul Prudhomme grew up affect his choice of jobs as an adult?

Students can research the lives of significant people by clicking on *Meet the People* at **www.sfsocialstudies.com**.

Chapter Summary

 Cause and Effect

On a separate sheet of paper, fill in the effect of each cause.

Cause	Effect
Coffee is not grown in Louisiana. →	
It would take too long for one person to perform every task to complete a job. →	

Vocabulary

Match each word with the correct definition or description.

1. goods (p. 180)
2. services (p. 180)
3. specialize (p. 191)
4. interdependence (p. 191)
5. technology (p. 192)

a. jobs that one person or group does for another

b. the use of tools and ideas to solve problems

c. to do one job or make one part of a product

d. depending on each other

e. things made or grown by people to sell to others

Facts and Main Ideas

❶ Why did railroads begin to replace steamboats in the middle 1800s?

❷ Why is interdependence important to Louisiana's economy?

❸ **Main Idea** Compare and contrast goods and services.

❹ **Main Idea** What are some of the different jobs held by people in Louisiana today?

❺ **Critical Thinking:** *Classify* What kinds of resources are the following items: an ambulance driver, the ambulance, and the gasoline that makes the ambulance run?

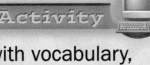

Internet Activity

To get help with vocabulary, people, and terms, select the dictionary or encyclopedia from *Social Studies Library* at **www.sfsocialstudies.com.**

Write About It

❶ **Make a list** of natural, human, and capital resources that you see every day.

❷ **Interview an adult** about his or her job. Ask questions about how the job is done and write down the answers.

❸ **Write a glossary** of terms that you learned in this chapter. List the terms and their definitions in alphabetical order.

Apply Skills

Use a Cutaway Diagram Look at the cutaway diagram. Tell what a baseball is made of from the center to the outside.

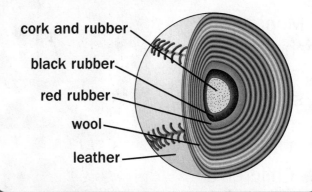

cork and rubber

black rubber

red rubber

wool

leather

Lesson 1

Crowley

Crowley is called the "Rice Capital of America."

Lesson 2

Monroe

Monroe has many interesting places to visit, such as the Northeast Louisiana Children's Museum.

CANADA

NORTH AMERICA

UNITED STATES

PACIFIC OCEAN

ATLANTIC OCEAN

1 **2**

LOUISIANA Monroe

Crowley

Gulf of Mexico

MEXICO

Why We Remember

You want to buy a bike. But how will you pay for it? You can do chores around the house to earn money. After you earn the money, which bike will you buy? There are many different kinds! How will you choose? People in Louisiana make decisions like this every day. In this chapter, you will learn how these decisions help our state's economy.

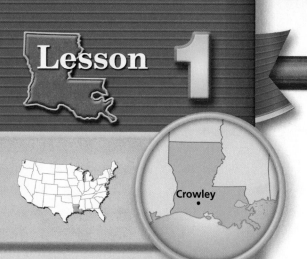

Crowley

Preview

Focus on the Main Idea
People take part in our state's economy by earning, spending, and saving money.

PLACE
Crowley

PEOPLE
Madam C. J. Walker
Todd Graves

VOCABULARY
earn
producer
consumer

Keeping Track of Money

You Are There It's a busy day for you and your soccer team. You are in the parking lot of your school. When cars drive by, you wave a big sign that says "CAR WASH!!!"

When a car turns into the parking lot, everyone on the team works together to wash every inch of the car. At the end of the day, you and your teammates count the money you have earned. Then you shout with joy. You have earned enough money to buy new uniforms for your team!

Cause and Effect As you read, think about how the economy of Louisiana affects people's lives.

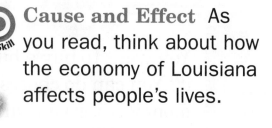

Earning Money

Have you ever sold lemonade, walked dogs, or washed cars? These are some ways to earn money. To **earn** means to get something, such as money, from working.

When you earn money, you have to think about what to do with it. People spend some of what they earn on services or goods they need, such as food. They might buy books or games too. Most people also try to save some of their money. People save their money to help pay for expensive goods, such as a car or a home. They also save money in case they need it in the future.

Madam C. J. Walker was very good at earning and saving money. She became one of the first African American women to become rich from starting a business. You will read more about her after this lesson.

REVIEW Why do people try to save some of the money they earn?
Main Idea and Details

▶ Some children earn money by delivering newspapers or selling lemonade.

201

Producers and Consumers

A person or group who makes products is called a **producer.** A person or group who uses products is called a **consumer.** Producers and consumers depend on one another. Let us look at the town of **Crowley** to see how this works.

Crowley is in southwest Louisiana. Many people in this region are rice farmers. Crowley is known as the "Rice Capital of America." In Crowley, rice producers and rice consumers need each other. Rice producers only earn money when consumers buy their rice. Consumers only have rice to eat when producers grow rice.

Consumers and producers are often the same people. For example, think about what happens when rice producers get paid. They become consumers when they buy goods for themselves.

► Rice is one of the farm products grown and sold in Louisiana. Fields of rice (below) are common in Crowley, the "Rice Capital of America."

REVIEW Why do rice producers and consumers need each other? **Summarize**

From Farm to Table

Suppose you live in a small town in southwestern Louisiana. Many farmers here grow rice. They send the rice to a rice mill, where the rice is prepared for sale. Then the rice is sent to stores. Study the map and answer the questions.

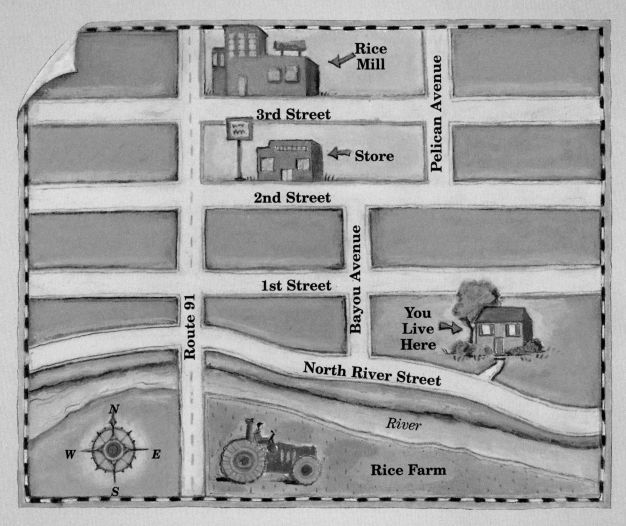

- The rice farmer needs to bring his rice to the rice mill. In what direction will the farmer drive?

- At the mill, the rice is cleaned and put in packages. A truck then takes the packages to the store. What roads could the truck use?

- You need to walk from your home to the store to buy rice. What is the shortest route to get there?

▶ Families take part in the economy when they shop for food.

Parts of the Economy

There are several parts to the economy. Businesses, such as factories and stores, are one part of the economy. As you have read, some businesses make goods. Others provide services.

Did you know that your home is another part of the economy? Think of all the goods and services your family buys. You can see why households are a very important part of our economy. A household is a family.

Banks are another important part of the economy. People often save money by putting it in a bank. Banks often lend people money to buy homes. Then the homeowners pay the banks back over time. Banks also lend money to people who want to start businesses.

▶ Many people save some of their money in banks.

After finishing college, **Todd Graves** decided to open his own restaurant in Baton Rouge. He knew this would be expensive. He needed a building, cooking equipment, furniture, and money to pay workers. Graves worked hard and saved money. He also got a loan.

Graves opened his first restaurant in 1996. By 2004 he had more than 20 restaurants! Like most people who are successful at starting a business, Graves does not mind hard work. "My biggest reward," he says, "is I'm living my dream every day."

REVIEW How do banks affect our economy? **Cause and Effect**

Summarize the Lesson

- People earn and save money to help them pay for goods and services.
- Producers and consumers depend on each other.
- Louisiana's economy includes households, businesses, and banks.

LESSON 1 REVIEW

Check Facts and Main Ideas

1. **Cause and Effect** Copy the chart on a separate sheet of paper. Describe two things that people can do with their money after they have **earned** it.

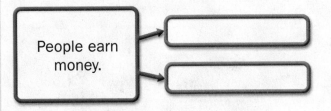

2. Do many people save some of their money? Explain why or why not.

3. Is a rice farmer a **producer,** a **consumer,** or both? Explain.

4. How do producers and consumers depend on each other?

5. **Critical Thinking:** *Express Ideas* Explain how businesses, households, and banks are all important parts of the economy.

Link to ◦◦ Geography

Map Your Neighborhood Look again at the Map Adventure on page 203. Draw a similar map of your own neighborhood. Include the place you live, a store, and any other places you think are important to the economy. Include the names of some streets.

Meet
Madam C. J. Walker
1867–1919 • Business owner

Madam C. J. Walker began life in a one-room cabin near Delta, Louisiana. When she grew up, she earned more money than almost any other woman of her time.

Walker started working when she was only five years old. She planted cotton on a Louisiana plantation.

When she was older, Walker wanted to improve how her hair looked. She made her own products to use on her hair. With money saved from her jobs, Walker made more of the products. She began to sell them door-to-door. African American women liked the beauty products she made for them.

Madam C. J. Walker added "Madame" to her name in 1906 to show that her products were of the highest quality.

BIOFACT

Later, Walker began selling her products by mail. With the money she earned, her business grew. She opened beauty schools. She trained thousands of people who sold her products in the United States and other countries. They were trained to take very good care of customers.

Walker became very wealthy. She said, "I am not ashamed of my humble [poor] beginning. Don't think that because you… [use] the washtub that you are any less a lady!"

> **"I got myself a start by giving myself a start."**

Learn from Biographies

Madam C. J. Walker learned to work very hard as a child. How do you think this habit helped her succeed?

Students can research the lives of significant people by clicking on *Meet the People* at **www.sfsocialstudies.com.**

People have used different forms of money for a long time. Money around the world might be made of different materials and have different shapes, sizes, and designs.

The ancient Egyptians used metal for money. This money was valued by weight, not shape.

Many years ago, people in Japan used coins called *koban*.

This is money from China long ago. People used this paper money instead of carrying the 1,000 coins it represented.

The pictures on these ancient coins represent the countries they are from: a lion for Turkey and a vase, squid, and turtle for the Aegean islands of Andros, Ceos, and Aegina.

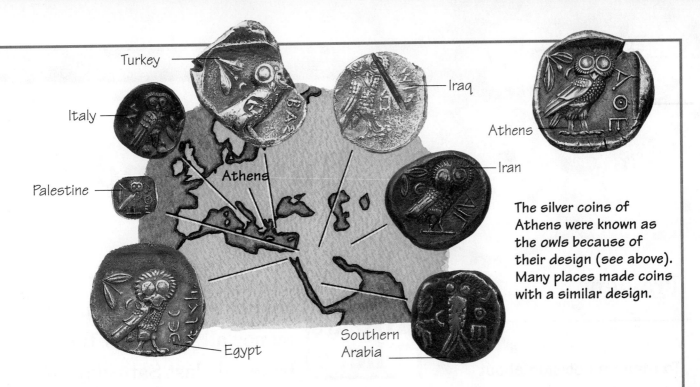

Turkey

Italy

Palestine

Athens

Iraq

Athens

Iran

Egypt

Southern Arabia

The silver coins of Athens were known as the *owls* because of their design (see above). Many places made coins with a similar design.

A silver penny called the **sterling** was first used in England in 1279.

Ancient Chinese coins were made of bronze in the shape of tools, like this hoe-shaped coin.

These rare coins are worth thousands of dollars each.

The Nigerian Ibo people used copper rings as money. These rings, called *manillas*, were used in West Africa from the 1400s until 1948.

209

Preview

Focus on the Main Idea
To make a decision about what to buy, people must make economic choices.

PLACE
Monroe

VOCABULARY
economic choice
opportunity cost
supply
demand
profit

▶ A lion at the Louisiana Purchase Gardens and Zoo

Buying and Selling

You Are There

Your class has been earning money all year. After the bake sale last Saturday, your class has finally saved enough money to take a class trip. You and your classmates are trying to decide where to go.

Since you live in Monroe, there are plenty of exciting places to visit. "Let's go to the Louisiana Purchase Gardens and Zoo," you suggest. "We can see zebras, monkeys, and lions!"

"I think we should go to the Northeast Louisiana Children's Museum," your friend Eddie says. "They have lots of fun activities and games." Your class only has enough money for one trip. Which place will you decide to visit?

Cause and Effect As you read, think about the things that can affect what a person decides to buy.

These students made an economic choice when they decided to go to the Northeast Louisiana Children's Museum.

What to Buy?

Which field trip do you think the class in Monroe should take? The students need to make an economic choice. An **economic choice** is a decision to buy one thing instead of another.

The students should think carefully before making their economic choice. They should compare how much each trip would cost and what they think they will get for their money. The students may decide to go to the museum because it is closer to their school. It would cost more to travel to the zoo.

In a way, going to the museum will cost the class a trip to the zoo. The zoo trip is the class's opportunity cost. **Opportunity cost** is what you give up when you choose one thing instead of another.

REVIEW What might cause the class from Monroe to decide to go to the museum?
Cause and Effect

Supply and Demand

Suppose you want to buy a new bicycle. You go to a few stores and compare prices. You start to notice that some bikes cost more than others. These differences in price are often due to supply and demand.

The amount of a product that producers want to sell is called **supply.** When the supply of a product increases, its cost usually goes down. For example, suppose a bike store had too many bikes. The store owner might put bikes on sale at a lower price.

The amount of a good or a service that people want and can pay for is called **demand.** When demand for a good or service increases, its price usually goes up too. Suppose everyone you know wants the same bike. With demand so high, the bike store owner might decide she could sell this bike at a higher price.

REVIEW What usually happens to the price of a good if the demand for the good is high?
◎ **Cause and Effect**

▶ Understanding supply and demand can help you make a wise economic choice.

Understanding Supply and Demand

This chart shows how supply and demand can work together to affect the prices of things you buy.

	Supply	Demand	Price
When supply is HIGH and demand is LOW, the price will usually be at its lowest.			$60.00
When supply is LOW and demand is LOW, the price will usually go up.			$80.00
When supply is LOW and demand is HIGH, the price will usually be at its highest.			$100.00
When supply is HIGH and demand is HIGH, the price will usually go down.			$80.00

▶ Supply and demand affect the prices of bikes and all other goods.

CHART SKILL *When is the price of bikes at its highest?*

Low prices on all bikes at Steve's Bike Shop

Best prices in town at Brenda's Bike Shop

▷ **Competition** between these two stores will cause the price of bikes to be lower. This is good news for you!

Making a Choice

Suppose you have saved enough money to buy a bike. You know exactly which bike you want. Now you need to decide where to buy it.

Like most people, you want to save money. You search for the store with the lowest prices. Luckily for you, there are several bike stores in your town. This is good for you, because the different stores have to compete with each other for business.

They all want consumers like you to buy their bikes. One way store owners might get your business is by lowering their prices. Competition between stores usually causes prices to be lower.

One morning you read the newspaper and notice that Brenda's Bike Shop is having a sale. You and your parents go to the shop. There is the bike you want at a great price! You decide to buy the bike.

Why did Brenda decide to have a sale? Like all business owners, Brenda is trying to earn a profit. **Profit** is the money a business has left over after all of its costs are paid.

When Brenda lowers prices, she might earn less money for each bike sold. However, she will probably sell more bikes. This helps her store make a profit.

REVIEW What caused you to buy the bike in the example above?
◉ **Cause and Effect**

Summarize the Lesson

- People make an economic choice when they decide to buy one thing rather than another.
- Opportunity cost is what a person gives up when he or she chooses one thing instead of another.
- Prices of products change as supply and demand change.
- Businesses try to make a profit.

LESSON 2 ▸ REVIEW

Check Facts and Main Ideas

1. ◉ **Cause and Effect** Copy this chart onto a separate sheet of paper. Describe how the prices of goods and services can change.

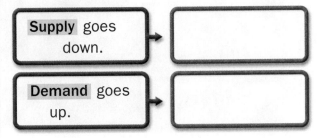

| Supply goes down. | → | |
| Demand goes up. | → | |

2. Describe one **economic choice** you made recently.
3. Explain **opportunity cost.**

4. What usually happens to prices when there is competition between stores?

5. **Critical Thinking:** *Draw Conclusions* Suppose farmers all over Louisiana have large amounts of cotton to sell. Would you expect the price of cotton to go up or down? Why?

Link to ⚭ Mathematics

Figure Out Your Profit Suppose your class holds a bake sale to raise money. You earn 25 cents **profit** for every cookie you sell. If you sell 30 cookies, how much profit do you earn?

Thinking Skills

Make a Decision

What? You make decisions every day. Decisions are choices that you make.

Why? It is important that you make careful choices and good decisions.

How? Following a step-by-step plan can help you make a wise decision. Robin used the plan below to help her choose a softball bat.

I want a new bat!

STEP 1
Figure out what you have to decide. Robin wanted to buy a softball bat. She had to decide which bat to buy at the sporting goods store.

What makes a good softball bat?

STEP 2
To make a good decision, you need to gather information. Robin asked her coach what made a good softball bat.

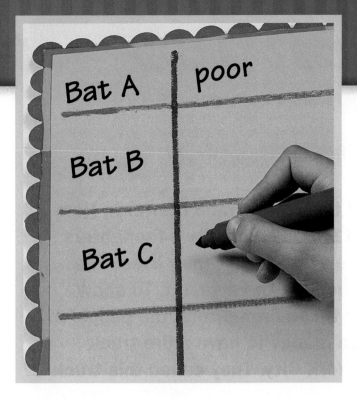

STEP 3

Before you make a decision, you need to identify, or figure out, what your choices are. Robin figured out her choices by talking to her coach and by looking at the bats at the store. She made a chart of choices.

This is the bat that I chose.

STEP 5

Finally, you are ready to make a decision. Robin decided to buy the bat that had the right length, weight, and color.

STEP 4

For each choice that you have, you need to think about what might happen if you make that choice. Robin looked at each bat before she decided which one to buy. She wanted to make sure that her decision was a good one.

Think and Apply

1. How did Robin gather information about softball bats?

2. What might happen if Robin chose a different bat?

3. How could you use this step-by-step plan to make a decision?

The Spirit of Louisiana

When terrorists attacked the World Trade Center in New York City on September 11, 2001, the city's firefighters came to the rescue. Some of them lost their lives. The city also lost many fire trucks in the disaster. To show respect for the bravery of these firefighters, the people of Louisiana decided to raise money to have a fire truck made especially for New York City. They called this truck *The Spirit of Louisiana.*

▶ *The Spirit of Louisiana* arrived in New York City and was put to use in the borough of Brooklyn.

"This brings together all the best about Louisiana," Governor Mike Foster said as he presented *The Spirit of Louisiana* to the Fire Department of New York City. Students, teachers, bankers, store clerks, firefighters, and other people from all around Louisiana donated money to buy the pumper truck. A factory in Holden, Louisiana, built the truck, which can pump a thousand gallons of water a minute. The factory's workers donated their time to do so. Almost four years later, New York firefighters drove *The Spirit of Louisiana* back to its home state to help after another disaster—Hurricane Katrina.

Around 300 firefighters came to Louisiana from New York to help the New Orleans Fire Department fight fires and rescue people after Hurricane Katrina and floodwaters destroyed

BUILDING CITIZENSHIP
Caring
Respect
Responsibility
Fairness
Honesty
Courage

parts of the city. They joined other firefighters from many other states. Some of the New York City firefighters also helped clean up the flood-damaged homes of New Orleans's firefighters.

Fire chief Frank Naglieri from the Bronx (a part of New York City) explained why many firefighters decided to come to Louisiana. "You sort of feel like you're repaying the debt," he said. "But if 9/11 never happened, we'd be down here."

▶ After Hurricane Katrina, New York City firefighters brought *The Spirit of Louisiana* back to New Orleans to help in rescue efforts.

Respect in Action

How did the people of Louisiana show respect for the firefighters of New York City? How did those same firefighters show respect for the citizens of Louisiana? How can you show respect for heroes in your community?

Chapter Summary

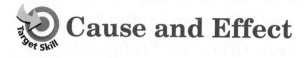 Cause and Effect

On a separate sheet of paper, fill in the effects of these changes to the economy.

| There are more producers of bikes than consumers. | → | |
| There are more consumers of bikes than producers. | → | |

Vocabulary

Fill in each blank with the letter of the vocabulary word that best completes the sentence.

1 A _____ is someone who uses products.

2 The money a business has left over after all of its costs are paid is its _____.

3 When you decide to buy one thing instead of another, you make an _____.

4 Someone who makes products is called a _____.

5 _____ is what you give up when you choose one thing instead of another.

a. producer (p. 202)

b. consumer (p. 202)

c. economic choice (p. 211)

d. opportunity cost (p. 211)

e. profit (p. 215)

Write About It

1 **Write a chart** to help you make an economic choice. In the chart, list two products you would like to buy. List the advantages and disadvantages of buying each product. Then decide which product to buy.

2 **Write a plan** that would help you to buy a product. Think of something you would like to buy. Make a plan showing how you will earn the money, how much you will save, and how much you will spend.

3 **Write an ad** for a bike store or other type of store. Make a poster advertising the sale of the product. Include the price in the ad. Also include other things that might bring consumers to the store.

Internet Activity

To get help with vocabulary, people, and terms, select the dictionary or encyclopedia from *Social Studies Library* at **www.sfsocialstudies.com.**

Facts and Main Ideas

1 How do people and households use banks?

2 What usually happens when the supply of a product increases?

3 **Main Idea** What are three ways that people take part in our economy?

4 **Main Idea** Why should you consider the opportunity cost when you make an economic choice?

5 **Critical Thinking:** *Predict* How might a television or magazine ad affect the economic choices you make?

Apply Skills

Make a Decision A large, new sporting goods store is moving to your town. This store will give many people jobs. This store will also take up a lot of land that was supposed to be a park. Should the new store come to town? Why or why not? Use the five-step decision-making process on pages 216 and 217 to help you decide.

End with a Recipe

Louisiana Red Beans and Rice

Many restaurants in our state sell red beans and rice. This is a popular southern Louisiana meal. In the past, people made red beans and rice on Mondays. They used leftovers from their Sunday dinner to make the meal tastier. Many cooks use their own special recipe. The following is one way to make this meal. Be sure to get help from an adult.

Ingredients You Need

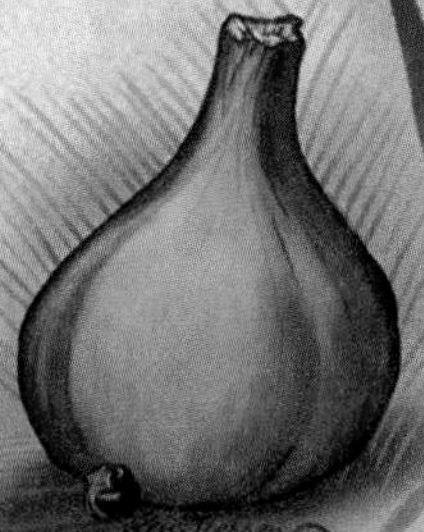

1 pound red beans, soaked in water overnight

3 celery stalks, chopped

1 medium green bell pepper, chopped

1 bay leaf

1 clove of garlic, minced

1 large onion, chopped

2 tablespoons of dried parsley flakes

A dash of ground cayenne pepper

1 package of smoked sausage
  cut in $\frac{1}{4}$-inch thick slices

How to Prepare

Rinse and drain soaked beans. Place them in a
5-to 6-quart Dutch oven and add about 6 cups
of fresh water. Bring it to a boil. Then reduce
the heat and simmer for about $1\frac{1}{2}$ hours, or
until beans are tender. Stir occasionally. Add
remaining ingredients. Simmer for about
1 hour, stirring occasionally. Add water
or salt if necessary. Serve over rice.
This serves 6 people.

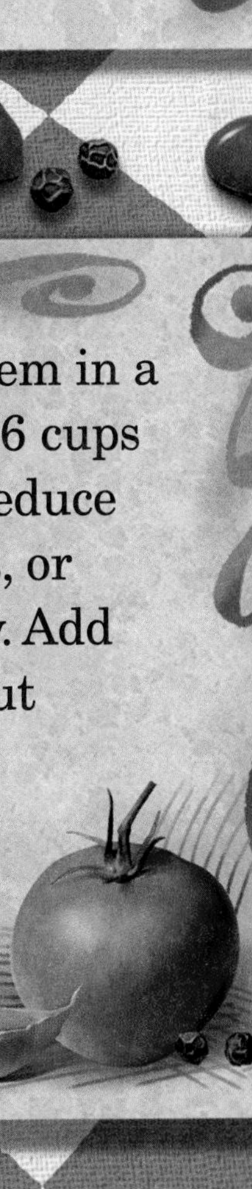

Review

Main Ideas and Vocabulary

TEST PREP

Read the passage. Then answer the questions.

People are part of the economy when they earn, spend, or save money. Businesses, households, and banks are parts of the economy.

Important goods in Louisiana today include oil, rice, and cotton. Some people have jobs making or growing goods. Other people provide services.

Some workers <u>specialize</u> in one job to help make a product. When workers depend on each other, it is called interdependence.

When you decide what to buy, you are making an economic choice. One thing to consider is cost. Prices are affected by supply and demand.

1 According to the passage, what affects prices?

  A households

  B oil, rice, and cotton

  C supply and demand

  D goods and services

2 In the passage, the word *specialize* means

  A to earn more money

  B to be someone special

  C to earn less money

  D to do one part of a job

3 What is the main idea of the passage?

  A Prices go down when supply is high.

  B People take part in our economy by earning, spending, and saving money.

  C Prices go down when demand is low.

  D Some people provide services.

Vocabulary

Write a letter to a friend telling him or her how a business works. Use five of these vocabulary words.

import (p. 182)

export (p. 182)

human resource (p. 190)

capital resource (p. 190)

earn (p. 201)

supply (p. 212)

demand (p. 212)

Apply Skills

Make a Decision Suppose your family wants your help in deciding where to take a summer vacation in Louisiana. Make a chart like the one on page 217. Gather information about three places you might like to go. Include details such as how far each place is from your home and fun things you could do there. After the chart is complete, use the information to decide where to go.

Read on Your Own

Look for books like these in the library.

Write and Share

Make a Work Poster Think of a product you would like to buy. Make a poster showing ways you could earn money to buy the product. Include drawings and captions that describe the work. Show your poster to the class.

UNIT 4 Project

On the Market

Create an advertisement for a good or service in Louisiana.

1 **Choose** a good or a service in Louisiana to advertise.

2 **Draw** pictures of the good or service.

3 **Make** your advertisement complete by including the name of the good or service and why people should buy or use it.

4 **Present** your advertisement to the class.

Internet Activity

For more information and activities, go to www.sfsocialstudies.com.

Citizens and the Government

How can you help your community?

Begin with
a Primary Source

"All government, of right, originates [begins] with the people. . . ."

— Louisiana State Constitution

This photograph shows Louisiana's capital, Baton Rouge. Many of Louisiana's government leaders work in this city, located on the Mississippi River.

Meet the People

Huey Long

1893–1935
Birthplace: Winnfield, Louisiana

Political leader

• Served as governor of Louisiana from 1928 to 1932

• Worked to improve roads and schools

• Served in the United States Senate from 1932 to 1935

Lindy Boggs

b. 1916
Birthplace: Pointe Coupee Parish, Louisiana

Political leader

• Related to William Claiborne, the first governor of our state

• Became the first woman from Louisiana elected to the U.S. House of Representatives, in 1973

• Worked to pass laws that help families and children

1895   1910   1925   1940

1893 • Huey Long   1935

1916 • Lindy Boggs

Students can research the lives of significant people by clicking on *Meet the People* at **www.sfsocialstudies.com**.

Kathleen Blanco

b. 1942

Birthplace: Iberia Parish, Louisiana

Political leader

- Taught at Breaux Bridge High School in southern Louisiana
- Has served in the government of Louisiana since 1984
- Became the first woman to serve as governor of Louisiana, in 2004

Ruby Bridges

b. 1954

Birthplace: Tylertown, Mississippi

Civil rights leader

- Was the first African American child to attend the William Frantz Elementary School in New Orleans, in 1960
- Founded the Ruby Bridges Foundation to teach children respect
- Wrote a book about her life, *Through My Eyes*

| 1955 | 1970 | 1985 | 2000 |

1942 • Kathleen Blanco

1954 • Ruby Bridges

Reading Social Studies

Government Services

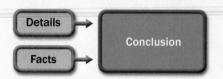

Draw Conclusions

Target Skill

- A conclusion is a decision you reach after you think about facts and details.

- You also use what you know to make a decision or form an opinion that makes sense of events.

Read this description of a government. Then look at the conclusion. The details that led to the conclusion are highlighted.

The government of Louisiana built a state library in 1925. It also gives money to help schools, museums, and universities.

Conclusion: Education is important to the Louisiana state government.

Word Exercise

Synonyms A synonym is a word that means the same or nearly the same as another word. It may help you understand new words. The passage reads, "You often use services that the state government *provides.*" Look in the dictionary and find some synonyms in the definition:

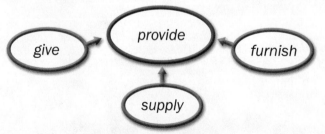

Look up each synonym to find the best one for *provide* as used in the passage.

Responsibilities of State Government

The state government meets our needs in many ways. You often use services that the state government provides. For example, the state maintains many roads, parks, and schools.

One project the government is working on is a new Calcasieu (KAL kuh soo) River Bridge. The bridge there now was built in the 1950s. The bridge cannot handle the traffic we have today. The government plans to have a new bridge in place by the year 2014.

The state government also built the State Library of Louisiana in 1925. The library is located in Baton Rouge. Both natives of Louisiana and visitors to the state can come to the library and learn more about Louisiana's history and traditions.

Use the reading skill of drawing conclusions to answer questions 1 and 2. Then answer the vocabulary question.

1. What conclusion can you draw about traffic on the Calcasieu River Bridge today compared to traffic in the 1950s? What sentence helped you draw this conclusion?

2. Why do you think the government built the State Library of Louisiana?

3. The passage reads, "For example, the state maintains many roads, parks, and schools." What is a synonym for *maintains*?

Lesson 1

New Orleans

Our state government helps run public schools in New Orleans and throughout Louisiana.

1

Lesson 2

Baton Rouge

Louisiana's state government meets in the capital, Baton Rouge.

2

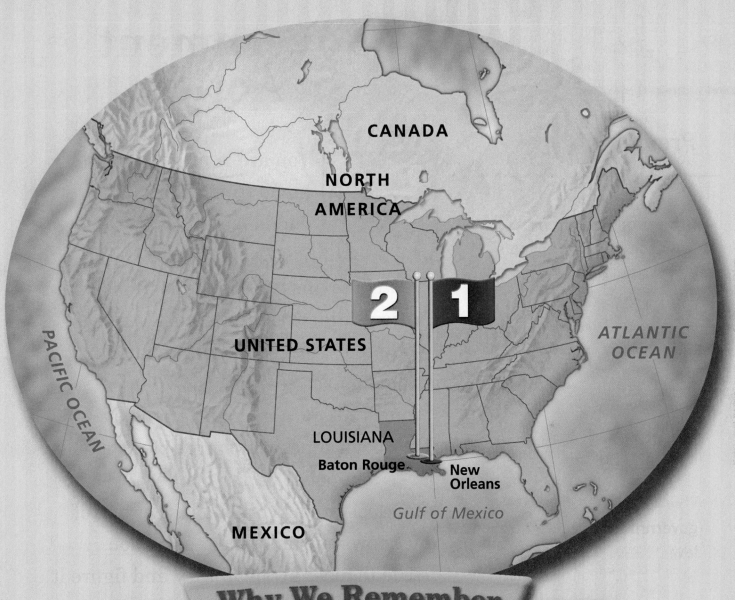

CANADA

NORTH AMERICA

PACIFIC OCEAN

UNITED STATES

ATLANTIC OCEAN

2 1

LOUISIANA

Baton Rouge

New Orleans

Gulf of Mexico

MEXICO

Why We Remember

Every day the Louisiana government is working to meet the needs of the state's people. The state government makes laws that provide for education, transportation, and recreation. Our government also passes laws and provides services to keep you safe. In this chapter you will learn about Louisiana's government.

Preview

Focus on the Main Idea
Governments help meet the basic needs of people by providing important services.

PLACE
New Orleans

PEOPLE
Huey Long

VOCABULARY
government
law

Government in Action

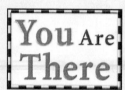
You Are There

You are riding the bus home from school. Your friend Jen asks, "Do you have a lot of homework?"

"I have to answer some questions about the government of Louisiana," you say.

"I do too," she says. "What exactly is government?"

You think for a moment, then say, "Isn't government in charge of things like parks and police departments?"

You look at each other. Neither one of you knows the answer for sure. You decide to meet at the library and figure it out together.

Draw Conclusions
As you read, think about why government is important. Write down some of your conclusions.

UNION, JUSTICE AND CONFIDENCE

What is Government?

A **government** is made up of the people and laws that operate a place, such as a city, state, or country. There are three levels of government. National government is the government of the country. State government is the government of a state. Local government is the government of a city, town, or parish.

The main job of the Louisiana state government is to run the state. This includes building roads and bridges, and maintaining parks, public schools, and libraries.

Huey Long served in both the Louisiana state government and the national government. You will read about him in the Biography after this lesson.

REVIEW How does our state government help Louisianans? ⟳ **Draw Conclusions**

▶ This building is a courthouse in East Baton Rouge Parish.

FACT FILE

Government Services

The government of Louisiana provides many important services. These services help meet the needs of people in our state.

State Parks

▶ The Louisiana government gave money to help create North Toledo Bend State Park.

Public Schools

▶ The state government helps run public schools like this elementary school in **New Orleans.**

State and National Highways

▶ Our state government helps maintain roads such as Interstate Highway 20 in northern Louisiana.

Veterans Hospitals

▶ The government helps run this hospital in Shreveport. The hospital provides medical care to veterans, or people who have served in the armed forces.

Rules and Laws

Are there special rules in your home? Maybe you have to do your homework before watching any television.

Rules may be made by families or schools. Laws are a little different. A **law** is a rule that is made by the government. Everyone must follow the law.

One of the main jobs of our state government is to make laws. For example, the state makes laws to protect our safety. Louisiana has a seatbelt law, which says that everyone in a car must wear a seatbelt.

REVIEW What is the main goal of the seatbelt law? ⟳ **Draw Conclusions**

Summarize the Lesson

- A government is made up of the people and laws that operate a place, such as a city, state, or country.
- The government of Louisiana provides important services which help meet the needs of people in our state.
- Our state government makes laws which everyone must follow.

LESSON 1 ‖ REVIEW

Check Facts and Main Ideas

1. ⟳ **Draw Conclusions** On a separate sheet of paper, draw a graphic organizer like the one shown. Use the details given to draw a conclusion about our state government.

State government maintains schools and libraries. →

State government makes laws to protect our safety. →

2. What is **government?** What is the state government's main job?

3. Name three important services provided by our state government.

4. Explain the difference between a rule and a **law.**

5. **Critical Thinking:** *Express Ideas* Look at the Fact File on page 238. Pick one of the government services in the Fact File. Why do you think this service is important to the people of Louisiana?

Link to ⟷ Writing

Describe a Law Find out more about one Louisiana state law. Write a short description of the law in which you explain its main goal. Also explain why the law is important.

Meet
Huey Long

1893–1935
Governor and Senator

Huey Long was born in Winnfield, Louisiana. He later said,

"Our community was a kindly one . . . . No one went hungry or in need of clothes if anyone in the neighborhood had things beyond his own immediate requirements [needs]. I was frequently sent by my parents with food and clothing of the best kind to some less fortunate [lucky] family living in the neighborhood."

After high school, Long took a job as a traveling salesman. He earned enough money to take classes in law. In 1915 he became a lawyer. When he was just 35, Long was elected governor of Louisiana.

Long never forgot the lessons he had learned as a child in Winnfield. As governor, he worked to help people who were not rich or powerful. One of his goals was to provide free schoolbooks to students. He also improved public hospitals and built new roads and bridges.

Not everyone supported Long while he was governor. Some people said he had too much power and did not respect people's rights.

In 1932 Long was began serving in the United States Senate, which is part of the national government.

Huey Long supported the creation of a medical school at Louisiana State University.

BIOFACT

Learn from Biographies
How do you think Huey Long's childhood affected his work as a government leader?

Students can research the lives of significant people by clicking on *Meet the People* at **www.sfsocialstudies.com.**

Baton Rouge

State Government

Preview

Focus on the Main Idea
The Louisiana state government has three branches, or parts, which work together to run the state and make laws.

PLACE
Baton Rouge

PEOPLE
Kathleen Blanco

VOCABULARY
capitol
capital
constitution
bill

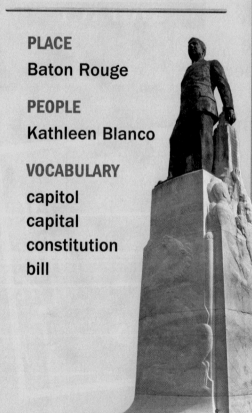

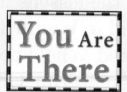

You Are There Your class is touring the amazing Louisiana State Capitol Building in Baton Rouge. Your teacher explains that a capitol building is a place where government leaders meet.

Outside the building, you see a large statue of Huey Long. Inside, you walk through the two huge rooms called "chambers." This is where state leaders meet to debate and vote on laws. Finally, your class rides the elevator up to the 27th floor. From way up here you can see almost all of Baton Rouge. At 450 feet tall, the Louisiana State Capitol is the tallest state capitol in the country!

Draw Conclusions As you read, draw conclusions about how the different parts of our state government work together.

242

Louisiana's Constitution

The words *capitol* and *capital* sound alike, but their meanings are different. As you just read, a **capitol** is a building in which government leaders meet. A **capital** is a city in which the government of a state or country is located. The capital of Louisiana is **Baton Rouge.**

When government leaders meet in Baton Rouge, they base their work on the Louisiana State Constitution. A **constitution** is a written plan of government. Our state constitution explains how to make laws and elect leaders. The constitution also protects the rights of the people.

▶ Louisiana's government leaders meet inside the State Capitol Building in Baton Rouge.

REVIEW On what do Louisiana government leaders base their work?
Main Idea and Details

Literature and Social Studies

The State Constitution

The Louisiana State Constitution begins by explaining the main purpose of state government:

"All government, of right, originates [begins] with the people, is founded on their will alone, and is instituted [set up] to protect the rights of the individual and for the good of the whole. Its only legitimate [lawful] ends [goals] are to secure justice for all, preserve peace, protect the rights, and promote the happiness and general welfare of the people."

243

Legislative Branch

The Louisiana State Constitution divides government into three branches, or parts. The three branches are the legislative branch, executive branch, and judicial branch. The constitution explains how these three branches must work together and share power.

The legislative branch is made up of two groups: the Louisiana House of Representatives and the Louisiana State Senate. Their main job is to make state laws.

A member of the legislative branch can write a **bill,** or a plan for a new law. Then leaders debate the bill. Before the bill can become a law, it must be approved by the House of Representatives and the Senate.

▶ James David Cain has served in both the Louisiana House of Representatives and the State Senate.

REVIEW How are the Louisiana House of Representatives and the Louisiana State Senate alike? **Compare and Contrast**

Three Branches of Louisiana's Government

Legislative

Leaders
- House of Representatives (105 members)
- Senate (39 members)

Main Job
Make laws

Executive

Leader
Governor

Main Job
Carry out laws

Judicial

Leaders
State Supreme Court

Main Job
Decide if laws have been broken and whether they are fair

▶ Before becoming governor, Kathleen Blanco served in the state legislature and was a teacher at Breaux Bridge High School.

How a Bill Becomes a Law

Legislative Branch
Bills are discussed in the legislative branch.

Executive Branch
The governor of Louisiana can approve or veto bills in the executive branch.

Judicial Branch
Judges can decide if laws should stay in place or not.

Executive Branch

After a bill is approved in the legislative branch, it goes to the executive branch. The leader of this branch is the governor. One of the governor's main jobs is to decide whether or not a bill should become a law. The governor may approve a bill by signing it. Then it becomes a law. He or she may also veto, or refuse to sign, a bill. Then the bill may go back to the legislative branch.

Once a new law is passed, it must be carried out, or enforced. The executive branch makes sure people follow the law.

In 2004 **Kathleen Blanco** became the first woman to serve as governor of Louisiana. What is it like to be governor? "My work day usually starts at 8 A.M. and continues until 7 or 8 P.M.," says Blanco. "The work is never finished."

REVIEW What happens to a bill after it is signed by the governor? **Sequence**

245

MAP ADVENTURE

Suppose your class is taking a tour of the state capital. Use this map to find some of the exciting places to visit in downtown Baton Rouge.

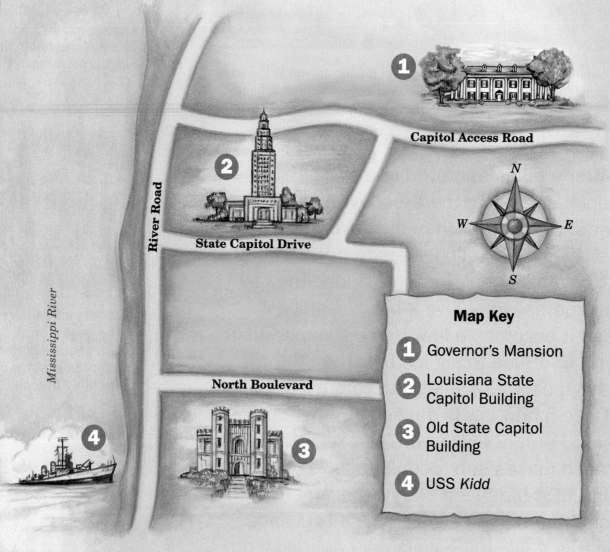

Map Key

1. Governor's Mansion
2. Louisiana State Capitol Building
3. Old State Capitol Building
4. USS *Kidd*

- Which building is shown by the number 1 on this map?

- Suppose you want to go from the Louisiana State Capitol Building to the Old State Capitol Building, which was used until 1932. Which direction would you walk?

- Next you want to visit the USS *Kidd*, a United States Navy ship that is now a museum. Where is the USS *Kidd* located?

Judicial Branch

The part of our state government that includes judges and courts is called the judicial branch. The judicial branch is led by the Louisiana Supreme Court. It is located in New Orleans.

Judges in the judicial branch decide what is right when there are disagreements about the law. Supreme Court judges have the power to decide whether a law is fair. If someone thinks a law is unfair, he or she can challenge the law in court. Judges then decide if the law should stay in place.

REVIEW Explain the powers of the judicial branch. **Summarize**

Summarize the Lesson

- Our state constitution explains how we can make laws and elect leaders in Louisiana.

- Louisiana's state government is divided into three branches: legislative, executive, and judicial.

- The three branches of government work together and share power.

LESSON 2 REVIEW

Check Facts and Main Ideas

1. **Draw Conclusions** On a separate sheet of paper, draw a graphic organizer like the one shown. Fill in details about each branch of government. The details should lead to the conclusion shown in the graphic organizer.

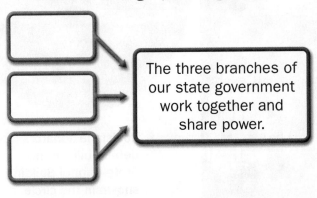

The three branches of our state government work together and share power.

2. Why is the Louisiana State **Constitution** important?

3. What is the main job of the legislative branch of government?

4. Who leads our state's executive branch?

5. **Critical Thinking:** *Compare and Contrast* How do the powers of the executive and judicial branches differ?

Link to ⚭ Art

Make a Poster Draw a poster that encourages people to visit Baton Rouge. You might want to include a drawing of the Louisiana State **Capitol** Building, or other exciting things to see in Baton Rouge. Give your poster a title.

Comparing Capitals

Baton Rouge and Washington, D.C.

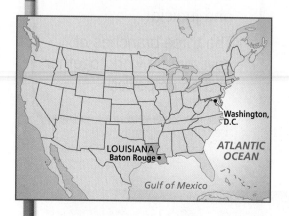

Our national capital has a lot in common with our state capital. Louisiana government leaders meet in the Louisiana State Capitol in Baton Rouge. The governor lives nearby in the Governor's Mansion.

Washington, D.C., is the capital of the United States. National government leaders meet in a building called the United States Capitol. The President lives in the White House. These pictures will help you compare and contrast the buildings in Baton Rouge and Washington, D.C.

▶ The current Louisiana Governor's Mansion was built in 1963, when country singer Jimmie Davis was governor.

▶ Louisiana senators debate bills in the State Capitol Building, shown in the circle above.

▶ The President of the United States lives and works in the White House in Washington, D.C. The office of the President is called the Oval Office (below). As its name suggests, the room is oval-shaped!

Visitors can tour many government buildings in Washington, D.C., including the United States Capitol. This is where members of the United States House of Representatives and Senate meet.

Identify Point of View

What? A point of view is the way a person feels about a problem or issue. For example, suppose the state has decided to build a new library in a town near you. Throughout the town, people are arguing about whether or not this is a good idea. They have different points of view about how the library will affect their community.

Why? Identifying different points of view can help you understand why people disagree.

▶ People can express their points of view about community issues at town meetings.

Miss Garza is a fourth-grade teacher. Here is what she said about the new library:

> *"I feel very glad the state is building a new library here. The students in my class do not have a place nearby to find books and do research. The new library would help them to complete assignments and find interesting books to read on their own."*

Mr. James has a different point of view. He owns a home down the street from where the library is supposed to be built. He is worried about how the new construction will affect his daily life:

> *"In my opinion, they should not build the new library. It will cause much more traffic, and this part of town is already too crowded. I am also worried that they will have to cut down many old trees to make room for the new building."*

How? To identify a person's point of view, ask yourself, "How does the issue affect the person?" With the library, it helped to know how Miss Garza and Mr. James felt about the project.

You can sometimes identify a point of view by reading things the person has said or written. People show their point of view when they use words such as "I think," "I feel," and "In my opinion."

Think and Apply

1. What is Miss Garza's **point of view** about the new library?

2. Why does Mr. James think building the library is a bad idea?

3. If you lived in this town, what would your point of view be about the library? Why?

251

Chapter Summary

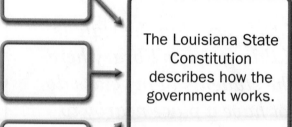

Draw Conclusions

On a separate sheet of paper, draw the diagram shown to the right. Fill in details about our state constitution that lead to the conclusion shown in the graphic organizer.

The Louisiana State Constitution describes how the government works.

Vocabulary

Match each word with the correct definition or description.

1 government (p. 237)

2 law (p. 239)

3 constitution (p. 243)

4 bill (p. 244)

a. a rule that is made by the government

b. a plan for a new law

c. the people and laws that operate a place

d. a written plan of government

Facts and Main Ideas

1 What are the three levels of government?

2 What is the difference between a *capitol* and a *capital?*

3 **Main Idea** How does the state government provide for the needs of the people?

4 **Main Idea** Summarize the main job that each branch of the state government has.

5 **Critical Thinking:** *Point of View* In which branch of the state government would you most like to work? Explain your reasons.

Write About It

1 **Write two interview questions** that you would ask one government leader in the legislative, executive, or judicial branch of the state government.

2 **Write a paragraph** explaining a new law you would pass if you worked in the Louisiana state government. Explain why you would pass this law.

3 **Write a newspaper article** about one of the services that the state government provides in your community. Choose a service such as a school, library, or public park. Write an article explaining how this service helps the community.

Internet Activity

To get help with vocabulary, people, and terms, select the dictionary or encyclopedia from *Social Studies Library* at **www.sfsocialstudies.com.**

Apply Skills

Identify Point of View Read a letter to the editor from a local newspaper. Explain the point of view of the writer to another classmate. What clues helped you to find the point of view?

Chapter 10

Citizens in Action

Lesson 1

Thibodaux

Citizens in Thibodaux helped their community by forming the Thibodaux Volunteer Fire Department.

1

Lesson 2

Shreveport

Every spring volunteers in Shreveport paint the houses of their older neighbors.

2

Why We Remember

Did you know that you are a very important part of Louisiana? You have the ability to make your community a better place. You can volunteer to help a neighbor or someone else in need. In this chapter, you will read about people in Louisiana who have made a difference in their communities and state.

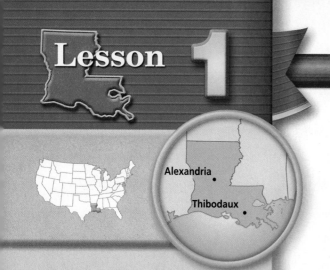

Alexandria

Thibodaux

Preview

Focus on the Main Idea
Citizens are the most important part of our government because they pick leaders and help improve communities.

PLACES
Alexandria
Thibodaux

PEOPLE
Lindy Boggs

VOCABULARY
democracy
republic
citizen

Living in a Democracy

You Are There "I'm not really nervous." At least, that's what you tell yourself as you walk up to the front of the class. You have decided to run for president of your class, and today is the day of your class election. Now it's your turn to tell the students why you think they should vote for you.

You realize that being a government leader must be pretty hard! You look down at the speech you have written in your notebook. "Well," you think, "if I'm going to be governor of Louisiana one day, this is good practice." Then you begin reading your speech.

 Draw Conclusions As you read, draw conclusions about the importance of citizens in our government.

Electing Leaders

Do you think you might like to be governor of Louisiana one day? If so, you will have to be elected by the people of our state. That is because our government is a democracy. A **democracy** is a government run by the people. In a democracy, voters have the power to choose their own leaders.

The United States is a special kind of democracy known as a republic. In a **republic,** people do not vote on every single decision that the government has to make. Instead people elect representatives to run the government and make laws. In 1973 **Lindy Boggs** became the first woman elected to represent Louisiana in our national government. You will read more about Boggs in the Biography after this lesson.

► Signs show support for different people running for government office.

REVIEW What important power do people have in a democracy? **Summarize**

► People vote for their government leaders on election day.

▶ The Thibodaux Volunteer Fire Department was formed by citizens who wanted to help people in their community.

▶ It is a student's responsibility to go to school. Chloe, a student from Alexandria, did not miss one day of school!

Responsible Citizens

What do you think is the most important job in a democracy? It is the job of citizen. A **citizen** is an official member of a country. People born in the United States are United States citizens. People born in other countries can also become United States citizens.

Citizens have important responsibilities. It is the job of citizens to help run the government and make communities better places to live. Citizens must also obey the law. Do you know what responsibility citizens get when they turn eighteen years old? At this age, citizens can vote in elections.

Younger citizens have the responsibility of going to school. A student named Chloe, from **Alexandria,** took this responsibility seriously. She did not miss a day of school from kindergarten through 12th grade! "I couldn't let anything get in the way of my perfect attendance," Chloe said.

Many citizens improve their community by volunteering. For example, citizens in **Thibodaux** formed the Thibodaux Volunteer Fire Department. This is one of many volunteer fire departments in Louisiana.

REVIEW Why are citizens the most important part of a democracy?
Draw Conclusions

Summarize the Lesson

- Our government is a special kind of democracy called a republic.
- In a republic, people elect representatives to run the government and make laws.
- Citizens help run the government and make communities better places to live.

LESSON 1 ⟩ REVIEW

Check Facts and Main Ideas

1. **Draw Conclusions** On a separate sheet of paper, draw a diagram like the one shown. Use the details given to draw a conclusion about citizens and the government.

> Citizens elect leaders and help run the government. →
>
> Citizens help make their communities better places to live. →

2. How are government leaders chosen in a **democracy?**

3. Explain how a **republic** works.

4. What are three important responsibilities of **citizens?**

5. **Critical Thinking: Apply Information** Why do you think it is important for citizens to vote in elections?

Link to ⟨⟩ **Writing**

Write a Speech Suppose your class is having an election and you want to be president. Write a speech that you could give to your classmates. Explain why you think you would be the best choice for class president.

Meet
Lindy Boggs

b. 1916
United States Congresswoman

Lindy Boggs comes from a family that has a long history of service in government. In fact, long ago one of her relatives was a member of Congress while George Washington was President!

"I grew up hearing the stories," she wrote. *"I learned the stories by heart, but I never expected that I would share directly in that heritage [tradition]. I never dreamed I would lead the life that I have led."*

Lindy grew up in New Roads, Louisiana. During college she met Hale Boggs. They were married in 1938.

In 1941 Hale Boggs was elected to the United States House of Representatives. Hale and Lindy moved to Washington, D.C. For the next 30 years, Lindy Boggs played an active part in the national government. She helped manage her husband's congressional office and helped him win elections. They also raised three children.

When Hale Boggs died in 1972, voters in Louisiana had to elect a new member of Congress. Lindy Boggs faced a difficult decision. Should she try to win this seat in Congress? Her children urged her to try.

Lindy Boggs won the election. She became the first woman from Louisiana to be elected to the United States House of Representatives. She served from 1973 to 1990. As an elected leader, she worked to pass laws that would help families and children.

Lindy Boggs once owned a very slow Shetland pony that she called Speedy.

BIOFACT

Learn from Biographies

What events in her life helped prepare Lindy Boggs to be a government leader?

Students can research the lives of significant people by clicking on *Meet the People* at **www.sfsocialstudies.com.**

As you know, Louisiana is one state of the United States of America. The American flag is a symbol of our nation. You will see it flying proudly throughout our state. The Stars and Stripes has gone through many changes over the years.

This is the most familiar version of the first Stars and Stripes.

Adopted for George Washington's Continental Army, this flag was also called the Continental Colors.

This battle flag was used in a square form by the Confederacy in the Civil War. The modern form is shown here.

This was the first flag of the Confederate States of America. It flew over Fort Sumter, in South Carolina, after the first shots in the war were fired there on April 12, 1861.

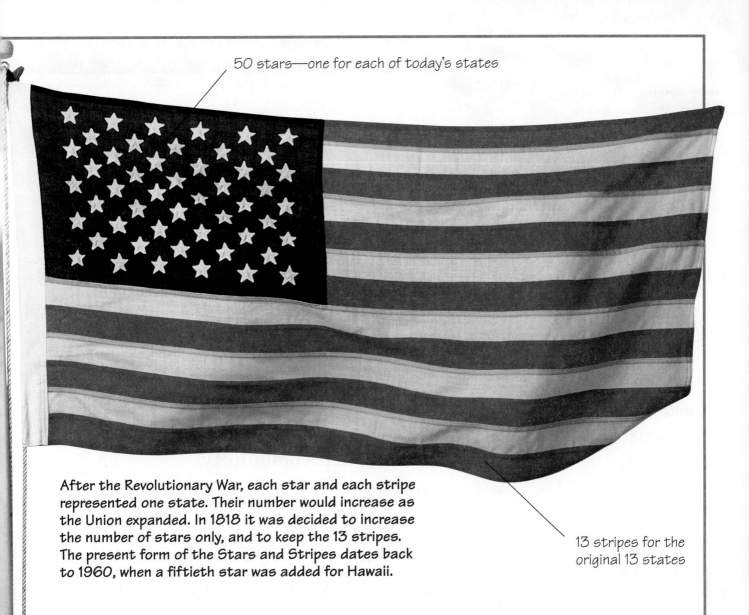

50 stars—one for each of today's states

13 stripes for the original 13 states

After the Revolutionary War, each star and each stripe represented one state. Their number would increase as the Union expanded. In 1818 it was decided to increase the number of stars only, and to keep the 13 stripes. The present form of the Stars and Stripes dates back to 1960, when a fiftieth star was added for Hawaii.

The famous photograph of marines raising the U.S. flag during World War II has been made into a memorial. The statue is an unusual instance of a real flag being combined with a piece of sculpture.

One of the uses of the national flag is to symbolize conquest—including scientific and peaceful conquest. American astronauts planted the flag when they landed on the moon.

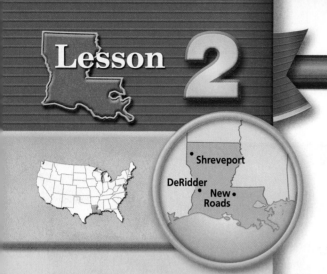

Shreveport

DeRidder

New Roads

Preview

Focus on the Main Idea
There are many things that citizens can do to make their communities better places to live.

PLACES
DeRidder
New Roads
Shreveport

PEOPLE
Ruby Bridges

VOCABULARY
volunteer

Improving Communities

You Are There Your homework assignment tonight is to look through the local newspaper. Your teacher wants you to find one article about something citizens are doing to improve their community.

You find a perfect article. It is about the students of East Beauregard Elementary School in DeRidder. They decided to raise money to buy dog and cat food. After getting lots of food, they donated it to animal shelters in DeRidder. The food they donated helped make sure that dogs and cats without homes did not go hungry. You can't wait to share this great story with your class!

 Draw Conclusions As you read, think about what makes a person a good citizen of his or her community.

Young Citizens

The story about students in **DeRidder** is true. This is just one of many things that young citizens are doing to help their communities. Another group of students in **New Roads** decided to send letters and care packages to American soldiers serving in other countries.

Think about what it means to be a good citizen. You know that good citizens obey the law and respect the rights and property of others. Good citizens also care about their neighbors and communities. Communities improve when people take time to help others.

REVIEW What are some qualities of good citizens? **Summarize**

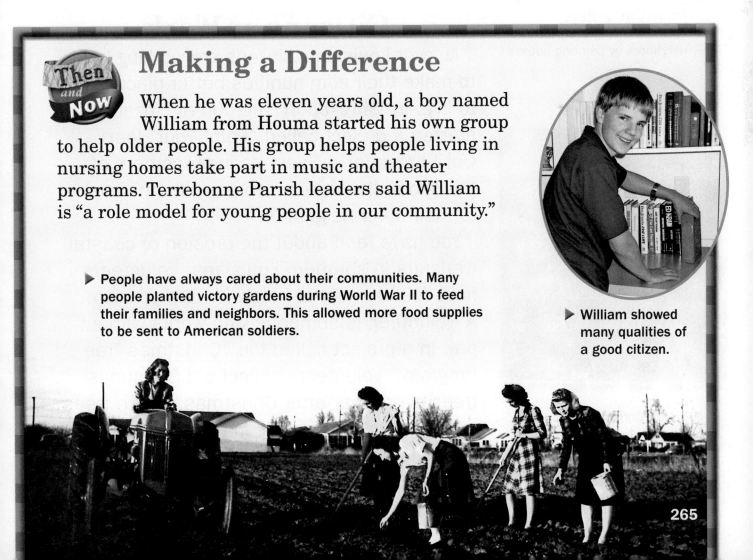

Then and Now

Making a Difference

When he was eleven years old, a boy named William from Houma started his own group to help older people. His group helps people living in nursing homes take part in music and theater programs. Terrebonne Parish leaders said William is "a role model for young people in our community."

▶ People have always cared about their communities. Many people planted victory gardens during World War II to feed their families and neighbors. This allowed more food supplies to be sent to American soldiers.

▶ William showed many qualities of a good citizen.

▶ In the "Paint Your Heart Out Shreveport" project, volunteers help their older neighbors by painting houses.

▶ In the "Christmas Tree Program," volunteers use old Christmas trees to slow down erosion.

Citizens at Work

All over Louisiana, citizens are working hard to make their communities better places to live. In **Shreveport** a group of citizens started a project called "Paint Your Heart Out Shreveport." Every spring members of this group get together to paint the houses of their older neighbors.

You have read about the erosion of coastal wetlands in southern Louisiana. Volunteers have found a way to help with this problem. A **volunteer** is someone who works without pay. In a project called the "Christmas Tree Program," volunteers collect old Christmas trees every year after Christmas. These trees are used to build fences in coastal wetlands. The fences help slow down coastal erosion.

Sometimes being a good citizen takes a lot of courage. The story of Ruby Bridges is a good example. For many years in Louisiana, black and white students had to attend segregated, or separate, schools. When Ruby Bridges was just six years old, she helped end segregation in Louisiana schools. You will read her story in Citizen Heroes after this lesson.

REVIEW What is the main goal of the Christmas Tree Program?
Main Idea and Details

Summarize the Lesson

- Young people are finding ways to make our state a better place to live.
- Good citizens obey the law, respect others, and care about their neighbors and communities.
- Citizens all over the state are working to solve problems and improve communities.

LESSON 2 REVIEW

Check Facts and Main Ideas

1. **Draw Conclusions** On a separate sheet of paper, draw a diagram like the one shown. Fill in details from the lesson that support this conclusion.

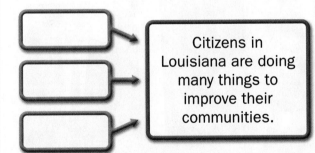

Citizens in Louisiana are doing many things to improve their communities.

2. Why did government leaders in Terrebonne Parish call William a "role model for young people"?

3. How are **volunteers** in Louisiana helping to slow down coastal erosion?

4. Think of one person you know who is a good citizen of your community. What makes this person a good citizen?

5. **Critical Thinking: *Make Decisions*** Suppose your class wanted to do something to help out in your community. What do you think your class should do?

Link to — **Reading**

Find an Article Suppose you have a homework assignment like the one described in You Are There on page 264. Look through a local newspaper. Find an article about something people are doing to improve your community. Share the story with your class.

Better Education For All

On November 14, 1960, six-year-old Ruby Bridges woke up in the morning and got ready for school. Since you do this every day, you might not think it would be a difficult thing to do. But for Ruby, going to William Frantz Elementary School that day took a lot of courage. She was about to become one of the first black students to attend an all-white school in New Orleans.

What exactly was going on? In 1954, the same year Bridges was born, the Supreme Court of the United States made an important decision. It said that public schools had to be open to all students. At that time, some schools were only for white students.

▶ Ruby Bridges reads to children from a book about her life (above). At right, six-year-old Ruby Bridges leaves school at the end of a day in 1960.

In 1960 the government made sure that schools in New Orleans were open to all students. Someone had to have the courage to be the first African American student at William Frantz Elementary. That someone was Ruby Bridges.

Some people did not want African Americans to attend the school. For an entire school year Ruby was the only student in her class because parents pulled their children from the school in protest. By the next year, though, the protests stopped. There were many children in Ruby's second-grade class—black and white students.

Bridges never forgot the challenges she faced in the first grade. As an adult, she went back to William Frantz Elementary as a volunteer. She also started an organization called the Ruby Bridges Foundation. This group helps parents get more involved in their children's education.

BUILDING CITIZENSHIP
Caring
Respect
Responsibility
Fairness
Honesty
Courage

▶ Years after she attended the William Frantz Elementary School, Ruby Bridges reunited with her first-grade teacher.

Courage in Action

Choose a person in Louisiana's history who showed courage. It could be someone in government or a citizen such as Ruby Bridges. Use the library to help you find out about this person. Write a paragraph about how he or she showed courage.

Use the Library

What? To get information about a topic you want to know more about, you can visit your local library.

Why? Libraries carry **periodicals,** which are magazines and newspapers that are printed regularly. Libraries also have **reference books,** such as dictionaries, atlases, encyclopedias, and almanacs. An almanac is a book published every year, with tables of facts and information on many subjects. Libraries have computers for doing **Internet searches.** They also have nonfiction books on just about any topic. Nonfiction books tell about real people, places, and events.

How? Suppose you want to do research about people who have made a difference in Louisiana's history. You might choose one of the people you have read about in this book, such as Bernardo de Gálvez, Sarah Morgan, or Louis C. Roudanez.

The more sources you use, the better the information will be. Using only one or two sources may not give you all the information that is important about a topic. Sources you might want to use for this project include the Internet, an encyclopedia, and a nonfiction book, such as a biography.

Search	Bernardo de Gálvez

- Do an Internet search to see if there is information about Bernardo de Gálvez. To use the Internet, you will need to do a **key word search.** In this case, the name of the person you want to research is the key word.

- Use the encyclopedia. Encyclopedias are arranged alphabetically. Look under "G" for "Gálvez."

- Ask the librarian to help you find a biography or other nonfiction book about Bernardo de Gálvez. If you cannot find a biography, look for a book about people in Louisiana's history.

Think and Apply

1. If you want to learn more about Sarah Morgan's Civil War diary, what **key word search** would you use on the Internet?

2. Why is it important to use more than one or two sources when researching a topic?

3. Suppose you want to find out more about Louis C. Roudanez. What are three types of sources that you could use?

Chapter Summary

Draw Conclusions

On a separate sheet of paper, draw the diagram shown below. Fill in a conclusion about younger citizens based on the details.

Young citizens have the responsibility of going to school.	→
Young citizens volunteer in many different ways to help their community.	→

Vocabulary

Write a paragraph explaining how people can help their government and communities. Use the vocabulary words below in your paragraph.

democracy (p. 257)   citizen (p. 258)

republic (p. 257)   volunteer (p. 266)

Facts and Main Ideas

1 What is an important responsibility of citizens under eighteen?

2 How did students in New Roads help American soldiers?

3 **Main Idea** In what way could you say that a citizen is a more important part of the government than a senator?

4 **Main Idea** What are some things that you can do to be a good citizen?

5 **Critical Thinking:** *Predict* How will going to school help you to vote when you turn eighteen?

Internet Activity

To get help with vocabulary, people, and terms, select the dictionary or encyclopedia from *Social Studies Library* at **www.sfsocialstudies.com.**

Write About It

1 **Make a list** of five volunteer projects you could do with your family or school to help your community.

2 **Write three interview questions** for Lindy Boggs or Ruby Bridges. Write a sentence explaining why you chose the person you did.

3 **Write a speech** explaining why it is important for every adult citizen over the age of eighteen to vote.

Apply Skills

Use the Library You have read that Ruby Bridges was one of the first black students to attend an all-white school in New Orleans. What library resources would you use to find more information about Ruby Bridges?

End with a Song

You Are My Sunshine

by Jimmie H. Davis and Charles Mitchell

"You Are My Sunshine" is another one of Louisiana's state songs. It was co-written by Jimmie Davis, who was a country music singer. He also served as Louisiana's governor from 1944 to 1948 and from 1960 to 1964.

274

Review

Main Ideas and Vocabulary

Read the passage. Then answer the questions.

You are the most important part of our government. As a citizen, you have a responsibility to go to school, help your community, and vote when you turn eighteen.

Our government is a special kind of democracy called a republic. People elect leaders to run the government.

The Louisiana state government provides many services. It helps maintain parks and public schools. The government also makes <u>laws</u> to keep us safe.

The state constitution explains how to make laws and elect leaders. It also divides the government into three branches: legislative, executive, and judicial.

You can do many things to help your community. People in Louisiana volunteer in many ways.

....

❶ According to the passage, our government
   A is a democracy and a republic
   B is not a democracy
   C has no constitution
   D has four branches

❷ In the passage, the word *law* means
   A government service
   B constitution
   C a rule made by the government
   D opportunity

❸ What is a main idea of this passage?
   A You should try to volunteer every year.
   B Citizens are the most important part of the government.
   C The government builds schools and parks.
   D Citizens have no say in the government.

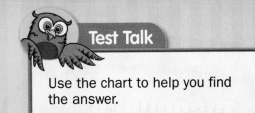

Vocabulary

Copy the sentences. Fill in each space with the correct letter.

   a. capitol (p. 243)
   b. capital (p. 243)
   c. citizen (p. 258)
   d. volunteer (p. 266)

❶ A _____ works without pay.

❷ Baton Rouge is the _____ of Louisiana.

❸ A _____ is an official member of a country.

❹ A _____ is a building where government leaders meet.

Apply Skills

Use the Library Use the library to write a short biography about a key person that you have read about in this book so far. Remember to think about what resources will be helpful and what keywords you will use in your search. Write a one-page biography using information you have found. List the resources you used at the bottom of the page.

Write and Share

Work as a Government To show how a law is created, divide the class into the three branches of state government. The legislative group will think of a new law and explain it in a paragraph. The executive branch will study the bill and write a paragraph explaining how they will enforce it. The judicial branch will write a paragraph explaining whether the law is fair or not. Turn to the charts on pages 244 and 245 for help.

Read on Your Own

Look for books like these in the library.

277

Discovery CHANNEL SCHOOL

UNIT 5 Project

Next Question!

Ask questions of a Louisiana state or local government leader at a press conference.

1 Choose students to play the roles of state or local government leaders and news reporters at a press conference in Louisiana.

2 Prepare a variety of questions to ask the government leaders about your state or community. Write answers to the questions.

3 Make press passes for the news reporters and official name tags for the government leaders.

4 Hold your press conference during class.

Press Pass
Daily World
Andy

Sheriff
Maria

Internet Activity

For more information and activities, go to www.sfsocialstudies.com.

People and Culture

Bouree

MBO SWEETS JAMBALAYA

What is special about Louisiana's culture?

Begin with
a Primary Source

KING
TOSS

TURKEY
Raffle
'5' '25'

TICKETS   GUMBO   SWEETS   JA

CRAWFISH

"There's a cultural mixture . . . [in Louisiana].
You still find this today in our culture, and
our food, and our way of speaking, and our
literature, and our songs."

— writer Ernest J. Gaines, 2003

Paul Schexnayder painted *The Fun
Festival* in 1993. It shows a school
festival in Louisiana in the 1930s.
Many festivals and fairs in Louisiana
celebrate our state's culture.

Meet the People

Jean Lafitte

c. 1780–1825

Birthplace: France

Pirate

- Sailed ships in the Gulf of Mexico and the Caribbean Sea
- Sold stolen goods in Louisiana
- Helped the Americans defeat the British at the Battle of New Orleans in 1815

Scholastique Picou Breaux

1796–1846

Birthplace: St. James, Louisiana

Founder of Breaux Bridge

- Founded the city of Breaux Bridge in 1829
- Drew up a city plan that included a diagram of the streets and a map of the area
- Is remembered today with a statue in Breaux Bridge

Louis Moreau Gottschalk

1829–1869

Birthplace: New Orleans, Louisiana

Pianist, composer

- Became a world-famous piano player when he was 13 years old
- Used Creole and Latin American music styles when writing his music
- Toured the United States, Europe, and South America playing piano

1750   1800   1850

1780 • Jean Lafitte   1825

1796 • Scholastique Picou Breaux   1846

1829 – 1869
Louis M. Gottschalk

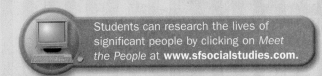
Students can research the lives of significant people by clicking on *Meet the People* at **www.sfsocialstudies.com**.

Louis Armstrong

1901–1971

Birthplace: New Orleans, Louisiana

Musician

- Sang in a boys quartet as a child
- Became famous for playing jazz music on the trumpet
- Appeared in many movies and on radio and television programs

Jake Delhomme

b. 1975

Birthplace: Breaux Bridge, Louisiana

Football player

- Played football in college at the University of Louisiana-Lafayette
- Plays professional football
- Raises racehorses with his father at his family's horse stable

1900   1950   2000

1901 • Louis Armstrong   1971

1975 • Jake Delhomme

Reading Social Studies

Music in Louisiana

Target Skill

Summarize

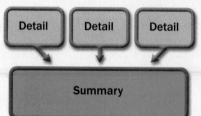

- A summary is a short statement that tells the main idea of an article or tells what happened in a story.

- When you summarize a paragraph, look at the details and the main idea.

- To summarize an article with many paragraphs, find the main idea of each paragraph. Then tell in a sentence or two what the whole article is about.

Read the paragraph. The first sentence tells the main idea. It is a good summary of this paragraph. The other sentences tell important details.

About the year 1900, musicians in New Orleans first began to play jazz music. One of the early jazz stars was a piano player named Ferdinand "Jelly Roll" Morton. Morton was one of the first great writers of jazz. His music is still played today.

Word Exercise

Parts of Speech Knowing if a word is being used as a noun or a verb can help you understand its meaning. Look at the different meanings for *play* below.

Noun	Verb
a story acted out on the stage	to perform on a musical instrument

Figure out the correct definition of *play* in this sentence: "Students acted in the play."

Celebrating Music in Louisiana

Louisiana is home to many different kinds of music. People from all over the world have brought their own styles of music to Louisiana.

When the Acadians arrived in the 1700s, they brought their songs and dances with them. People still play Cajun music in Louisiana today, usually using fiddles and accordions.

The city of New Orleans is known as the birthplace of jazz. Louis Armstrong, who was born in New Orleans in 1901, helped make jazz popular all over the world.

Other popular styles of music in Louisiana include blues, country, rock and roll, gospel, Dixieland, and zydeco. Louisiana is famous for its great music and musicians!

Apply it!

Use the reading skill of summarizing to answer questions 1 and 2. Then answer the vocabulary question.

1 What is the main idea of the first paragraph?

2 Which statement is the best summary of the entire article?

   a. Many Louisiana musicians still play jazz today.

   b. Louisiana is famous for its great variety of music.

3 In the second paragraph, is *play* being used as a noun or a verb?

The People of Louisiana

CANADA

NORTH AMERICA

UNITED STATES

LOUISIANA

Breaux Bridge

St. Bernard Parish

Gulf of Mexico

MEXICO

PACIFIC OCEAN

ATLANTIC OCEAN

2 **1**

Why We Remember

The people of Louisiana are what make our state wonderful. People from Africa, Asia, Europe, and Latin America have come to live in Louisiana. Every group of people has brought their own culture to make Louisiana special. In this chapter you will read about the people and cultures of Louisiana.

287

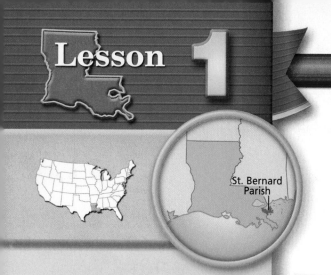
Louisiana Cultures

Preview

Focus on the Main Idea
People from all over the world have brought their own special cultures to our state.

PLACE
St. Bernard Parish

VOCABULARY
culture
immigrant

▶ Traditional Isleño clothing

You Are There This is a field trip you have really been looking forward to. Today your class is exploring Los Isleños (ees LAYN yos) Museum in St. Bernard Parish.

"*Isleños* is a Spanish word that means 'islanders,'" your teacher explains. "The group of people known as the Isleños came to Louisiana in the late 1700s. They came from the Canary Islands, which were part of Spain."

Inside the museum, exhibits tell the story of the Isleños. You will see real clothes, tools, and musical instruments that were used by Isleños long ago. This is a great way to learn about the people of Louisiana!

 Summarize As you read, think of a one-sentence summary for each paragraph.

Louisiana's Population

More than four million people live in Louisiana today. The graph on this page shows you how much our state's population has grown since 1900.

Louisiana's population is made up of many groups of people. Each group has a special culture. A **culture** is the way a group of people lives. Culture includes a group's language, music, religion, food, clothing, and holidays.

You just read about a group of people called the Isleños. This is one example of a cultural group. Isleños speak Spanish and have their own styles of clothing and dance. Today there are Isleño communities in **St. Bernard Parish** in southeastern Louisiana. The Isleños are one of the many groups of people that make our state special.

▶ Performers show onlookers a traditional Isleño style of dance.

REVIEW What is the main idea of the second paragraph? ↻ **Summarize**

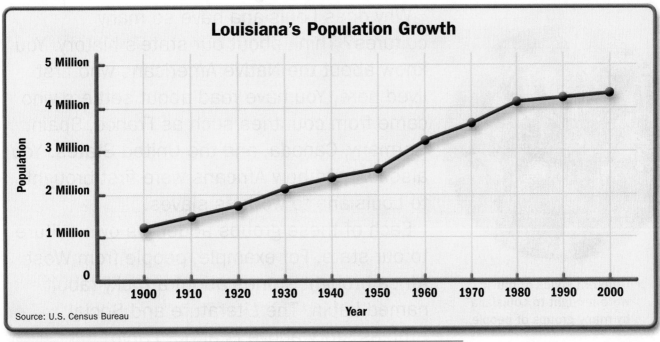

Louisiana's Population Growth

Population / Year

Source: U.S. Census Bureau

GRAPH SKILL Use a Line Graph *In what year was Louisiana's population slightly more than three million people?*

289

Why Lapin's Tail Is Short
by Sharon Arms Doucet

In this story, Lapin wants to get across a bayou. So he tricks a group of alligators by saying he wants to count them. The alligators line up in the bayou to be counted. Then Lapin jumps on their backs and laughs as he crosses the water.

"Ha, ha! I don't care a fig about counting you ole gators. I just wanted to get to this side of the bayou so's I could have myself some lunch!" And he jumped for the grassy green bank.

But this time he'd laughed too soon. Compère [friend] Alligator snapped open his gigantic jaws and chomped down on Compère Lapin's long, bushy tail. . . .

R-r-r-i-i-i-p! went his backside.

Lapin made it to the other side, all right. But most of his beautiful, prideful tail stayed back there in Alligator's razor-sharp teeth.

And that's why, to this very day, Compère Lapin's tail is as short and stumpy as a cotton boll [part of a cotton plant].

Many Cultures

Why does Louisiana have so many cultures? Think about our state's history. You know about the Native Americans who first lived here. You have read about settlers who came from countries such as France, Spain, Germany, Canada, and the United States. You also learned how Africans were first brought to Louisiana to work as slaves.

Each of these groups added its own culture to our state. For example, people from West Africa brought stories about a tricky rabbit named Lapin. The Literature and Social Studies story above is about Lapin.

▶ Different styles of music were brought to Louisiana by many groups of people.

Each year immigrants from countries all over the world come to live in Louisiana. An **immigrant** is a person who moves to a country and lives there. In Louisiana today, the largest numbers of immigrants come from countries in Latin America and Asia.

Each group of immigrants adds something special to the culture of our state. At the same time, all Louisianans share the culture of the United States. We all respect our country's past and celebrate our country's holidays.

REVIEW What is one way people from West Africa added to the culture of Louisiana? 🎯 **Summarize**

Summarize the Lesson

- More than four million people live in Louisiana today.

- People from all over the world have brought their cultures to Louisiana.

- Immigrants continue to settle in Louisiana today.

LESSON 1 REVIEW

Check Facts and Main Ideas

1. 🎯 **Summarize** On a separate sheet of paper, fill in two details that support the lesson summary.

People from all over the world have brought their cultures to Louisiana.

2. What are some things that can be part of a group's **culture?**

3. Why does Louisiana have so many cultures?

4. The largest numbers of **immigrants** to Louisiana today come from which two places?

5. **Critical Thinking: *Interpret Graphs*** Look back at the line graph on page 289. Write a one-sentence summary of the information in this graph.

Link to ⌖ Writing

Write a Family Story Ask a family member or neighbor how they or their relatives first came to Louisiana. Write down the information. Then share what you have learned with the rest of your class.

Making a New Home

Louisiana and Vietnam

About 25,000 immigrants from the Southeast Asian nation of Vietnam live in Louisiana today. They traveled thousands of miles from Vietnam to Louisiana in search of a better life for themselves and their families. Like other immigrants, they brought their language, music, and cooking styles to our state. They also brought important skills. In both Vietnam and Louisiana, farming and fishing are important activities. Many immigrants who used to farm or catch fish in Vietnam were able to continue this work in Louisiana.

▶ These Vietnamese men are docking their fishing boat in Louisiana.

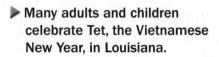

▶ Many adults and children celebrate Tet, the Vietnamese New Year, in Louisiana.

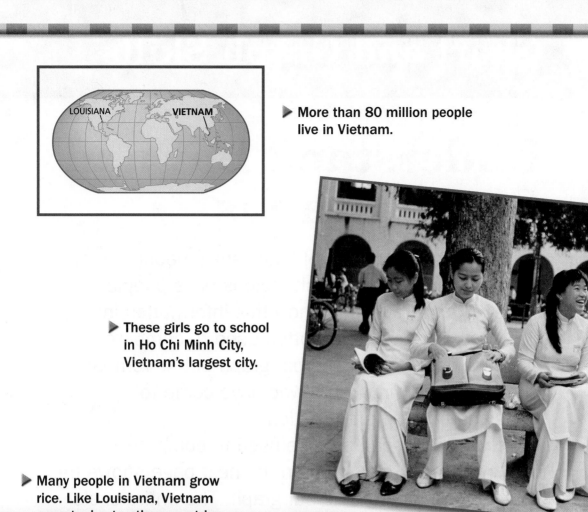

▶ **More than 80 million people live in Vietnam.**

▶ **These girls go to school in Ho Chi Minh City, Vietnam's largest city.**

▶ **Many people in Vietnam grow rice. Like Louisiana, Vietnam exports rice to other countries.**

Understand Bar and Circle Graphs

What? About 116,000 of Louisiana's people today are immigrants. From which regions have people come? A **bar graph** can show this information in a clear way. Bar graphs are often used to compare numbers or amounts. The bar graph below compares the number of immigrants who have come to Louisiana from different regions.

A **circle graph** can also be used to compare amounts. The circle graph on the next page shows the same information as the bar graph. The entire circle represents all the immigrants in Louisiana. Each slice of the circle stands for the people from one region.

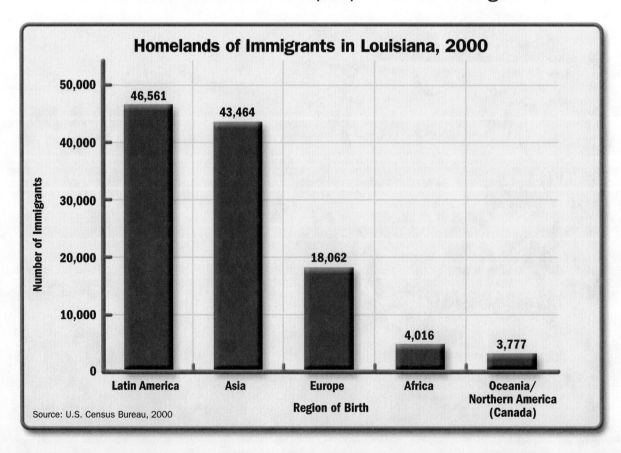

Homelands of Immigrants in Louisiana, 2000

Source: U.S. Census Bureau, 2000

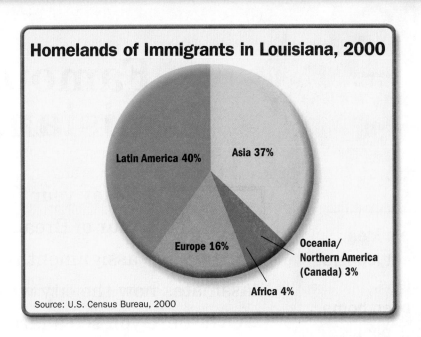

Homelands of Immigrants in Louisiana, 2000

Latin America 40%

Asia 37%

Europe 16%

Oceania/
Northern America
(Canada) 3%

Africa 4%

Source: U.S. Census Bureau, 2000

Why? Bar graphs and circle graphs show facts in a clear, simple picture. They also help you compare information.

How? Look at the bar graph on page 294. The words at the bottom of the graph tell you which region each bar stands for. The numbers above and to the left of each bar tell you how many people are represented.

Now look at the circle graph on this page. The words tell you which region each slice of the graph stands for. The numbers tell you what percentage each slice represents. The graph says that 37 percent of the immigrants came from Asia. In other words, 37 out of every 100 immigrants came from Asia.

Think and Apply

1 About how many people have come to Louisiana from Asia? Which graph did you use to find this answer?

2 What percentage of all immigrants came from Africa? Which graph did you use?

3 Have more immigrants come from Europe or Latin America? How did you find the answer?

Breaux
Bridge •

Famous Louisianans

Preview

Focus on the Main Idea
From government leaders to great musicians, Louisiana has been home to many famous people.

PLACE
Breaux Bridge

PEOPLE
Scholastique Picou
  Breaux
Jean-Baptiste Le Moyne
  de Bienville
Jean Lafitte
Louis Moreau
  Gottschalk
Louis Armstrong

VOCABULARY
jazz

► Scholastique Picou
  Breaux statue

You Are There Today your class is taking a tour of Breaux Bridge. Your assignment is to tell your classmates how the city was started.

"Over here you see a large statue," you tell the class. "This is an Acadian woman named Scholastique Picou Breaux. Breaux founded this city in 1829.

"Many years later, a group of women here decided to build a statue to honor Breaux. But no one knew what she looked like. They hired a local artist to make the statue. When the artist studied Breaux's life, she learned that she was Breaux's great-great granddaughter! So she used her daughter as a model for the statue."

 Summarize As you read, look for details that can help you to summarize the main ideas of this lesson.

People from the Past

Scholastique Picou Breaux founded the town of **Breaux Bridge** when she was just 33 years old. She also had five children at the time. So you know she must have been very busy!

Breaux is just one of many interesting people from Louisiana's history. Another person who began a city is **Jean-Baptiste Le Moyne de Bienville.** As governor of Louisiana, he founded the city of New Orleans in 1718.

Have you heard of **Jean Lafitte?** Lafitte was a famous pirate in the early 1800s. He used to hide in the swamps south of New Orleans. He is also known for helping Louisiana in the War of 1812. When the British attacked New Orleans, Lafitte joined the American side. He helped the Americans win the Battle of New Orleans in 1815.

▶ Jean-Baptiste Le Moyne de Bienville was governor of the colony of Louisiana and founder of New Orleans.

REVIEW What do we remember about Scholastique Picou Breaux and Jean-Baptiste Le Moyne de Bienville? ↻ **Summarize**

▶ The pirate Jean Lafitte helped the Americans during the War of 1812.

Louisiana's Famous People

You have already met some of the famous people from our state. Here are some more Louisianans you may have heard about.

▶ **Kate Chopin (1850–1904)** was a famous writer who wrote stories about the Creole and Cajun cultures of New Orleans.

▶ **Bryant Gumbel (b. 1948)** has been a news anchor on national television. He has interviewed government leaders from all over the world.

▶ **Jimmie Davis (1899–2000)** served twice as Louisiana's governor and co-wrote one of our state songs. He often sang at campaign stops when he ran for governor.

▶ **Mahalia Jackson (1911–1972)** was one of the most famous gospel music singers of all time. She was called the "Queen of Gospel Song."

Making Music

Louisiana has always had great musicians. In the 1800s **Louis Moreau Gottschalk** became a famous piano player when he was just 13! Around 1900, a new style of music called **jazz** was born in New Orleans. Trumpet player and singer **Louis Armstrong** helped make jazz popular.

Today, our state is still a great place to hear music. Each year thousands of visitors attend the New Orleans Jazz and Heritage Festival. This ten-day festival celebrates the music of New Orleans and Louisiana.

REVIEW Identify the sentence above that best summarizes the information on this page. **Summarize**

Summarize the Lesson

- Scholastique Picou Breaux and Jean-Baptiste Le Moyne de Bienville are famous for founding cities.

- Louisiana has produced many great musicians, including Louis Armstrong and Louis Moreau Gottschalk.

LESSON 2 REVIEW

Check Facts and Main Ideas

1. **Summarize** On a separate sheet of paper, fill in three details that support the lesson summary.

People from Louisiana have become famous for doing many different things.

2. What do Scholastique Picou Breaux and Jean-Baptiste Le Moyne de Bienville have in common?

3. Why is Bryant Gumbel a famous Louisianan?

4. What is **jazz?** When and where did it begin?

5. **Critical Thinking: *Express Ideas*** Which person from this lesson is the most interesting to you? Explain your opinion.

Link to Reading

Read a Biography Go to the library and find a biography about a famous person from Louisiana. Read the book and think about how to summarize it. Then share the main ideas with your class.

Meet
Louis Armstrong

1901–1971 • Musician

Louis Armstrong grew up in New Orleans, the city where jazz was born. As a young boy, he listened to many of the great early jazz musicians. Louis was determined to become a musician himself. "I had an awful urge to learn the cornet," he remembered. The cornet is a brass horn similar to a trumpet.

Louis learned to play by watching older musicians. Most of his time, though, was spent working. He delivered coal and sold newspapers to help make sure his family had enough money.

All the while, Louis was getting better and better at playing the cornet. By the time he was sixteen, he had formed a small band with some friends. They were able to earn money by playing jazz at parades, dances, and picnics in New Orleans.

Armstrong got a big break in 1922. He was invited to play with a famous band in Chicago, Illinois. Armstrong later said,

"I was so happy I did not know what to do. I had hit the big time. . . . My boyhood dream had come true at last."

Armstrong eventually switched to playing the trumpet. He quickly became one of the most famous musicians in the country. He traveled from city to city, playing concerts and recording albums. Today, Armstrong is remembered as one of the greatest American musicians.

Learn from Biographies

From a young age, Louis Armstrong wanted to be a musician. How did he show determination in achieving this dream?

Armstrong's first cornet is in the Smithsonian Museum in Washington, D.C.

BIOFACT

➤ "Saint Louis Blues" was one of Louis Armstrong's popular songs.

Students can research the lives of significant people by clicking on *Meet the People* at **www.sfsocialstudies.com**.

Chapter Summary

Summarize

On a separate sheet of paper, fill in the details to complete the summary of Chapter 11.

Many people and groups have added to Louisiana's special culture.

Vocabulary

Write a paragraph using each vocabulary word below. Include details you learned from this chapter in each sentence.

culture (p. 289)

jazz (p. 299)

immigrant (p. 291)

Facts and Main Ideas

1. What is special about Isleños culture?

2. What is Jean Lafitte famous for?

3. **Main Idea** What are some groups that have added their cultures to our state?

4. **Main Idea** For what kinds of music have Louisiana musicians become famous?

5. **Critical Thinking:** *Draw Conclusions* Why do you think the people of Breaux Bridge chose to build a statue to honor Scholastique Picou Breaux?

Write About It

1. **Write a thank-you note** to the Los Isleños Museum after a class trip you may have taken. Include details about what you learned at the museum.

2. **Write a "You Are There"** describing what you think it was like for Louis Moreau Gottschalk to become a famous piano player at 13.

3. **Take a survey** to see which famous Louisianan from the chapter your classmates think is most important to our state's history and culture.

Apply Skills

Understand Bar and Circle Graphs
Study the graphs on pages 294 and 295. Then answer the questions below.

1. Which graph shows percentages?

2. What region do most immigrants come from? Which graph can give you this information?

3. Why are bar and circle graphs useful?

Internet Activity

To get help with vocabulary, people, and terms, select the dictionary or encyclopedia from *Social Studies Library* at www.sfsocialstudies.com.

303

Chapter 12

Celebrations and Traditions

Lesson 1

New Orleans

New Orleans is one of the cities where Mardi Gras celebrations are held every year.

1

Lesson 2

Ponchatoula

Visitors can sample the fruit at the Ponchatoula Strawberry Festival.

2

CANADA

NORTH AMERICA

UNITED STATES

PACIFIC OCEAN

ATLANTIC OCEAN

LOUISIANA

Ponchatoula

New Orleans

Gulf of Mexico

MEXICO

2 1

Why We Remember

Did you know that Louisiana has festivals to honor crawfish, strawberries, and even frogs? Festivals and historic sites help us remember the past and celebrate different cultures. Plus, we have the outdoors. Louisiana is great for fishing or hiking. In this chapter, you will learn about fun activities to do around the state.

305

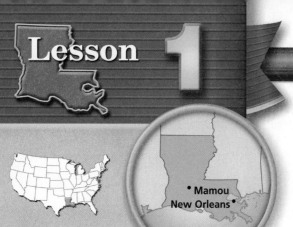
• Mamou
New Orleans •

Preview

Focus on the Main Idea
The cultural groups of
Louisiana have brought
many different kinds
of food, music, and
celebrations to our state.

PLACES
New Orleans
Mamou

VOCABULARY
custom
tradition
Mardi Gras

Celebrating Cultures

You Are There What do you call a spicy
dish made of rice, onions,
garlic, pepper, and meats
such as ham, chicken, sausage, and
shrimp? Here's a hint: this is a classic
Louisiana recipe. It's called jambalaya
(jahm bah LIE yah)!

You and your family are spending
the day at the Jambalaya Festival in
Gonzales. There are carnival rides, races,
and music. And don't forget all the great
food. Some of Louisiana's best chefs are
here to compete in the World Champion
Jambalaya Cooking Contest. Each chef
has to cook his or her jambalaya with the
same exact ingredients. You can't wait to
judge the results for yourself!

 Summarize As you read, think
of ways to summarize the main
idea in each paragraph.

▶ Jambalaya

Cultures and Customs

You know that Louisiana is home to many different cultures. Cultural groups often have their own **customs,** or special ways of doing things. Customs can include different ways of cooking, dressing, and celebrating. For example, you just read about a food called jambalaya. Cooking this dish is a custom of people from Cajun and Creole backgrounds. Many other cultural groups have brought their own recipes to Louisiana.

Customs can also include different ways of playing music. A singer and accordion player named Boozoo Chavis helped make zydeco (ZEYE de coh) famous. Zydeco is a style of Creole dance music that was first played by African Americans in southwestern Louisiana. Today it is popular around the world!

▶ Zydeco is one of the music styles played at the Louisiana Swamp Festival in New Orleans.

REVIEW What are two examples of customs in Louisiana? ↻ **Summarize**

▶ Some instruments used to play zydeco music include the accordion and the frattoir, a metal instrument worn on the chest.

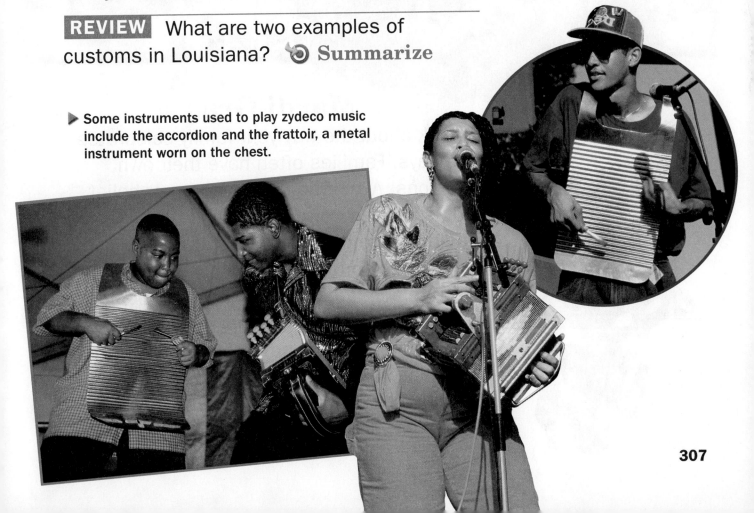

Mardi Gras in New Orleans

Louisiana's first Mardi Gras was celebrated in New Orleans in 1766. Today, more than one million people celebrate Mardi Gras in New Orleans. Look at the pictures below to see how Mardi Gras traditions today are similar to those from long ago.

▶ Today, colorful costumes and parades are still a part of Mardi Gras celebrations in New Orleans.

▶ The picture below was taken in 1933. It shows that Mardi Gras parades with large floats have been a New Orleans tradition for many years.

▶ Some people wear masks like these to celebrate Mardi Gras.

Mardi Gras

Think about the way your family celebrates birthdays. Families often have their own traditions. A **tradition** is a custom or belief that is handed down over the years. Traditions are often repeated as a part of yearly celebrations.

The celebration of **Mardi Gras** has been a Louisiana tradition since the 1700s. French settlers brought Roman Catholic holidays to Louisiana. One tradition was to throw a big party before the beginning of Lent. Lent is a time of prayer and fasting for Roman Catholics.

This party was known as Mardi Gras. Soon other cultures began contributing their own music, dance, and costumes to Mardi Gras.

Today, Mardi Gras is a celebration held in **New Orleans** and other cities. In New Orleans, people watch parades and dance to the music of marching bands. Other cities have their own traditions. In **Mamou,** people dress up in costumes and ride horses from house to house. They sing, dance, and collect ingredients for a huge meal that everyone can share!

REVIEW How is Mardi Gras celebrated in Louisiana? ⊙ **Summarize**

Summarize the Lesson

- The cultural groups of Louisiana have brought a variety of customs to our state.

- Customs can include different ways of cooking food, playing music, and celebrating special events.

- French settlers began the tradition of Mardi Gras in Louisiana in the 1700s.

LESSON 1 REVIEW

Check Facts and Main Ideas

1. ⊙ **Summarize** On a separate sheet of paper, fill in details that support the lesson summary.

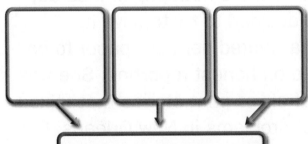

Louisiana is home to many customs and traditions.

2. What is one **custom** of people from Cajun and Creole backgrounds?

3. How did Boozoo Chavis contribute to the culture of Louisiana?

4. How did **Mardi Gras** become a **tradition** in Louisiana?

5. **Critical Thinking: *Draw Conclusions*** You know that Louisiana is home to people from a wide variety of cultural backgrounds. Do you think this has led to the wide variety of customs and traditions in Louisiana? Explain.

Link to ⊶ Music

Research Music Styles Find out more about one style of music that is popular in Louisiana. How did this music begin? What kinds of instruments are used? Who are some musicians who play this kind of music today?

Getting the Word Out

A good way to learn about local customs and traditions in your area of Louisiana is to read a newspaper. But what would you do if you were suddenly put in charge of a major newspaper? Eliza Nicholson faced that question when she was just 26 years old.

The year was 1876. Eliza had experience as a newspaper writer. In fact, she was the first woman in Louisiana to earn a living by writing for a newspaper. Now she faced an even bigger challenge: how to run *The Daily Picayune* (pik a YOON) by herself! *The Daily Picayune* newspaper was losing money at the time. Many people told her to sell the newspaper. Instead, Eliza decided to try to save it.

Eliza wanted her newspaper to be based on honest reporting. She was not afraid to print stories that talked about problems in New Orleans. For example, *The Daily Picayune* often spoke out against cruelty to animals. The newspaper also called for improving education and for building a special hospital for children.

▶ Before she was put in charge of *The Daily Picayune*, Eliza Nicholson wrote poetry under the name Pearl Rivers.

BUILDING CITIZENSHIP

Caring

Respect

Responsibility

Fairness

Honesty

Courage

At the same time, Eliza worked to increase sales of the newspaper. She had many ideas that were new at the time. She added sections for women and children to the newspaper. *The Daily Picayune* soon became a very popular and successful newspaper.

The success of *The Daily Picayune* was important to Eliza Nicholson. She did not measure success simply by how much money her newspaper earned, however. She wanted the newspaper to make a positive contribution to her community. Eliza's commitment to honest reporting is still remembered today.

▶ Eliza Nicholson added features to *The Daily Picayune*, such as comics and advice columns.

Honesty in Action

How did Eliza Nicholson show honesty?
Why is honesty an important part of good citizenship?

Use Map Scales

What? The map below shows just some of the interstate highways that cross Louisiana. On the map, these highways are only a few inches long. Suppose you want to know how long the roads really are. You could use a map scale to figure this out. A **map scale** is a tool that helps you measure distances on a map. It tells you what a certain small distance on a map equals in actual miles on Earth.

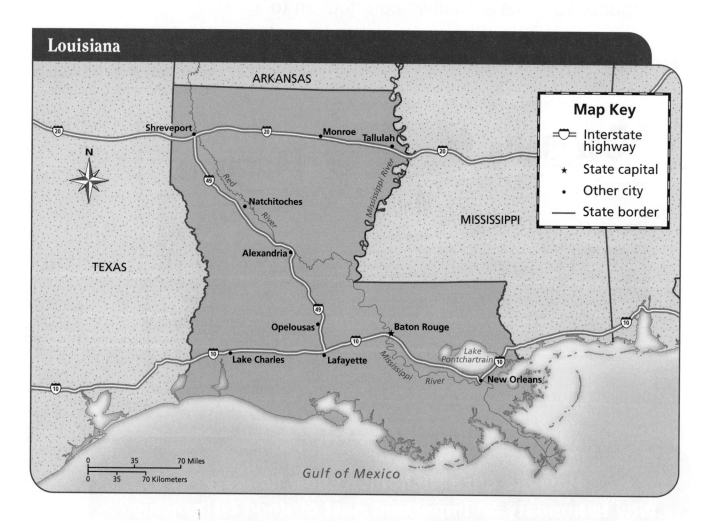

Why? Suppose your family is planning to drive from Shreveport to Natchitoches. You will want to know the distance between these two cities so you can figure out how long the trip will take. A map scale helps you figure out the actual distance in miles or kilometers between two places.

How? To use a map scale, put a ruler under the scale. The scale will have marks on it. Each mark stands for a real distance. With your ruler, measure the distance between marks. Then look at the scale. How many miles does that measurement stand for?

On the map on page 312, one inch stands for 70 miles. To measure the distance between Shreveport and Natchitoches, place your ruler so that one end touches Shreveport. Make sure the ruler touches Natchitoches as well. Count the number of inches between Shreveport and Natchitoches (one inch). Since each inch equals 70 miles, the distance between the two communities is about 70 miles.

▶ Shreveport is about 210 miles from Lafayette. How many inches is that on the map?

Think and Apply

1 What is a **map scale?** How is it useful?

2 About how many miles is the distance from Lafayette to Natchitoches?

3 Which highway is longer in Louisiana, Interstate 10 or Interstate 20? How do you know?

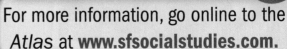

Internet Activity

For more information, go online to the *Atlas* at **www.sfsocialstudies.com**.

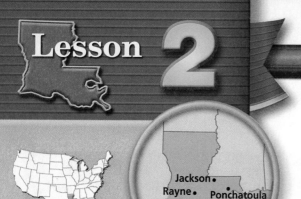

Places to See

Preview

Focus on the Main Idea
There is plenty to see in Louisiana, including historic sites, festivals, and sporting events.

PLACES
Jackson
Rayne
Ponchatoula

PEOPLE
Jake Delhomme

VOCABULARY
festival

You Are There

Your class is exploring the Cabildo, a building in New Orleans. "The Cabildo was built in the 1790s," your teacher says. "Spanish government leaders used to meet here when Spain controlled the Louisiana colony. Then, one day in 1803, a crowd of people gathered outside. Can anyone guess why? The year 1803 is a clue."

"Does it have to do with the Louisiana Purchase?" you ask.

"That's right," your teacher says. "The Americans officially took over Louisiana in this building. Just outside, the American flag was raised for the first time."

You have learned a lot about Louisiana history this year in school. And now you are seeing some of this history up close!

 Summarize As you read, think about how each main topic could be summarized in one sentence.

▶ The Cabildo

Living History

One great way to learn about history is to see it for yourself. The state government protects historic sites all over Louisiana. Historic sites include real homes, farms, and schools from Louisiana's past. Suppose you wanted to see what life was like for students in the 1800s. At Centenary State Historic Site in **Jackson,** you can walk through the small rooms where college students slept, ate, and studied.

In New Orleans you can ride on the streetcars. These are the exact same streetcars that carried people around New Orleans in the early 1900s. Back then, streetcars shared the roads with horses and just a few cars. Today, the streets are crowded with cars, trucks, and buses!

REVIEW How have the streets of New Orleans changed since the early 1900s? How have they remained the same?
Compare and Contrast

▶ The Centenary State Historic Site and the Riverfront Streetcar Line still exist. They show how people lived and traveled long ago.

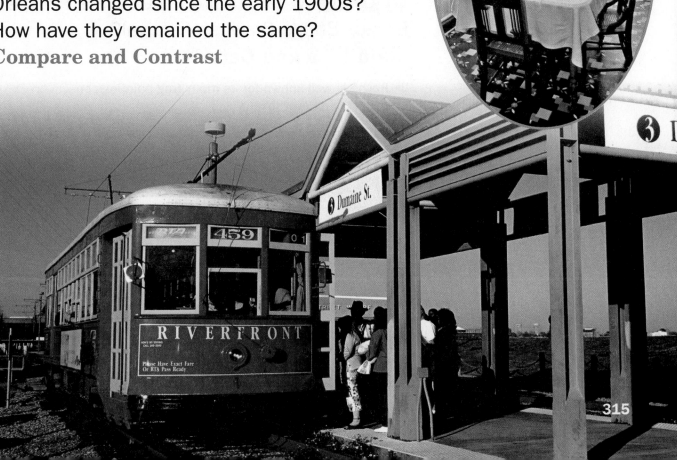

Fairs and Festivals

There are more than 400 fairs and festivals in Louisiana each year. A **festival** is a program of entertainment that is often held every year. These events celebrate our state's rich variety of cultures and traditions. At the Louisiana Folklife Festival in Monroe, people can learn about Native American, African American, Creole, and Cajun customs such as different styles of art, music, and storytelling. The Breaux Bridge Crawfish Festival celebrates crawfish and the Cajun culture of southern Louisiana.

At the Frog Festival in **Rayne,** you can watch the World Champion Frog Jumping Contest. You also might want to visit the Ponchatoula Strawberry Festival in the city of **Ponchatoula.** Here you can taste the sweet fruit that is grown and sold by local farmers.

▶ The Ponchatoula Strawberry Festival has rides, music, games, and, of course, strawberries!

REVIEW What culture is celebrated at the Breaux Bridge Crawfish Festival?
Main Idea and Details

▶ Rayne is well-known for its many frog paintings on buildings all over town.

MAP ADVENTURE

You have decided to visit several festivals in Louisiana. You will need a map to plan your trip. Study the map below and answer the questions.

Map Key

- Louisiana State Fair
- Louisiana Folklife Festival
- Louisiana Corn Festival
- Ponchatoula Strawberry Festival
- Breaux Bridge Crawfish Festival
- Rayne Frog Festival

Shreveport

Monroe

LOUISIANA

Bunkie

Breaux Bridge

Ponchatoula

Rayne

N W E S

Gulf of Mexico

- Which of the festivals on the map is located nearest to the center of the state?

- Which festival is the furthest south?

- Suppose you are at the Louisiana State Fair. If you travel east, which festival will you soon reach?

- Picture where New Orleans would be on this map. Which festival is closest to New Orleans?

► People of all ages can enjoy outdoor activities in Louisiana.

► Thousands of people come to Baton Rouge to watch football games at Louisiana State University.

Outdoor Action

Louisiana is famous for its exciting outdoor life. Our state is great for hiking, biking, boating, fishing, and all kinds of sports. In fact, people come from all over the country to enjoy the outdoors in Louisiana. This is good news for our state's economy. For example, think about what happens when people come here to go fishing. They spend money to stay in hotels, eat in restaurants, and buy fishing supplies. All that spending helps support local businesses.

Many people in Louisiana love playing and watching sports. Do you have a favorite sports team? The women's basketball team at Louisiana Tech University is often one of the best in the country. At Louisiana State University, more than 90,000 fans pack Tiger Stadium to watch the football team play! **Jake Delhomme** was a star football player at the University of Louisiana-Lafayette. You will read his story in the Biography after this lesson.

REVIEW What are some popular outdoor activities in Louisiana? **Summarize**

Summarize the Lesson

- At historic sites, you can explore real homes, farms, and schools from Louisiana's past.
- Many festivals celebrate our state's cultures and traditions.
- People in Louisiana enjoy outdoor activities, including hiking, boating, fishing, and sports.

LESSON 2 REVIEW

Check Facts and Main Ideas

1. **Summarize** On a separate sheet of paper, fill in a sentence to summarize this lesson.

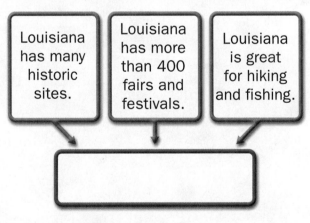

Louisiana has many historic sites.

Louisiana has more than 400 fairs and festivals.

Louisiana is great for hiking and fishing.

2. Why are historic sites important?
3. What is one **festival** that celebrates Louisiana culture?

4. How do outdoor activities such as fishing help the economy of Louisiana?
5. **Critical Thinking: *Express Opinions*** Which one of the places or events from this lesson would you most want to see? Explain your reasons.

Link to ⚭ Art

Design a Poster Pick one of the festivals described in this lesson. Draw a poster that would make people want to come to this festival. Include the name of the festival and a picture that would make people interested in it.

Meet
Jake Delhomme

b. 1975 • Football Player

What is it like to play football for a living? It is not easy, as Jake Delhomme can tell you. Growing up in Breaux Bridge, Jake dreamed of becoming a football player. He was a star player for the "Ragin' Cajuns," his college team at the University of Louisiana-Lafayette. Was he good enough to play for a professional football team? Many coaches did not think so.

Delhomme remembers,

> *"Sometimes if you're not the tallest guy or have the strongest arm, you get pushed off to the side. One thing you can't measure . . . you can't measure someone's heart. I thought I had a lot of heart, and given an opportunity, I could maybe do well."*

Each year, professional football teams "draft," or choose, players from colleges all over the country. No one drafted Jake Delhomme after he finished college in 1997. Still, he refused to give up. He tried out for many different teams.

By 1998 Delhomme was on a professional football team. In 2003 he surprised everyone by leading his team to victory after victory. Delhomme's team went all the way to the Super Bowl, the most important game in football!

Jake Delhomme gained many new fans. As always, his biggest fans are in Breaux Bridge. He still spends his free time back home with his family and friends.

A Breaux Bridge restaurant named a sandwich "The Jake" in honor of Delhomme. It is a hamburger with onions, hot peppers, and bacon.

BIOFACT

Learn from Biographies

Many coaches thought Jake Delhomme was not good enough to play professional football. Why did he feel he could succeed?

Students can research the lives of significant people by clicking on *Meet the People* at **www.sfsocialstudies.com.**

Jazz had its beginnings in New Orleans. Bands there began playing in an improvised style around 1900. To *improvise music* means to invent tunes and rhythms as you go along. New Orleans is still known for its jazz musicians and style.

The soprano sax is the smallest and highest-pitched saxophone in common use. All saxes have the same keywork, which means that players can change from one sax to another.

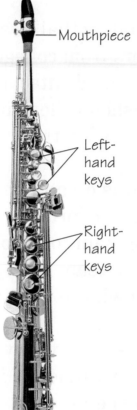

Mouthpiece

Left-hand keys

Right-hand keys

The tenor sax is the most-played of all the saxophones. Adolphe Sax made saxophones in 14 sizes, but only four are now common—the soprano, alto, tenor, and baritone saxes.

Sidney Bechet was one of the first jazz musicians to play soprano sax.

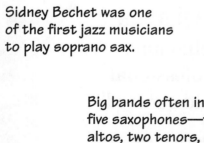

Big bands often include five saxophones—two altos, two tenors, and a baritone sax. This is a famous band led by Count Basie.

The trumpet plays both high and loud, leading all other softer and deeper instruments.

Side sections of tubing

The deepest member of the string family is the double bass. This huge instrument rests on the floor with the bass player standing behind.

Jazz drummer Buddy Rich began drumming at the age of 18 months when, known as Baby Traps, he appeared with his parents' stage act. He was a drummer all his life.

Louis Armstrong was one of the first trumpet soloists to improvise with only the rhythm section to back him.

F-shaped sound-hole typical of violin family

Frog

Chapter Summary

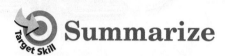 **Summarize**

On a separate sheet of paper, fill in a sentence to summarize these details about Chapter 12.

| Mardi Gras is a celebration based on Roman Catholic traditions. | The St. Charles Avenue Streetcar shows how people traveled in the early 1900s. | The Crawfish Festival celebrates Cajun culture. |

Vocabulary

Fill in each blank with the letter of the vocabulary word that best completes the sentence.

1 A _____ is a custom or belief that is handed down over the years.

2 A _____ is a program of entertainment and is often held every year.

3 Cultural groups often have their own _____, or special ways of doing things.

4 _____ has been celebrated in Louisiana since the 1700s.

a. customs (p. 307)

b. tradition (p. 308)

c. Mardi Gras (p. 308)

d. festival (p. 316)

Facts and Main Ideas

1. How do people in Mamou celebrate Mardi Gras?

2. What can you learn at the Centenary State Historic Site in Jackson?

3. **Main Idea** What kinds of customs have cultural groups brought to Louisiana?

4. **Main Idea** What different kinds of activities can people do in Louisiana?

5. **Critical Thinking:** *Draw Conclusions* How do fans support the football team at Louisiana State University?

Write About It

1. **Write a description** of a Mardi Gras celebration to someone who has never seen one.

2. **Write an invitation** to a friend from out of state to a festival near your home. Explain some of the fun things you will be able to do at the festival.

3. **Write a travel brochure** to attract visitors to Louisiana. List outdoor activities that tourists can do, such as hiking and fishing.

Apply Skills

Use Map Scales Study the map and map scale on page 312. Then answer the questions. You will need a ruler.

1. What is the purpose of a map scale?

2. What distance does 1 inch represent on this map?

3. About how many miles is the distance from Lake Charles to Lafayette?

Internet Activity

To get help with vocabulary, people, and terms, select the dictionary or encyclopedia from *Social Studies Library* at **www.sfsocialstudies.com.**

Fiddle Fever

By Sharon Arms Doucet

The following story is about a Cajun boy named Félix who lives on his family's farm in Louisiana. His dream is to play the fiddle, so he works hard to play well. In this passage, Félix tells what it feels like to play in front of a crowd.

I stepped out onto the porch. All eyes turned toward me, and people started clapping and whistling. "Come on, Félix!" they called, and "*Jouez, jouez!*" [Play, play!] I looked at the other musicians and at Chance, who'd taken a seat at the far end of the group. Two guitar players stood, waiting for me to pick a song.

I set the fiddle onto my tender collarbone and lifted the bow above the strings. "I'd like to play a song I made up for my maman [mother], Marie Olivier LeBlanc," I said. "*Bien merci pour tous*. Thank you for everything." Maman looked up at me from the yard and blew me a kiss.

As I pulled the bow across the strings, the music began to spin out of me like silk out of a spider. The song was a lively two-step. In between the notes lay all that had happened in the last few months—the anger and the joy, the heartbreak and the hope. And under that blew the breath of my uncle, of my grandfather, and of all those who'd come before us, all the way back to *Acadie* [Acadia].

Maman and Papa danced a slow swirl together. Pretty soon other couples formed up in the yard, and friends and neighbors smiled and waved encouragement. Finally, I felt like everybody who looked at me could really see me for who I was, who I was still becoming. . . .

Review

Main Ideas and Vocabulary

Read the passage. Then answer the questions.

People from all over the world have brought their own cultures to Louisiana to make it a special place. Most immigrants to Louisiana today come from Latin America and Asia.

Jazz is a style of music that began in New Orleans around 1900. Louis Armstrong helped make jazz popular.

Many cultural groups have their own customs. For example, cooking jambalaya is a custom of people from Cajun and Creole backgrounds.

Mardi Gras celebrations are a Louisiana tradition in cities all over the state. In some cities, people hold parades.

There are many places to learn about Louisiana's culture and history. Festivals in places like Breaux Bridge and Monroe teach people about different cultural groups.

1 What does the word *immigrants* mean in this passage?

A Mardi Gras parades

B jazz musicians

C people who move into a country and live there

D Cajun cooking

2 What does *tradition* mean in this passage?

A a history lesson

B a name for the area around Breaux Bridge

C a style of music

D a custom or belief that is handed down over the years

3 What is the main idea of this passage?

A Festivals are held in many cities.

B People have brought their own cultures to Louisiana to make it a special place.

C Jazz began in New Orleans.

D Cooking jambalaya is a Cajun and Creole custom.

Write and Share

Research a Culture Think about a culture in Louisiana that interests you. Research the culture and make a poster about it. Make several drawings with captions to tell about it. Explain your poster to your classmates.

Apply Skills

Use Map Scales Look at the map of Louisiana on page 312. Find the distance from one Louisiana city to another. Measure the distance in inches between the two cities. Describe how to use this number and the map's scale to find the actual distance between the two cities.

Read on Your Own

Look for books like these in the library.

Vocabulary

Write a journal entry describing what you learned about Louisiana's culture in this unit. Use the following vocabulary words in your entry.

immigrant (p. 291)

custom (p. 307)

festival (p. 316)

Celebrate!

In a group, give a report about a festival or celebration in Louisiana.

1 **Choose** a local festival or celebration held in our state.

2 **Find out** about the history and reasons for the festival or celebration. Write questions and answers about it.

3 **Choose** a person who will play the role of TV news reporter. This person will interview group members.

4 **Make** a backdrop for your interview.

5 **Present** your eyewitness news report to the class.

Internet Activity

For more information and activities, go to www.sfsocialstudies.com.

Reference Guide

Table of Contents

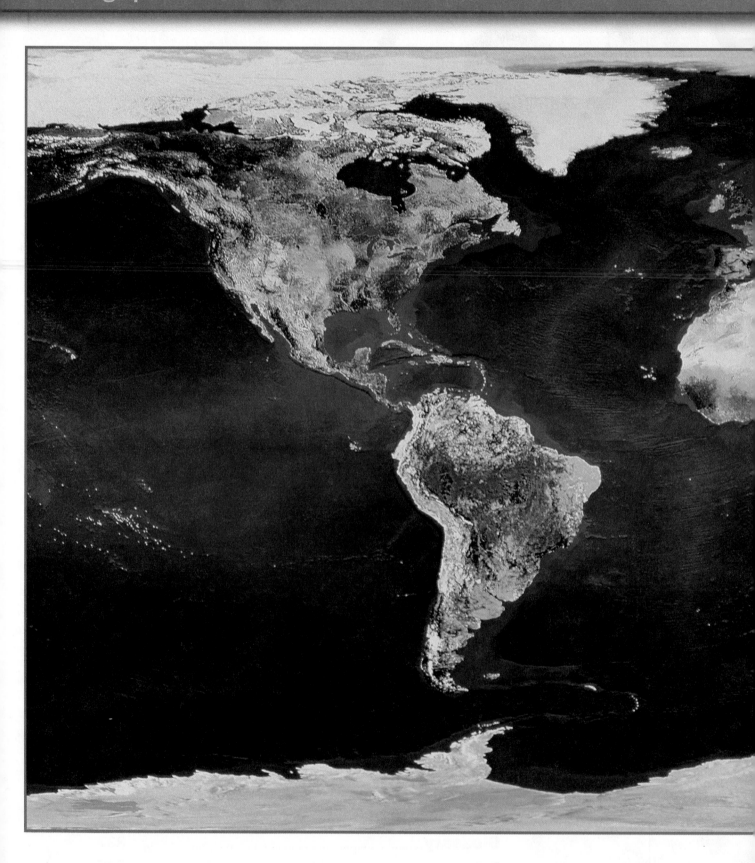

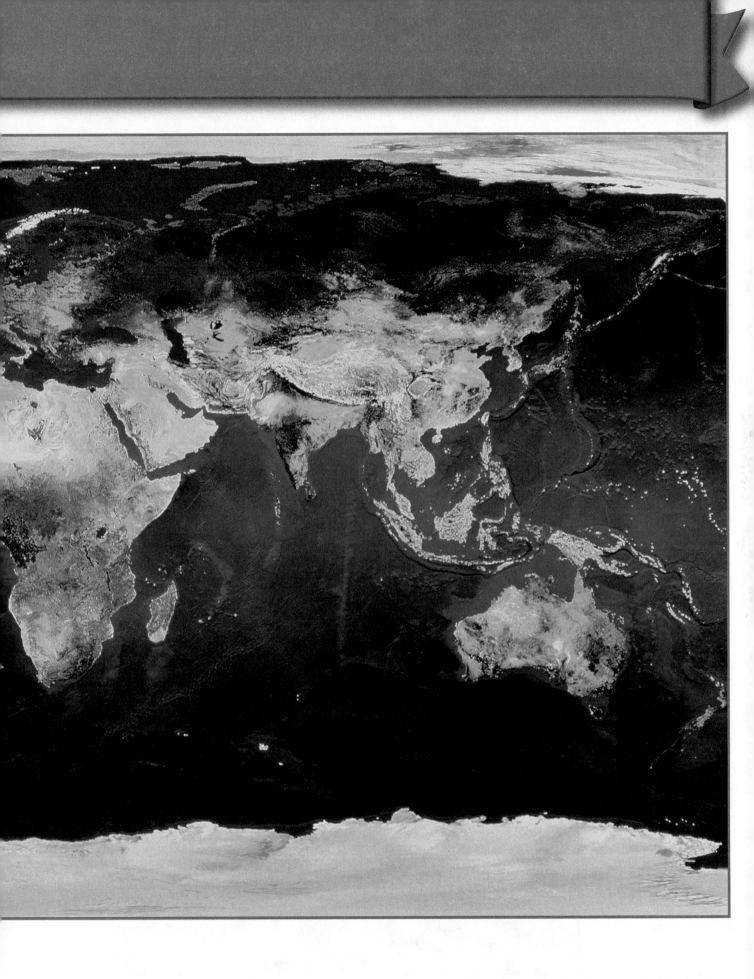

Atlas
Map of the World: Political

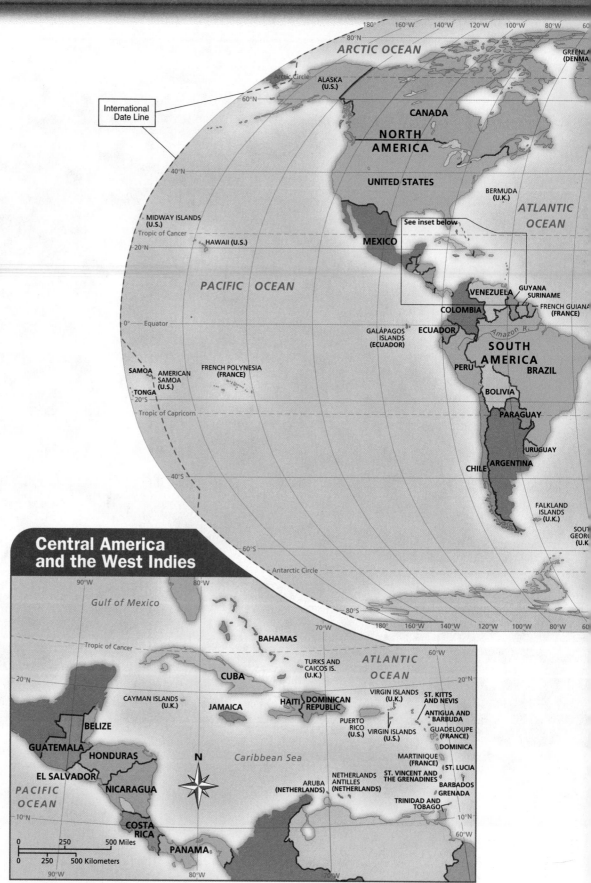

ARCTIC OCEAN

Arctic Circle

ALASKA (U.S.)

80°N

60°N

International Date Line

CANADA

NORTH AMERICA

GREENLAND (DENMARK)

40°N

UNITED STATES

BERMUDA (U.K.)

ATLANTIC OCEAN

MIDWAY ISLANDS (U.S.)

Tropic of Cancer

HAWAII (U.S.)

20°N

MEXICO

See inset below

PACIFIC OCEAN

VENEZUELA

GUYANA

SURINAME

FRENCH GUIANA (FRANCE)

COLOMBIA

0° Equator

GALÁPAGOS ISLANDS (ECUADOR)

ECUADOR

Amazon R.

SOUTH AMERICA

SAMOA

AMERICAN SAMOA (U.S.)

FRENCH POLYNESIA (FRANCE)

PERU

BRAZIL

TONGA

BOLIVIA

20°S

Tropic of Capricorn

PARAGUAY

URUGUAY

CHILE

ARGENTINA

40°S

FALKLAND ISLANDS (U.K.)

SOUTH GEORGIA (U.K.)

60°S

Antarctic Circle

80°S

180° 160°W 140°W 120°W 100°W 80°W 60°W

Central America and the West Indies

90°W

80°W

Gulf of Mexico

BAHAMAS

Tropic of Cancer

CUBA

TURKS AND CAICOS IS. (U.K.)

70°W

60°W

ATLANTIC OCEAN

20°N

20°N

CAYMAN ISLANDS (U.K.)

JAMAICA

HAITI

DOMINICAN REPUBLIC

VIRGIN ISLANDS (U.K.)

ST. KITTS AND NEVIS

BELIZE

PUERTO RICO (U.S.)

VIRGIN ISLANDS (U.S.)

ANTIGUA AND BARBUDA

GUADELOUPE (FRANCE)

GUATEMALA

DOMINICA

HONDURAS

N

Caribbean Sea

MARTINIQUE (FRANCE)

ST. LUCIA

EL SALVADOR

ST. VINCENT AND THE GRENADINES

BARBADOS

PACIFIC OCEAN

NICARAGUA

ARUBA (NETHERLANDS)

NETHERLANDS ANTILLES (NETHERLANDS)

GRENADA

TRINIDAD AND TOBAGO

10°N

10°N

COSTA RICA

0 250 500 Miles

0 250 500 Kilometers

PANAMA

60°W

90°W

80°W

70°W

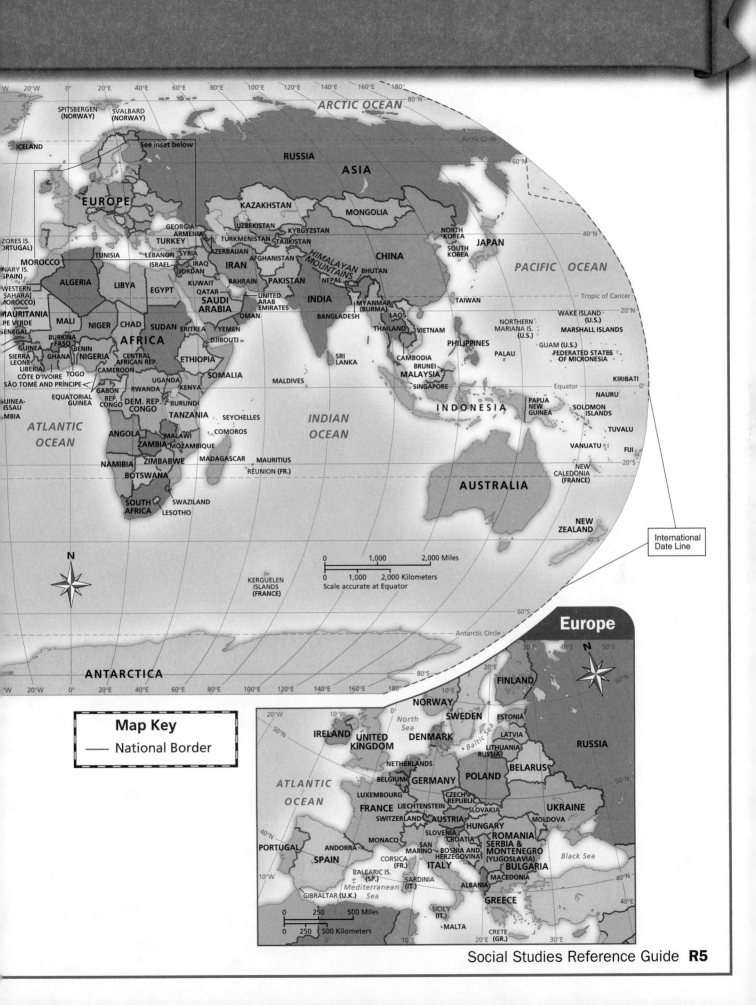

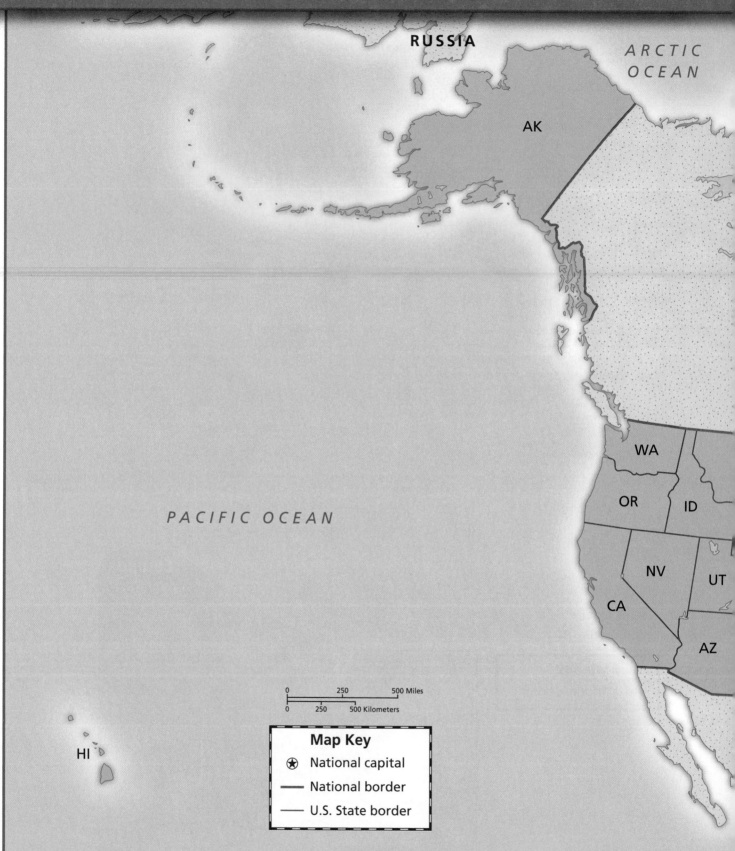

RUSSIA

ARCTIC OCEAN

AK

PACIFIC OCEAN

WA

OR

ID

NV

UT

CA

AZ

HI

0   250   500 Miles
0   250   500 Kilometers

Map Key

⊛ National capital

━ National border

─ U.S. State border

Greenland
(DENMARK)

CANADA

MEXICO

Gulf of Mexico

N

CUBA

BAHAMAS

ATLANTIC

OCEAN

HAITI

DOM.
REP.

JAMAICA

MT ND MN WI MI ME
SD VT NH NY MA
WY NE IA IL IN OH PA NJ CT RI
CO KS MO KY WV VA DE MD DC
NM OK AR TN NC
TX MS AL GA SC
LA FL

State or area	Abbreviation
Alabama	AL
Alaska	AK
Arizona	AZ
Arkansas	AR
California	CA
Colorado	CO
Connecticut	CT
Delaware	DE
District of Columbia	DC
Florida	FL
Georgia	GA
Hawaii	HI
Idaho	ID
Illinois	IL
Indiana	IN
Iowa	IA
Kansas	KS
Kentucky	KY
Louisiana	LA
Maine	ME
Maryland	MD
Massachusetts	MA
Michigan	MI
Minnesota	MN
Mississippi	MS
Missouri	MO
Montana	MT
Nebraska	NE
Nevada	NV
New Hampshire	NH
New Jersey	NJ
New Mexico	NM
New York	NY
North Carolina	NC
North Dakota	ND
Ohio	OH
Oklahoma	OK
Oregon	OR
Pennsylvania	PA
Rhode Island	RI
South Carolina	SC
South Dakota	SD
Tennessee	TN
Texas	TX
Utah	UT
Vermont	VT
Virginia	VA
Washington	WA
West Virginia	WV
Wisconsin	WI
Wyoming	WY

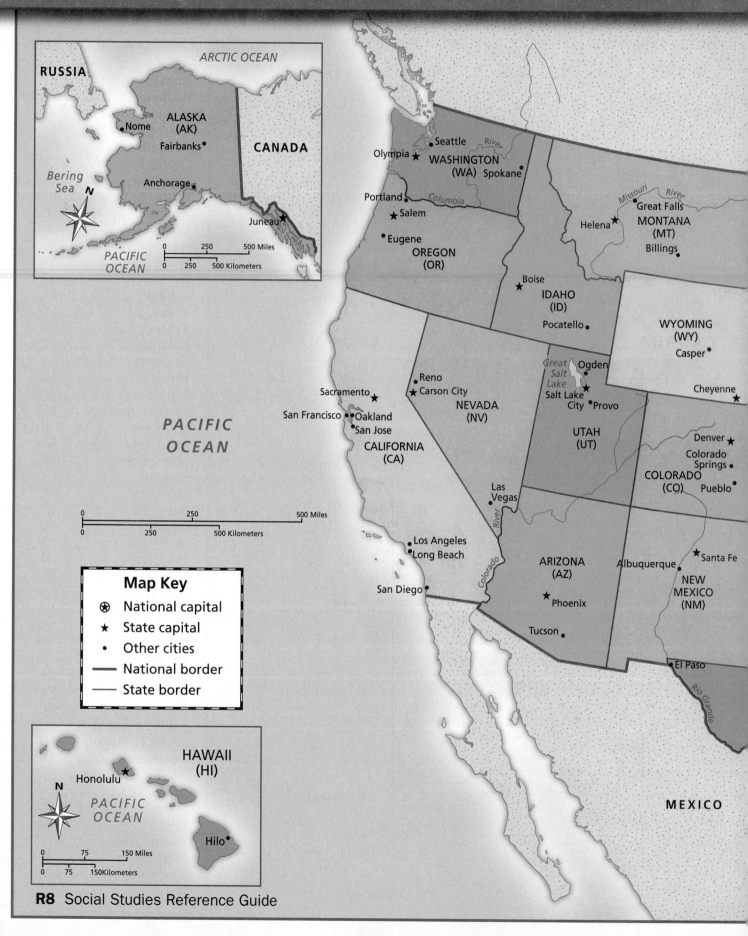

Map Key

⊛ National capital

★ State capital

• Other cities

— National border

— State border

RUSSIA

ARCTIC OCEAN

ALASKA (AK)

• Nome

Fairbanks •

CANADA

Bering Sea

Anchorage •

Juneau ★

PACIFIC OCEAN

0   250   500 Miles

0   250   500 Kilometers

HAWAII (HI)

Honolulu ★

PACIFIC OCEAN

Hilo •

0   75   150 Miles

0   75   150 Kilometers

• Seattle

Olympia ★   **WASHINGTON (WA)**   • Spokane

River

Portland •

★ Salem

• Eugene

OREGON (OR)

Columbia

Missouri   River

Great Falls •

Helena ★   **MONTANA (MT)**

• Billings

★ Boise   **IDAHO (ID)**

Pocatello •

WYOMING (WY)

Casper •

Cheyenne ★

• Reno

Carson City ★

Sacramento ★

San Francisco • • Oakland

• San Jose

NEVADA (NV)

CALIFORNIA (CA)

Great Salt Lake

Ogden •

Salt Lake City ★ • Provo

UTAH (UT)

Denver ★

Colorado Springs •

COLORADO (CO)   Pueblo •

Las Vegas •

River

• Los Angeles

• Long Beach

San Diego •

Colorado

ARIZONA (AZ)

Phoenix ★

Tucson •

Albuquerque •   ★ Santa Fe

NEW MEXICO (NM)

• El Paso

Rio Grande

PACIFIC OCEAN

0   250   500 Miles

0   250   500 Kilometers

MEXICO

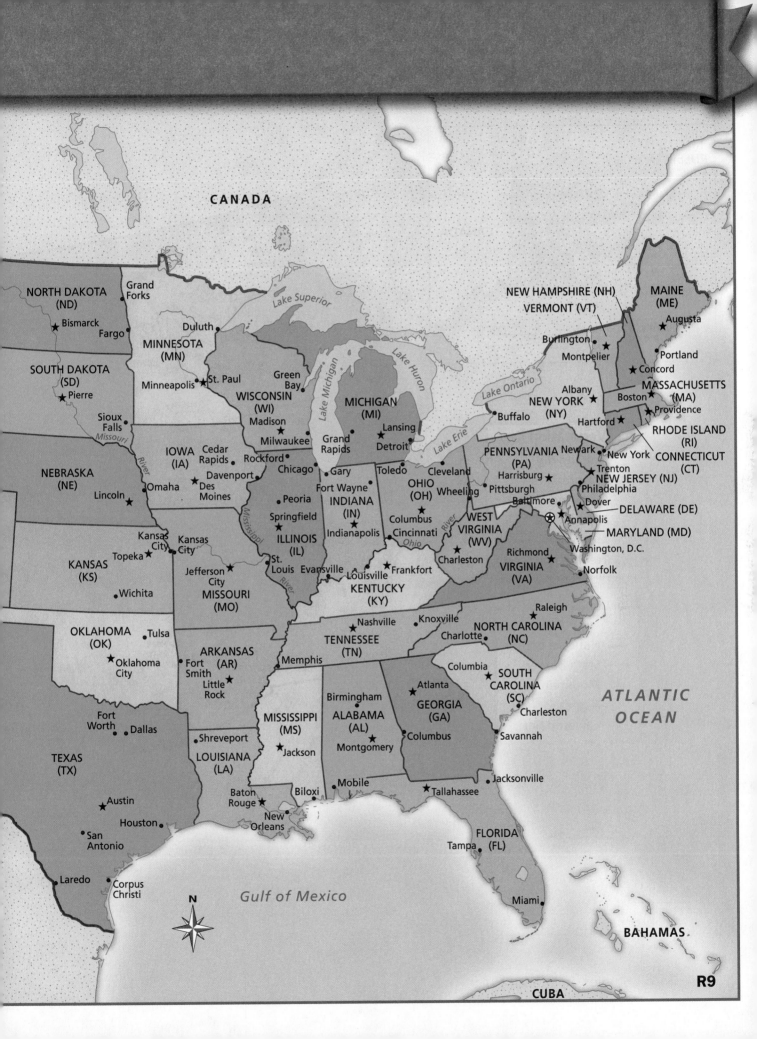

CANADA

NORTH DAKOTA (ND)
Grand Forks
Bismarck
Fargo

SOUTH DAKOTA (SD)
Pierre

MINNESOTA (MN)
Duluth
Minneapolis
St. Paul

WISCONSIN (WI)
Green Bay
Madison
Milwaukee

Lake Superior

MICHIGAN (MI)
Lansing
Grand Rapids
Detroit

Lake Michigan
Lake Huron
Lake Ontario
Lake Erie

NEW HAMPSHIRE (NH)
VERMONT (VT)
MAINE (ME)
Augusta
Burlington
Montpelier
Portland
Concord

Albany
NEW YORK (NY)
Buffalo
Boston
MASSACHUSETTS (MA)
Providence
Hartford
RHODE ISLAND (RI)
CONNECTICUT (CT)

SIoux Falls
IOWA (IA)
Cedar Rapids
Rockford
Davenport
Des Moines

NEBRASKA (NE)
Lincoln
Omaha

Missouri River
Mississippi River

Chicago
Peoria
Springfield
ILLINOIS (IL)

Gary
Fort Wayne
INDIANA (IN)
Indianapolis

Toledo
Cleveland
OHIO (OH)
Columbus
Cincinnati
Wheeling

PENNSYLVANIA (PA)
Harrisburg
Pittsburgh

Newark
Trenton
New York
NEW JERSEY (NJ)
Philadelphia
Baltimore
Dover
DELAWARE (DE)
Annapolis
MARYLAND (MD)
Washington, D.C.

WEST VIRGINIA (WV)
Charleston

Ohio River

VIRGINIA (VA)
Richmond
Norfolk

KANSAS (KS)
Kansas City
Topeka
Wichita

Kansas City

MISSOURI (MO)
Jefferson City
St. Louis

KENTUCKY (KY)
Louisville
Frankfort
Evansville

OKLAHOMA (OK)
Tulsa
Oklahoma City

ARKANSAS (AR)
Fort Smith
Little Rock

TENNESSEE (TN)
Nashville
Memphis
Knoxville

NORTH CAROLINA (NC)
Raleigh
Charlotte

FORT WORTH
Dallas

TEXAS (TX)
Austin
Houston
San Antonio
Laredo
Corpus Christi

LOUISIANA (LA)
Shreveport
Baton Rouge
New Orleans

MISSISSIPPI (MS)
Jackson

ALABAMA (AL)
Birmingham
Montgomery
Mobile

GEORGIA (GA)
Atlanta
Columbus

Columbia
SOUTH CAROLINA (SC)
Charleston
Savannah

Biloxi
Tallahassee
Jacksonville

FLORIDA (FL)
Tampa
Miami

ATLANTIC OCEAN

N

Gulf of Mexico

BAHAMAS

CUBA

Atlas

Map of Our Fifty States: Physical

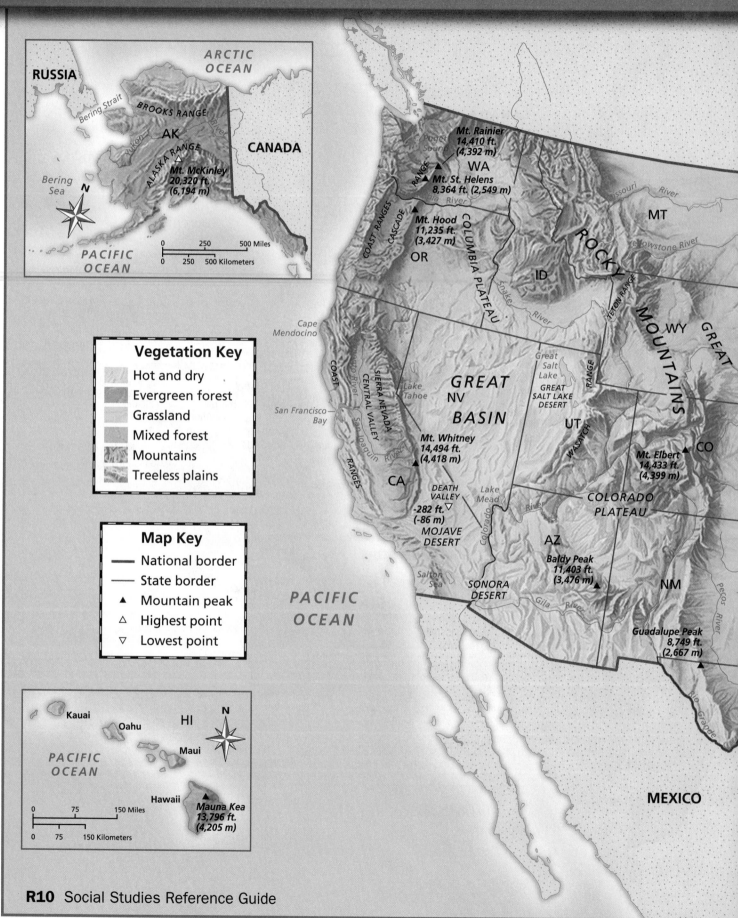

RUSSIA

ARCTIC OCEAN

BROOKS RANGE

AK

ALASKA RANGE

△ Mt. McKinley
20,320 ft.
(6,194 m)

Yukon River

CANADA

Bering Strait

Bering Sea

N

PACIFIC OCEAN

| 0 | 250 | 500 Miles |
| 0 | 250 | 500 Kilometers |

Vegetation Key

- Hot and dry
- Evergreen forest
- Grassland
- Mixed forest
- Mountains
- Treeless plains

Map Key

— National border
— State border
▲ Mountain peak
△ Highest point
▽ Lowest point

Mt. Rainier
14,410 ft.
(4,392 m)

WA

▲ Mt. St. Helens
8,364 ft. (2,549 m)

COAST RANGES

CASCADE RANGE

▲ Mt. Hood
11,235 ft.
(3,427 m)

Columbia River

COLUMBIA PLATEAU

OR

Puget Sound

Cape Mendocino

COAST RANGES

Sacramento River

CENTRAL VALLEY

SIERRA NEVADA

Lake Tahoe

San Joaquin River

San Francisco Bay

Mt. Whitney
14,494 ft.
(4,418 m) ▲

CA

COAST RANGES

DEATH VALLEY
-282 ft. ▽
(-86 m)

MOJAVE DESERT

Lake Mead

Salton Sea

SONORA DESERT

PACIFIC OCEAN

Snake River

ID

ROCKY MOUNTAINS

TETON RANGE

WY

Missouri River

Yellowstone River

MT

GREAT

Great Salt Lake

GREAT SALT LAKE DESERT

WASATCH RANGE

UT

GREAT
NV
BASIN

COLORADO PLATEAU

Colorado River

AZ

Baldy Peak
11,403 ft.
(3,476 m) ▲

Gila River

Mt. Elbert
14,433 ft. ▲
(4,399 m)

CO

NM

Pecos River

Guadalupe Peak
8,749 ft.
(2,667 m)
▲

Rio Grande

MEXICO

Kauai

Oahu

HI
N

Maui

PACIFIC OCEAN

Hawaii

▲ Mauna Kea
13,796 ft.
(4,205 m)

| 0 | 75 | 150 Miles |
| 0 | 75 | 150 Kilometers |

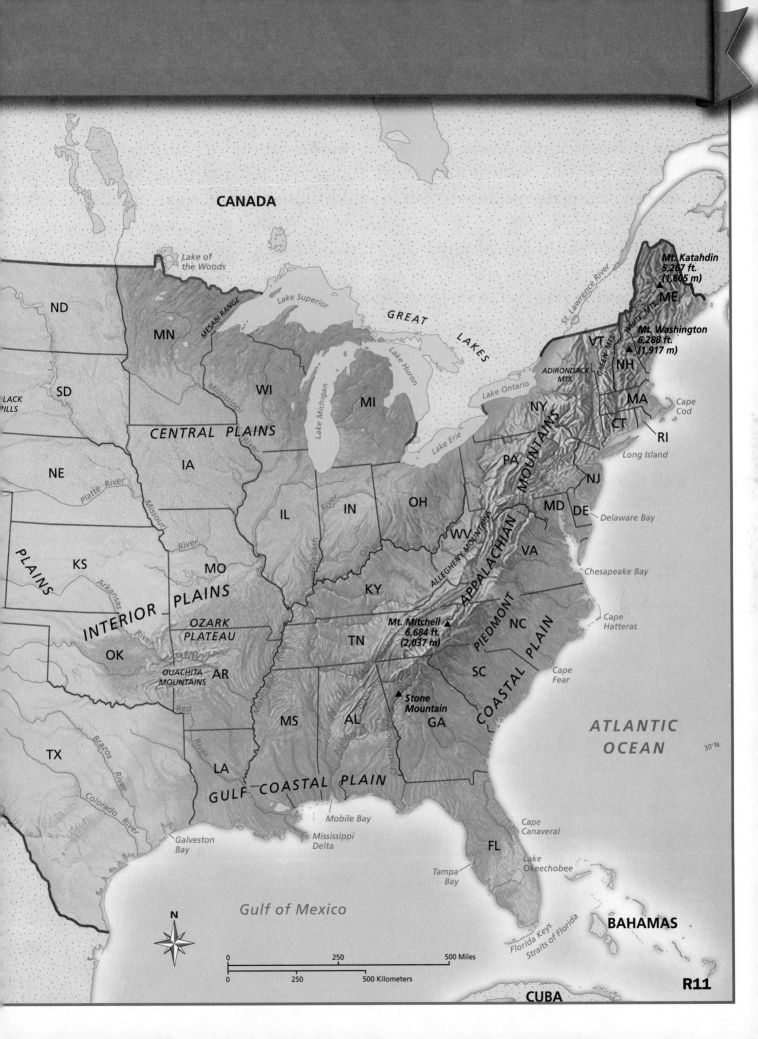

CANADA

Lake of the Woods

Lake Superior

GREAT LAKES

St. Lawrence River

Mt. Katahdin
5,267 ft.
(1,605 m)
ME

ND

MESABI RANGE

MN

Lake Huron

WHITE MTS.

Mt. Washington
6,288 ft.
(1,917 m)

VT

GREEN MTS.

NH

Mississippi River

WI

Lake Michigan

MI

Lake Ontario

ADIRONDACK MTS.

SD

BLACK HILLS

CENTRAL PLAINS

NY

MA

Cape Cod

CT

RI

Lake Erie

IA

PA

Long Island

NE

Platte River

IL

IN

OH

MOUNTAINS

NJ

MD

DE

Delaware Bay

Missouri River

WV

ALLEGHENY MOUNTAINS

APPALACHIAN

VA

KS

Arkansas River

MO

INTERIOR PLAINS

OZARK PLATEAU

KY

Chesapeake Bay

PLAINS

Mt. Mitchell
6,684 ft.
(2,037 m)

TN

PIEDMONT

NC

Cape Hatteras

OK

OUACHITA MOUNTAINS

AR

Mississippi River

SC

COASTAL PLAIN

Cape Fear

Red River

▲ Stone Mountain

Savannah River

MS

AL

GA

Alabama River

Chattahoochee River

ATLANTIC OCEAN

30°N

TX

Brazos River

LA

GULF COASTAL PLAIN

Colorado River

Galveston Bay

Mobile Bay

Mississippi Delta

Cape Canaveral

FL

Lake Okeechobee

Tampa Bay

Gulf of Mexico

N

Florida Keys

Straits of Florida

BAHAMAS

0   250   500 Miles

0   250   500 Kilometers

R11

CUBA

Geography Terms

bay narrower part of a large body of water that cuts into land

canyon steep, narrow valley with high sides

cliff steep wall of rock or earth, sometimes called a bluff

coast land at the edge of a large body of water such as an ocean

desert very dry land with few plants

foothills hilly land at the bottom of a mountain

forest large area of land where many trees grow

gulf body of water, smaller than a sea, with land around part of it

harbor sheltered body of water where ships safely tie up to land

hill rounded land higher than the land around it

island land with water all around it

lake large body of water with land all or nearly all around it

mesa hard-to-climb flat-topped hill, with steep sides

mountain highest land on Earth

mountain range long row of mountains

ocean any of four largest bodies of water on Earth

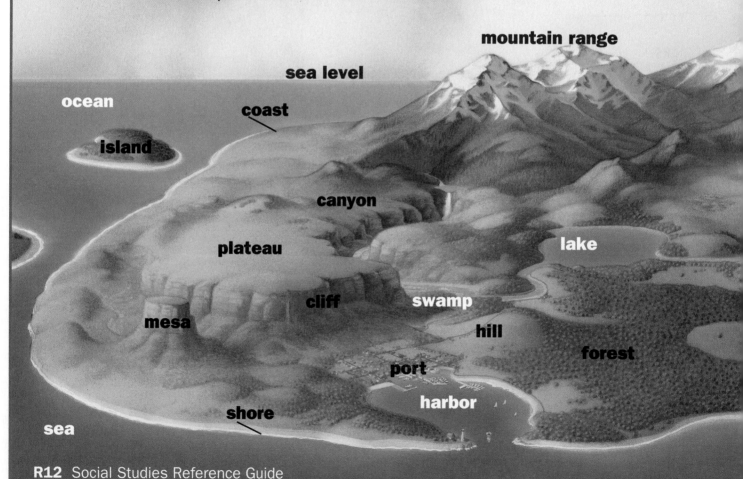

peak pointed top of a mountain

peninsula land with water on three sides

plain very large area of flat land

plateau high, wide area of flat land, with steep sides

port place, usually in a harbor, where ships safely load and unload goods and people

river large stream of water leading to a lake, other river, or ocean

sea large body of water somewhat smaller than an ocean

sea level an ocean's surface, compared to which land can be measured either above or below

shore land along a river, lake, sea, or ocean

swamp very shallow water covering low land filled with trees and other plants

valley low land between mountains or hills

volcano mountain with opening at the top formed by violent bursts of steam and hot rock

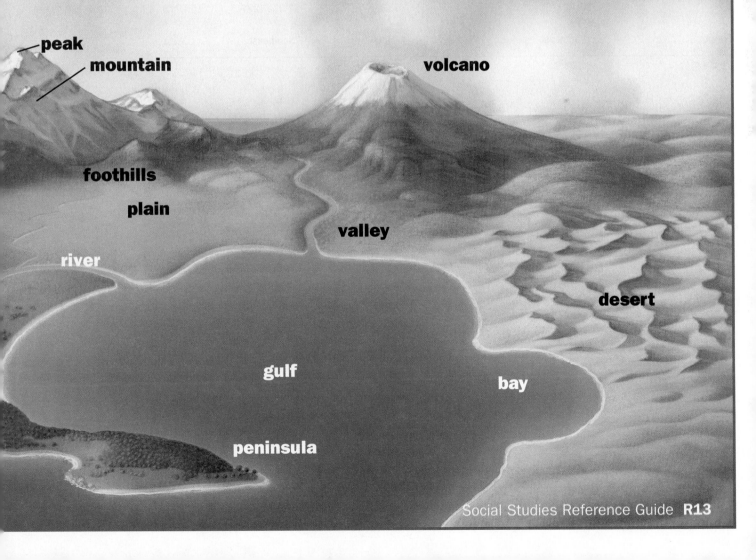

peak
mountain
volcano
foothills
plain
valley
river
desert
gulf
bay
peninsula

Facts About Our Fifty States

	AL Alabama	AK Alaska	AZ Arizona	AR Arkansas	CA California	CO Colorado
Capital	Montgomery	Juneau	Phoenix	Little Rock	Sacramento	Denver
Date and order of statehood	1819 (22)	1959 (49)	1912 (48)	1836 (25)	1850 (31)	1876 (38)
Nickname	Heart of Dixie	The Last Frontier	Grand Canyon State	Land of Opportunity	Golden State	Centennial State
Population	4,447,100	626,932	5,130,632	2,673,400	33,871,648	4,301,261
Square miles and rank in area	50,750 (28)	570,374 (1)	113,642 (6)	52,075 (27)	155,973 (3)	103,730 (8)
Region	Southeast	West	Southwest	Southeast	West	West

	IN Indiana	IA Iowa	KS Kansas	KY Kentucky	LA Louisiana	ME Maine
Capital	Indianapolis	Des Moines	Topeka	Frankfort	Baton Rouge	Augusta
Date and order of statehood	1816 (19)	1846 (29)	1861 (34)	1792 (15)	1812 (18)	1820 (23)
Nickname	Hoosier State	Hawkeye State	Sunflower State	Bluegrass State	Pelican State	Pine Tree State
Population	6,080,485	2,926,324	2,688,418	4,041,769	4,468,976	1,274,923
Square miles and rank in area	35,870 (38)	55,875 (23)	81,823 (13)	39,732 (36)	43,566 (33)	30,865 (39)
Region	Midwest	Midwest	Midwest	Southeast	Southeast	Northeast

CT Connecticut	DE Delaware	FL Florida	GA Georgia	HI Hawaii	ID Idaho	IL Illinois
Hartford	Dover	Tallahassee	Atlanta	Honolulu	Boise	Springfield
1788 (5)	1787 (1)	1845 (27)	1788 (4)	1959 (50)	1890 (43)	1818 (21)
Constitution State	Diamond State; First State	Sunshine State	Peach State	Aloha State	Gem State	Land of Lincoln
3,405,565	783,600	15,982,378	8,186,453	1,211,537	1,293,953	12,419,293
4,845 (48)	1,955 (49)	53,997 (26)	57,919 (21)	6,423 (47)	82,751 (11)	55,593 (24)
Northeast	Northeast	Southeast	Southeast	West	West	Midwest

MD Maryland	MA Massachusetts	MI Michigan	MN Minnesota	MS Mississippi	MO Missouri	MT Montana
Annapolis	Boston	Lansing	St. Paul	Jackson	Jefferson City	Helena
1788 (7)	1788 (6)	1837 (26)	1858 (32)	1817 (20)	1821 (24)	1889 (41)
Free State	Bay State	Wolverine State	North Star State	Magnolia State	Show Me State	Treasure State
5,296,486	6,349,097	9,938,444	4,919,479	2,844,658	5,595,211	902,195
9,775 (42)	7,838 (45)	56,809 (22)	79,617 (14)	46,914 (31)	68,898 (18)	145,556 (4)
Northeast	Northeast	Midwest	Midwest	Southeast	Midwest	West

Facts About Our Fifty States

	NE Nebraska	NV Nevada	NH New Hampshire	NJ New Jersey	NM New Mexico	NY New York
Capital	Lincoln	Carson City	Concord	Trenton	Santa Fe	Albany
Date and order of statehood	1867 (37)	1864 (36)	1788 (9)	1787 (3)	1912 (47)	1788 (11)
Nickname	Cornhusker State	Silver State	Granite State	Garden State	Land of Enchantment	Empire State
Population	1,711,263	1,998,257	1,235,786	8,414,350	1,819,046	18,976,457
Square miles and rank in area	76,644 (15)	109,806 (7)	8,969 (44)	7,419 (46)	121,365 (5)	47,224 (30)
Region	Midwest	West	Northeast	Northeast	Southwest	Northeast

	SC South Carolina	SD South Dakota	TN Tennessee	TX Texas	UT Utah	VT Vermont
Capital	Columbia	Pierre	Nashville	Austin	Salt Lake City	Montpelier
Date and order of statehood	1788 (8)	1889 (40)	1796 (16)	1845 (28)	1896 (45)	1791 (14)
Nickname	Palmetto State	Mount Rushmore State	Volunteer State	Lone Star State	Beehive State	Green Mountain State
Population	4,012,012	754,844	5,689,283	20,851,820	2,233,169	608,827
Square miles and rank in area	30,111 (40)	75,898 (16)	41,220 (34)	261,914 (2)	82,168 (12)	9,249 (43)
Region	Southeast	Midwest	Southeast	Southwest	West	Northeast

North Carolina	North Dakota	Ohio	Oklahoma	Oregon	Pennsylvania	Rhode Island
NC	**ND**	**OH**	**OK**	**OR**	**PA**	**RI**
Raleigh	Bismarck	Columbus	Oklahoma City	Salem	Harrisburg	Providence
1789 (12)	1889 (39)	1803 (17)	1907 (46)	1859 (33)	1787 (2)	1790 (13)
Tar Heel State	Sioux State	Buckeye State	Sooner State	Beaver State	Keystone State	Ocean State
8,049,313	642,200	11,353,140	3,450,654	3,421,399	12,281,054	1,048,319
48,718 (29)	68,994 (17)	40,953 (35)	68,679 (19)	96,003 (10)	44,820 (32)	1,045 (50)
Southeast	Midwest	Midwest	Southwest	West	Northeast	Northeast

Virginia	Washington	West Virginia	Wisconsin	Wyoming
VA	**WA**	**WV**	**WI**	**WY**
Richmond	Olympia	Charleston	Madison	Cheyenne
1788 (10)	1889 (42)	1863 (35)	1848 (30)	1890 (44)
Old Dominion	Evergreen State	Mountain State	Badger State	Equality State
7,078,515	5,894,121	1,808,344	5,363,675	493,782
39,598 (37)	66,582 (20)	24,087 (41)	54,314 (25)	97,105 (9)
Southeast	West	Southeast	Midwest	West

Our National Flag

The flag of the United States of America is an important symbol for our country. The flag should be shown respect at all times. When we say the Pledge of Allegiance to the flag, we are saying that we will be good citizens of the United States of America.

When saying the Pledge of Allegiance, stand, face the flag, and place your right hand over your heart.

The Pledge of Allegiance

I pledge allegiance to the flag
Of the United States of America
And to the Republic for which it stands,
One Nation under God, indivisible,
With liberty and justice for all.

Displaying the Flag

- Display the flag only from sunrise to sunset, except when bad weather might damage the flag.

- No other flag or pennant should be placed above the U.S. flag. If another flag is displayed on the same level, it should be to the right of the flag of the United States of America.

- When the flag passes in a parade, stand and put your right hand over your heart.

- When singing the National Anthem, everyone should rise and stand at attention. A man should remove his hat with his right hand and place the palm of his right hand over his heart.

Flag Holidays

The flag of the United States should be flown every day, but especially on these holidays:

New Year's Day	January 1
Inauguration Day	January 20
Lincoln's Birthday	February 12
Washington's Birthday	third Monday in February
Easter Sunday	varies
Mother's Day	second Sunday in May
Armed Forces Day	third Saturday in May
Memorial Day	last Monday in May (half-staff until noon)
Flag Day	June 14
Independence Day	July 4
Labor Day	first Monday in September
Constitution Day	September 17
Columbus Day	second Monday in October
Navy Day	October 27
Veteran's Day	November 11
Thanksgiving Day	fourth Thursday in November
Christmas Day	December 25

By Public Law or Executive Order, the flag flies 24 hours a day at the following locations:

The White House, Washington, D.C.

The United States Capitol, Washington, D.C.

Iwo Jima Memorial to U.S. Marines, Arlington, Virginia

Battleground in Lexington, MA (site of the first shots in the Revolutionary War)

Winter Encampment Cabins, Valley Forge, Pennsylvania

Fort McHenry, Baltimore, Maryland (A flag flying over Fort McHenry after a battle during the War of 1812 provided the inspiration for "The Star-Spangled Banner.")

The Star-Spangled Banner Flag House, Baltimore, Maryland (This is the site where the famous flag over Fort McHenry was sewn.)

Washington Monument, Washington, D.C.

Many other places fly the flag at night as a patriotic gesture by custom.

Atlas
Louisiana Cities and Towns

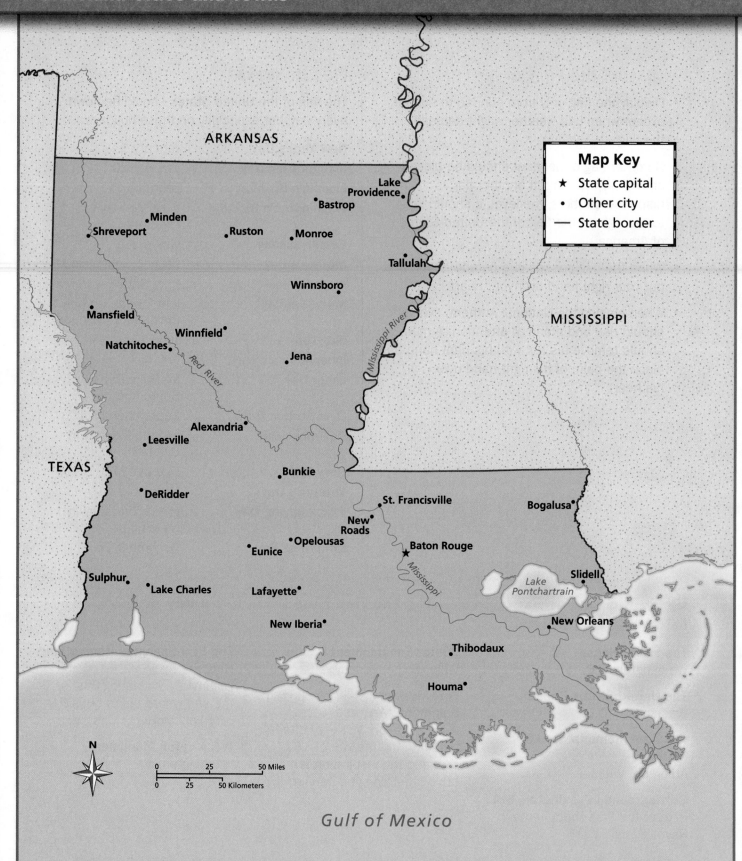

ARKANSAS

Map Key
★ State capital
• Other city
— State border

MISSISSIPPI

Lake Providence
Bastrop
Minden
Shreveport
Ruston
Monroe
Tallulah
Winnsboro
Mansfield
Winnfield
Natchitoches
Jena
Red River
Mississippi River

Alexandria
Leesville
TEXAS
Bunkie
St. Francisville
Bogalusa
DeRidder
New Roads
Eunice
Opelousas
Baton Rouge
Mississippi
Sulphur
Lake Charles
Lafayette
Lake Pontchartrain
Slidell
New Iberia
New Orleans
Thibodaux
Houma

N

0   25   50 Miles
0   25   50 Kilometers

Gulf of Mexico

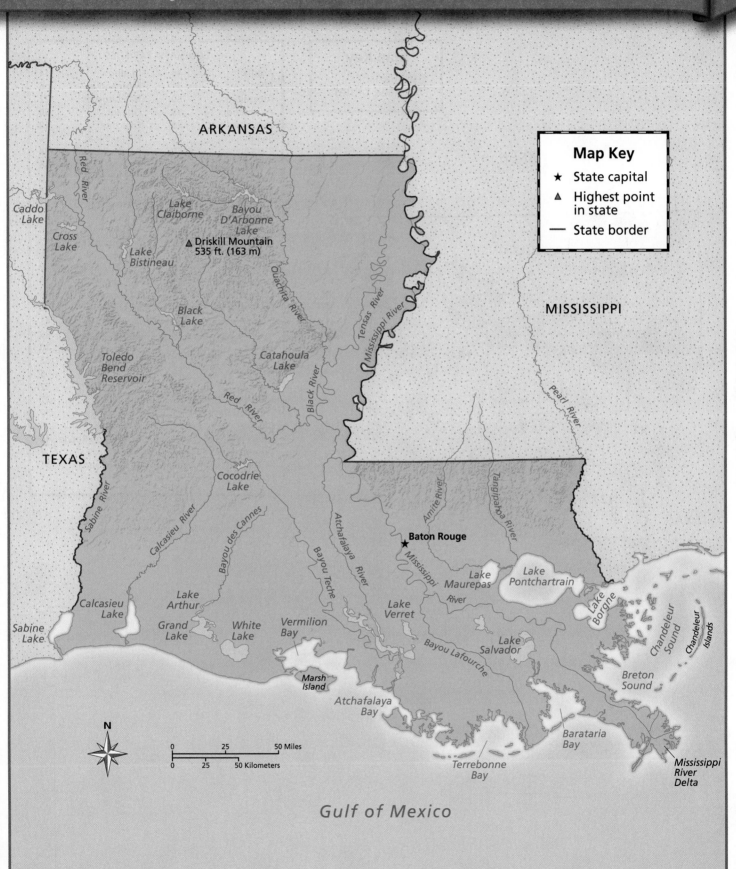

Louisiana Physical Features

ARKANSAS

Red River

Caddo Lake

Cross Lake

Lake Claiborne

Bayou D'Arbonne Lake

▲ Driskill Mountain 535 ft. (163 m)

Lake Bistineau

Black Lake

Ouachita River

Tensas River

Mississippi River

Map Key
★ State capital
▲ Highest point in state
— State border

MISSISSIPPI

Toledo Bend Reservoir

Catahoula Lake

Black River

Red River

Pearl River

TEXAS

Sabine River

Cocodrie Lake

Calcasieu River

Bayou des Cannes

Atchafalaya River

Bayou Teche

Amite River

Tangipahoa River

★ Baton Rouge

Mississippi River

Lake Maurepas

Lake Pontchartrain

Calcasieu Lake

Lake Arthur

Grand Lake

White Lake

Vermilion Bay

Lake Verret

Lake Borgne

Chandeleur Sound

Chandeleur Islands

Sabine Lake

Marsh Island

Bayou Lafourche

Lake Salvador

Breton Sound

Atchafalaya Bay

Barataria Bay

Terrebonne Bay

Mississippi River Delta

N

0   25   50 Miles
0   25   50 Kilometers

Gulf of Mexico

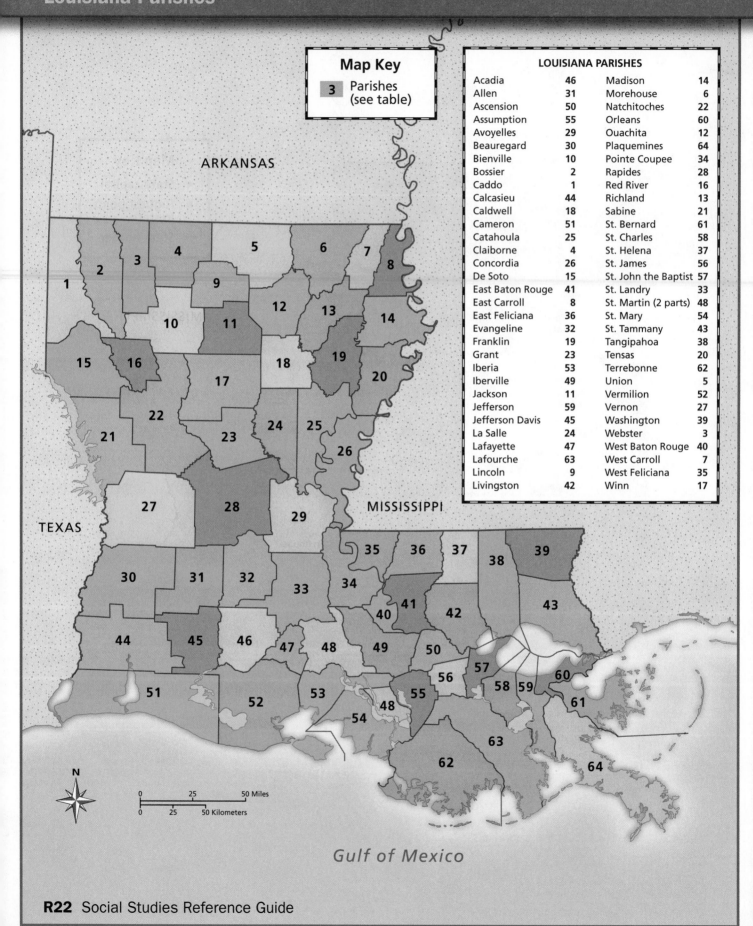

Map Key

3 Parishes (see table)

LOUISIANA PARISHES

Parish	#	Parish	#
Acadia	46	Madison	14
Allen	31	Morehouse	6
Ascension	50	Natchitoches	22
Assumption	55	Orleans	60
Avoyelles	29	Ouachita	12
Beauregard	30	Plaquemines	64
Bienville	10	Pointe Coupee	34
Bossier	2	Rapides	28
Caddo	1	Red River	16
Calcasieu	44	Richland	13
Caldwell	18	Sabine	21
Cameron	51	St. Bernard	61
Catahoula	25	St. Charles	58
Claiborne	4	St. Helena	37
Concordia	26	St. James	56
De Soto	15	St. John the Baptist	57
East Baton Rouge	41	St. Landry	33
East Carroll	8	St. Martin (2 parts)	48
East Feliciana	36	St. Mary	54
Evangeline	32	St. Tammany	43
Franklin	19	Tangipahoa	38
Grant	23	Tensas	20
Iberia	53	Terrebonne	62
Iberville	49	Union	5
Jackson	11	Vermilion	52
Jefferson	59	Vernon	27
Jefferson Davis	45	Washington	39
La Salle	24	Webster	3
Lafayette	47	West Baton Rouge	40
Lafourche	63	West Carroll	7
Lincoln	9	West Feliciana	35
Livingston	42	Winn	17

ARKANSAS

TEXAS

MISSISSIPPI

Gulf of Mexico

N

0   25   50 Miles

0   25   50 Kilometers

Louisiana Road Map

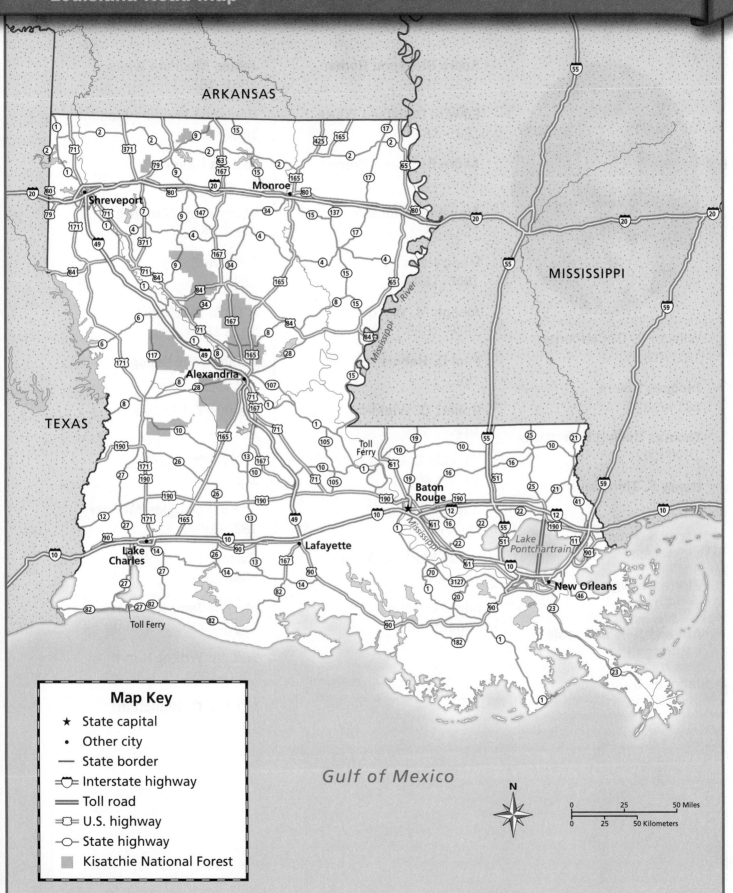

Map Key

★ State capital

• Other city

— State border

Interstate highway

Toll road

U.S. highway

State highway

Kisatchie National Forest

Louisiana Governors

William C. C. Claiborne
1812–1816

Jacques Villeré
1816–1820

Thomas Bolling Robertson
1820–1824

Henry S. Thibodaux
1824

Henry S. Johnson
1824–1828

Pierre Derbigny
1828–1829

Armand Julie Beauvais
1829–1830

Jacques Dupré
1830–1831

Andre Bienvenu Roman
1831–1835

Edward Douglass White
1835–1839

Andre Bienvenu Roman
1839–1843

Alexandre Mouton
1843–1846

Isaac Johnson
1846–1850

Joseph M. Walker
1850–1853

Paul O. Hebert
1853–1856

Robert C. Wickliffe
1856–1860

Thomas Overton Moore
1860–1864

George F. Shepley
1862–1864

Henry Watkins Allen
1864–1865

Michael Hahn
1864–1865

James Madison Wells
1865–1867

Benjamin Franklin Flanders
1867–1868

Joshua Baker
1868

Henry Clay Warmoth
1868–1872

John McEnery
1872

P. B. S. Pinchback
1872-1873

William Pitt Kellogg
1873–1877

Francis T. Nicholls
1877–1880

Louis Alfred Wiltz
1880–1881

Samuel Douglas McEnery
1881–1888

Francis T. Nicholls
1888–1892

Murphy James Foster
1892–1900

William Wright Heard
1900–1904

Newton C. Blanchard
1904–1908

Jared Y. Sanders
1908–1912

Luther E. Hall
1912–1916

Ruffin G. Pleasant
1916–1920

John M. Parker
1920–1924

Henry L. Fuqua
1924–1926

Oramel H. Simpson
1926–1928

Huey P. Long
1928–1932

Alvin O. King
1932

Oscar K. Allen
1932–1936

James A. Noe
1936

Richard W. Leche
1936–1939

Earl K. Long
1939–1940

Sam H. Jones
1940–1944

Jimmie H. Davis
1944–1948

Earl K. Long
1948–1952

Robert F. Kennon
1952–1956

Earl K. Long
1956–1960

Jimmie H. Davis
1960–1964

John J. McKeithen
1964–1972

Edwin W. Edwards
1972–1980

David C. Treen
1980–1984

Edwin W. Edwards
1984–1988

Charles E. Roemer, III
1988–1992

Edwin W. Edwards
1992–1996

Murphy J. Foster
1996–2004

Kathleen Blanco
2004–

Louisiana Symbols

State Flag

State Bird
Brown Pelican

State Flower
Magnolia

State Musical Instrument
Diatonic Accordion

State Mammal
Louisiana Black Bear

State Dog
Catahoula Leopard Dog

State Crustacean
Crawfish

State Wildflower
Iris

State Insect
Honeybee

State Amphibian
Green Tree Frog

Facts About Louisiana's Parishes

Parish Name	Parish Seat	Population (2000)	Area in Square Miles
Acadia	Crowley	58,861	663
Allen	Oberlin	25,440	774
Ascension	Donaldsonville	76,627	301
Assumption	Napoleonville	23,388	356
Avoyelles	Marksville	41,481	832
Beauregard	DeRidder	32,986	1,184
Bienville	Arcadia	15,752	832
Bossier	Benton	98,310	849
Caddo	Shreveport	252,161	899
Calcasieu	Lake Charles	183,577	1,105
Caldwell	Columbia	10,560	551
Cameron	Cameron	9,991	1,441
Catahoula	Harrisonburg	10,920	742
Claiborne	Homer	16,851	763
Concordia	Vidalia	20,247	718
De Soto	Mansfield	25,494	904
East Baton Rouge	Baton Rouge	412,852	459
East Carroll	Lake Providence	9,421	436
East Feliciana	Clinton	21,360	454
Evangeline	Ville Platte	35,434	669
Franklin	Winnsboro	21,263	648
Grant	Colfax	18,698	670
Iberia	New Iberia	73,266	589
Iberville	Plaquemine	33,320	627
Jackson	Jonesboro	15,397	582
Jefferson	Gretna	455,466	331
Jefferson Davis	Jennings	31,435	658
Lafayette	Lafayette	190,503	283
Lafourche	Thibodaux	89,974	1,141
La Salle	Jena	14,282	643
Lincoln	Ruston	42,509	469
Livingston	Livingston	91,814	654

Parish Name	Parish Seat	Population (2000)	Area in Square Miles
Madison	Tallulah	13,728	661
Morehouse	Bastrop	31,021	804
Natchitoches	Natchitoches	39,080	1,295
Orleans	New Orleans	484,674	205
Ouachita	Monroe	147,250	638
Plaquemines	Pointe a la Hache	26,757	1,030
Pointe Coupee	New Roads	22,763	563
Rapides	Alexandria	126,337	1,318
Red River	Coushatta	9,622	406
Richland	Rayville	20,981	576
Sabine	Many	23,459	1,029
St. Bernard	Chalmette	67,229	514
St. Charles	Hahnville	48,072	288
St. Helena	Greensburg	10,525	420
St. James	Convent	21,216	253
St. John the Baptist	Edgard	43,044	250
St. Landry	Opelousas	87,700	932
St. Martin	St. Martinville	48,583	736
St. Mary	Franklin	53,500	624
St. Tammany	Covington	191,268	925
Tangipahoa	Amite City	100,588	807
Tensas	St. Joseph	6,618	626
Terrebonne	Houma	104,503	1,368
Union	Farmerville	22,803	906
Vermilion	Abbeville	53,807	1,205
Vernon	Leesville	52,531	1,357
Washington	Franklinton	43,926	665
Webster	Minden	41,831	615
West Baton Rouge	Port Allen	21,601	203
West Carroll	Oak Grove	12,314	356
West Feliciana	St. Francisville	15,111	405
Winn	Winnfield	16,894	950

Gazetteer

This Gazetteer is a geographic dictionary that will help you locate and pronounce the names of places in this book. Lines of latitude and longitude are given for cities. The page numbers tell you where each place appears on a map (m) or in the text (t).

Alexandria (al ig zan' drē ə) A city located in central Louisiana, near parts of the Kisatchie National Forest: 31°N, 92°W. (m. 13, t. 259)

Atchafalaya Swamp (ə chə fə li' ə swämp) A swamp that surrounds much of the Atchafalaya River in southern Louisiana. (m. 40, t. 41)

Athens (ath' ənz) A small town in Claiborne Parish in northern Louisiana: 33°N, 93°W. (m. 66, t. 68)

Avery Island (ā' və rē ī' lənd) A salt dome in marshy land near the southern coast of central Louisiana. It is where where a popular pepper sauce was invented and is still made: 30°N, 92°W. (m. 88, t. 89)

Avondale (a' vən dāl) A town in southeastern Louisiana where many people work building ships: 30°N, 91°W. (m. 188, t. 191)

Baton Rouge (bat' ən rüzh) The capital of Louisiana. It is located in southeastern Louisiana: 30°N, 91°W.
(m. 13, t. 32, 243)

Bayou Teche (bī' ü tesh) A slow-moving stream in southern Louisiana that is a popular place for visitors. (m. 182, t. 42)

Bodcau Bayou (bȯd' caw bī' ü) A slow-moving stream in the West Gulf Coastal Plain region of Louisiana. (m. 19, t. 20)

Breaux Bridge (brō brij) A town in southern Louisiana that was founded by Scholastique Picou Breaux in 1829: 30°N, 92°W. (m. 296, t. 297)

Crowley (kraù' lē) A town in southern Louisiana that is known as the "Rice Capital of America": 30°N, 92°W. (m. 200, t. 202)

DeRidder (də rid' ər) A city located in western Louisiana near the Texas border: 31°N, 93°W. (m. 264, t. 265)

Driskill Mountain (dris' kəl moun' tən) A mountain in Louisiana. It has the highest elevation in the state, at 535 feet. (m. 40, t. 44)

East Gulf Coastal Plain (ēst gulf kōs' təl plān) One of Louisiana's three main land regions. It covers the land east of the Mississippi River and north of Lake Pontchartrain. (m. 19, t. 19)

Forest Hill (fôr' əst hil) A small town in central Louisiana, where author Kimberly Willis Holt lived as a child: 31°N, 93°W. (m. 66, t. 69)

Gulf of Mexico (gulf əv mek' sə kō) A large body of water located south of Louisiana, into which the Mississippi River empties. (m. 13, t. 34)

Jackson (jak' sən) A town in southeastern Louisiana where people can see how students lived and studied long ago at the Centenary State Historic Site: 31°N, 91°W. (m. 314, t. 315)

Jefferson Parish (jef' ər sən pâr' ish) A parish located south of New Orleans. The suburban community of Marrero is located here. (m. 66, t. 70)

Jennings (je' ningz) A small town in southern Louisiana where oil was first discovered in Louisiana in 1901: 30°N, 92°W. (m. 88, t. 90)

Kisatchie National Forest (ki sä' chē nash' ə nəl fôr' ist) Louisiana's only national forest, located in central and northern parts of the state. (m. 44, t. 44)

Lake Charles (lāk chärlz) A large city in southwestern Louisiana, known for its beaches and outdoor festivals: 30°N, 93°W. (m. 13, t. 67)

Louisiana (lü zē an' ə) One of the 50 states of the United States, located in the southern part of the country. The capital is Baton Rouge. (m. 13, t. 11)

Mamou (mə mü') A town in southern Louisiana with a Mardi Gras tradition that includes people riding horses from house to house to collect ingredients for a meal: 31°N, 92°W. (m. 306, t. 309)

Mississippi River (mis ə sip' ē ri' vər) A major river in the United States. It flows from Minnesota through Louisiana, and into the Gulf of Mexico. (m. 13, t. 31)

Mississippi River Delta (mis ə sip' ē ri' vər del' tə) A landform made of silt located at the mouth of the Mississippi River in the Gulf of Mexico. (m. 19, t. 21)

Mississippi River Plain (mis ə sip' ē ri' vər plān) One of Louisiana's three main land regions. It follows the path of the Mississippi River to the Gulf of Mexico. (m. 19, t. 19)

Monroe (mən rō') A city in northeastern Louisiana that is well known for its many tourist attractions, including the Louisiana Folklife Festival: 33°N, 92°W. (m. 13, t. 180, 211)

Natchitoches (na' kə tish) The oldest permanent settlement in Louisiana. It was founded in 1714 near the Red River: 32°N, 93°W. (m. 312, t. 132)

New Orleans (nü ôr' lənz) A famous city in Louisiana located in the southeastern part of the state. It is one of the busiest ports in the United States: 29°N, 90°W. (m. 13, t. 32, 134, 145, 238, 309)

New Roads (nü rōdz) A town located in southern Louisiana near the Mississippi border: 31°N, 91°W. (m. 264, t. 265)

Pronunciation Key

a in hat	ō in open	sh in she
ā in age	ȯ in all	th in thin
â in care	ô in order	ᴛʜ in then
ä in far	oi in oil	zh in measure
e in let	ou in out	ə = a in about
ē in equal	u in cup	ə = e in taken
ėr in term	ù in put	ə = i in pencil
i in it	ü in rule	ə = o in lemon
ī in ice	ch in child	ə = u in circus
o in hot	ng in long	

Gazetteer

Opelousas (ä pə lü' səs) A city in southern Louisiana near Lafayette: 31°N, 92°W. (m. 188, t. 189)

Ponchatoula (pän chə tü' lə) A town in southeastern Louisiana where the Ponchatoula Strawberry Festival is held: 30°N, 90°W. (m. 314, t. 316)

Port Hudson (pôrt həd' sən) A fort located north of Baton Rouge that was the site of a 48-day battle between Confederate and Union soldiers during the Civil War. The Union gained control of Port Hudson in 1863. (m. 150, t. 152)

Poverty Point (pä' vər tē point) A settlement in northeastern Louisiana that was built long ago by early Native Americans. (m. 124, t. 125)

Rayne (rān) A town in southern Louisiana where the Frog Festival is held: 30°N, 92°W. (m. 314, t. 316)

Shreveport (shrēv' pôrt) A city in northwestern Louisiana, on the Red River. It is named after Henry Miller Shreve, who cleared the Red River in the 1830s: 32°N, 94°W. (m. 13, t. 75, 266)

St. Bernard Parish (sānt bər närd' par' ish) A parish in southeastern Louisiana where many Isleño communities are located. (m. 288, t. 289)

Tensas River National Wildlife Refuge (ten' sò ri' vər nash' ə nəl wīld' līf ref' yüj) An area of land in northeastern Louisiana that is set aside to protect plants and animals. (m. 98, t. 99)

Thibodaux (ti' bə dō) A city located in southeastern Louisiana: 30°N, 91°W. (m. 256, t. 259)

United States (yü nī' tid stāts) A country made up of 50 states that is located in North America. (m. 9, t. 12)

West Gulf Coastal Plain (west gulf kōs' təl plān) One of Louisiana's three main land regions. It covers the land west of the Mississippi River Plain. (m. 19, t. 19)

Pronunciation Key

a in hat	ō in open	sh in she
ā in age	ȯ in all	th in thin
â in care	ô in order	ŦH in then
ä in far	oi in oil	zh in measure
e in let	ou in out	ə = a in about
ē in equal	u in cup	ə = e in taken
ėr in term	u̇ in put	ə = i in pencil
i in it	ü in rule	ə = o in lemon
ī in ice	ch in child	ə = u in circus
o in hot	ng in long	

Biographical Dictionary

This Biographical Dictionary tells you about the people in this book and how to pronounce their names. The page numbers tell you where the person first appears in the text.

★ A ★

Armstrong, Louis (ärm' stróng) 1901–1971 He was a musician whose trumpet playing helped make jazz popular. (p. 299)

Audubon, John James (ôd' ə bän) 1785–1851 He was an artist who is famous for his lifelike drawings of birds. (p. 99)

★ B ★

Beauregard, P. G. T. (bō' rə gärd) 1818–1893 He was a Confederate general during the Civil War. He led Confederate soldiers to victory at Fort Sumter. (p. 152)

Beriwal, Madhu (bâr' ə wəl) b. 1956 She runs a company in Louisiana that helps prepare communities for emergencies. She was given the Technology Leader of the Year award by Louisiana in 2003. (p. 193)

Blanco, Kathleen (blän' kō) b. 1942 She became the first woman to serve as governor of Louisiana, in 2004. (p. 245)

Boggs, Lindy (bägs) b. 1916 She was the first woman from Louisiana elected to the United States House of Representatives, in 1973. (p. 257)

Breaux, Scholastique Picou (brō) 1796–1846 She founded the town of Breaux Bridge in 1829. She drew up a plan of the city that included a diagram of the streets and a map of the area. (p. 297)

Bridges, Ruby (brij' əz) b. 1954 She was the first African American child to attend the William Frantz Elementary School in New Orleans, in 1960. (p. 267)

Pronunciation Key

a in hat	ō in open	sh in she
ā in age	ȯ in all	th in thin
â in care	ô in order	ŦH in then
ä in far	oi in oil	zh in measure
e in let	ou in out	ə = a in about
ē in equal	u in cup	ə = e in taken
ėr in term	u̇ in put	ə = i in pencil
i in it	ü in rule	ə = o in lemon
ī in ice	ch in child	ə = u in circus
o in hot	ng in long	

Biographical Dictionary

★ D ★

De Soto, Hernando (di sō' tō) 1496?–1542 He was a Spanish explorer who led a group of the first Europeans to reach the Mississippi River. (p. 131)

Delhomme, Jake (də lōm') b. 1975 He is a professional football player. He also played football in college at the University of Louisiana-Lafayette. (p. 319)

Dormon, Caroline (dôr' mən) 1888–1971 She helped form Kisatchie National Forest to protect trees and other plants so people can enjoy them in the future. (p. 44)

★ F ★

Fisher-Blassingame, Rose ('fisher bla' sing gām) b. 1962 She teaches traditional Choctaw cane basket weaving. (p. 79)

★ G ★

Gálvez, Bernardo de (gäl' vās) 1746–1786 He was the governor of the Spanish colony of Louisiana. He helped the American colonists during the American Revolution. (p. 135)

Gottschalk, Louis Moreau (got' shälk) 1829–1869 He became a world-famous piano player when he was 13 years old. He used Creole and Latin American styles in the music he wrote. (p. 299)

Graves, Todd (grāvz) b. 1972 He is the owner of a chain of restaurants called Raising Cane's. He opened his first restaurant in Baton Rouge in 1996 and now has more than 20 locations. (p. 205)

★ H ★

Holt, Kimberly Willis (hōlt) b. 1960 She is an author of books for young readers. Many of her stories take place in Louisiana. (p. 69)

Hunter, Clementine (hun' tėr) 1886?–1988 She was the first African American artist to have a show in the New Orleans Museum of Art. (p. 45)

★ J ★

Jefferson, Thomas (jef' ər sən) 1743–1826 He was the third President of the United States, serving from 1801 to 1809. He was responsible for the Louisiana Purchase in 1803. (p. 145)

★ L ★

La Salle, Robert (lə sal') 1643–1687 He was a French explorer who traveled down the Mississippi River to the Gulf of Mexico in 1682. He claimed the land around the Mississippi River for France and named it Louisiana. (p. 15)

Lafitte, Jean (lə fēt') c. 1780–1825 He was a pirate who helped the Americans fight the Battle of New Orleans during the War of 1812. He became a pirate again after the war. (p. 297)

Le Moyne, Jean-Baptiste, de Bienville (lə mwän') 1680–1767 He founded New Orleans and served as the governor of the French colony of Louisiana. (p. 297)

Long, Huey (lȯng) 1893–1935 He was elected governor of Louisiana in 1928 and served in the United States Senate from 1932 to 1935. (p. 237)

★ M ★

McIlhenny, Edmund (mak' əl hen ē) 1815–1890 He invented a popular pepper sauce using red peppers and salt from Avery Island. (p. 89)

Morgan, Sarah (môr' gən) 1842–1909 She kept a diary of her experiences living in Baton Rouge during the Civil War. (p. 153)

Pronunciation Key

a	in hat	ō	in open	sh	in she
ā	in age	ȯ	in all	th	in thin
â	in care	ô	in order	ᴛʜ	in then
ä	in far	oi	in oil	zh	in measure
e	in let	ou	in out	ə	= a in about
ē	in equal	u	in cup	ə	= e in taken
ėr	in term	u̇	in put	ə	= i in pencil
i	in it	ü	in rule	ə	= o in lemon
ī	in ice	ch	in child	ə	= u in circus
o	in hot	ng	in long		

Biographical Dictionary

Poncho, Lovelin (pon' chō) He is one of the leaders of the Coushatta Native American group, in Louisiana. (p. 127)

Prudhomme, Paul (prə dŏm') b. 1940 He is a chef and restaurant owner in New Orleans who uses local ingredients to make traditional Louisiana recipes. (p. 189)

Roudanez, Louis Charles (rü' də nā) 1823–1890 He was a doctor who published the first daily newspaper in the United States to be owned by African Americans, in the 1800s. (p. 154)

Shreve, Henry Miller (shrēv) 1785–1851 He was a river captain and steamboat builder. He helped clear the Red River so people could travel by water more easily to northern Louisiana. (p. 75)

Twain, Mark (twān) 1835–1910 Born Samuel Clemens, he was a riverboat pilot who wrote many books, including *The Adventures of Tom Sawyer.* (p. 31)

Walker, Madam C. J. (wo' kər) 1867–1919 She made hair products for African American women. She founded the Madam C. J. Walker Manufacturing Company and became a millionaire. (p. 201)

Pronunciation Key

a	in hat	ō	in open	sh	in she
ā	in age	o	in all	th	in thin
â	in care	ô	in order	ŦH	in then
ä	in far	oi	in oil	zh	in measure
e	in let	ou	in out	ə	= a in about
ē	in equal	u	in cup	ə	= e in taken
ėr	in term	ủ	in put	ə	= i in pencil
i	in it	ü	in rule	ə	= o in lemon
ī	in ice	ch	in child	ə	= u in circus
o	in hot	ng	in long		

Glossary

This Glossary will help you understand the meanings and pronounce the vocabulary words in this book. The page number tells you where the word first appears.

abundance (ə bun' dəns) a large supply of something (p. 92)

adapt (ə dapt') to change the way you do something (p. 78)

bar graph (bär graf) a graph that uses bars to show and compare information (p. 294)

bayou (bī' ü) a slow moving stream (p. 20)

bill (bil) a plan for a new law (p. 244)

capital (kap' ə təl) a city in which the government of a state or country is located (p. 243)

capital resource (kap' ə təl ri sôrs') a machine, tool, or building used to make goods or provide services (p. 190)

capitol (kap' ə təl) a building in which government leaders meet (p. 243)

cardinal directions (kärd' n əl də rek' shəns) the north, south, east, and west directions on a map (p. 96)

century (sen' chər ē) 100 years (p. 128)

circle graph (sėr' kəl graf) a circular drawing divided into sections that compares information (p. 294)

citizen (sit' ə zən) an official member of a country (p. 258)

Civil War (siv' əl wôr) the war between the Northern and Southern states from 1861 to 1865 (p. 151)

classify (klas' ə fī) to place things that have similar features together in the same group (p. 72)

colony (kol' ə nē) a place that is ruled by another country (p. 131)

community (kə myü' nə tē) a place where people live, work, and have fun together (p. 67)

compass rose (kum' pəs rōz) a symbol on a map that shows directions (p. 96)

Pronunciation Key

a in hat	ō in open	sh in she
ā in age	ȯ in all	th in thin
â in care	ô in order	ᴛʜ in then
ä in far	oi in oil	zh in measure
e in let	ou in out	ə = a in about
ē in equal	u in cup	ə = e in taken
ėr in term	ů in put	ə = i in pencil
i in it	ü in rule	ə = o in lemon
ī in ice	ch in child	ə = u in circus
o in hot	ng in long	

Glossary

Confederate States of America
(kən' fed' ər it stāts əv ə mer' ə kə)
the government formed in 1861 by the
11 Southern states that left the United
States after Abraham Lincoln was
elected President (p. 151)

conserve (kən sėrv') to use resources
carefully (p. 93)

constitution (kon stə tü' shən) a written
plan of government (p. 243)

consumer (kən sü' mər) a person or
group who uses products (p. 202)

culture (kul' chər) the way a group of
people lives, including language,
music, religion, food, clothing, and
holidays (p. 289)

custom (kus' təm) a special way
that a cultural group does something,
including cooking, dressing, and
celebrating (p. 307)

cutaway diagram (kut' ə wā dī' ə gram)
a diagram that shows the inside and
outside of a building or object (p. 186)

decade (dek' ād) ten years (p. 128)

delta (del' tə) the land that is made from
silt dropped at the mouth of a river
(p. 21)

demand (di mand') the amount of a good
or a service that people want and can
pay for (p. 212)

democracy (di mok' rə sē) a government
that is run by the people (p. 257)

earn (ern) to get something, such as money, from working (p. 201)

economic choice (ə kə nom' ik chois) a decision to buy one thing instead of another (p. 211)

economy (ə kon' ə mē) a system for making, managing, and delivering goods and services (p. 179)

elevation (el ə vā' shən) the height of something above or below sea level (p. 44)

environment (en vī' rən mənt) all the things that surround us and affect the growth of living things, such as air, water, and land (p. 75)

erosion (i rō' zhən) the slow wearing away of land by water, wind, and other natural forces (p. 101)

explorer (ek splôr' ər) a person who travels looking for new lands and discoveries (p. 15)

export (ek spôrt') to send goods from one country to another for sale (p. 182)

fertile (fėr' təl) good for growing crops (p. 31)

festival (fes' tə vəl) a program of entertainment that is often held every year (p. 316)

floodplain (flud plān) lands along a river that are flooded by the river's waters during heavy rain or when snow melts (p. 31)

geography (jē og' rə fē) the study of Earth and the ways people use it (p. 14)

goods (gu̇dz) things made or grown by people to sell to others (p. 180)

government (guv' ərn mənt) the people and laws that run a place, such as a country, state, or city (p. 237)

Pronunciation Key

a in hat	ō in open	sh in she
ā in age	ȯ in all	th in thin
â in care	ô in order	ŦH in then
ä in far	oi in oil	zh in measure
e in let	ou in out	ə = a in about
ē in equal	u in cup	ə = e in taken
ėr in term	u̇ in put	ə = i in pencil
i in it	ü in rule	ə = o in lemon
ī in ice	ch in child	ə = u in circus
o in hot	ng in long	

Glossary

★ H ★

hemisphere (hem' ə sfir) one half of Earth; there are northern, southern, eastern, and western hemispheres (p. 12)

human resource (hyü' mən ri sôrs') a person who makes goods or provides a service (p. 190)

★ I ★

immigrant (im' ə grənt) a person who moves to a country and lives there (p. 291)

import (im pôrt') to bring goods from one country into another for sale (p. 182)

interdependence (in' tər di pen' dens) depending on each other (p. 191)

intermediate direction (in tər mē' də it də rek' shən) a direction in the middle of two cardinal directions, such as northeast or southwest (p. 96)

Internet search (in' tər net sėrch) a way to look for information on the Internet (p. 270)

★ J ★

jazz (jaz) a style of music that began in New Orleans in the early 1900s (p. 299)

★ K ★

key word search (kē' wėrd sėrch) an Internet search using a word or words to find information on a subject (p. 271)

★ L ★

landform (land' fôrm) a natural shape on Earth's surface, such as a mountain (p. 20)

law (lò) a rule that is made by the government (p. 239)

levee (lev' ē) a high bank or wall that is built along the sides of a river to keep it from overflowing (p.77)

line graph (līn graf) a graph that shows how something changes over time (p. 24)

Louisiana Purchase (lü zē an' ə pėr' chəs) the sale in 1803 of a large amount of land west of the Mississippi River by France to the United States for 15 million dollars (p. 145)

M

map scale (map skal) a tool that helps you measure distances in miles and kilometers on a map (p. 312)

Mardi Gras (mär' dē grä) a time before Lent that is celebrated with parades, costumes, and music; a tradition in Louisiana since the 1700s (p. 308)

N

natural resource (nach' ər əl ri sôrs') a material found in nature that people can use (p. 89)

northeast (nôrth ēst') an intermediate direction halfway between north and east (p. 96)

northwest (nôrth west') an intermediate direction halfway between north and west (p. 97)

O

opportunity cost (op ər tü' nə tē kȯst) what you give up when you choose one thing instead of another (p. 211)

P

periodical (pir ē od' ə kəl) a magazine or newspaper that is printed regularly (p. 270)

plantation (plan tā' shən) a large farm where crops such as cotton and sugarcane are grown (p. 133)

point of view (point əv vyü) the way a person feels about a problem or issue (p. 250)

population (pop yə lā' shən) the number of people living in an area (p. 32)

Pronunciation Key

a in hat	ō in open	sh in she
ā in age	ȯ in all	th in thin
â in care	ô in order	ŦH in then
ä in far	oi in oil	zh in measure
e in let	ou in out	ə = a in about
ē in equal	u in cup	ə = e in taken
ėr in term	ù in put	ə = i in pencil
i in it	ü in rule	ə = o in lemon
ī in ice	ch in child	ə = u in circus
o in hot	ng in long	

Glossary

population map (pop yə lā′ shən map) a map that shows the number of people living in different areas (p. 38)

port (pôrt) a place where ships can load and unload goods from all over the world (p. 32)

primary source (prī′ mâr ē sôrs) a description of an event written by a person who was there (p. 148)

producer (prə dü′ sər) a person or group who makes products (p. 202)

profit (prof′ it) the money a business has left over after all of its costs are paid (p. 215)

Reconstruction (rē′ kən struk′ shən) the period of rebuilding after the Civil War during which the Southern states rejoined the United States (p. 154)

reference book (ref′ ər ens bủk) a book containing helpful facts or information, such as an almanac, encyclopedia, or atlas (p. 270)

region (rē′ jən) a large land area with special features that make it different from other areas (p. 19)

republic (ri pub' lik) a government in which the citizens elect representatives to run the government and make laws (p. 257)

rural community (rùr' əl kə myü' nə tē) a community in the countryside where towns are small and far apart (p. 68)

scarcity (skâr' sə tē) not enough of something to meet people's needs and wants (p. 92)

secondary source (sek' ən dâr' ē sôrs) a description of an event written by someone who was not there (p. 148)

services (sėr' vis əs) jobs that one person or group does for another (p. 180)

settlement (set' l mənt) a place where people live (p. 125)

slavery (slā' vər ē) a system in which people are forced to work for other people (p. 133)

southeast (south ēst') an intermediate direction halfway between south and east (p. 97)

southwest (south west') an intermediate direction halfway between south and west (p. 96)

specialize (spesh' ə līz) to do one job or make one part of a product (p. 191)

suburban community (sə bėr' bən kə myü' nə tē) a community located near a large city (p. 70)

supply (sə plī') the amount of a product that producers want to sell (p. 212)

Pronunciation Key		
a in hat	ō in open	sh in she
ā in age	ȯ in all	th in thin
â in care	ô in order	ᴛʜ in then
ä in far	oi in oil	zh in measure
e in let	ou in out	ə = a in about
ē in equal	u in cup	ə = e in taken
ėr in term	ù in put	ə = i in pencil
i in it	ü in rule	ə = o in lemon
ī in ice	ch in child	ə = u in circus
o in hot	ng in long	

Glossary

technology (tek nol' ə jē) the use of tools and ideas to solve problems (p. 192)

trade (trād) the buying or selling of goods and services (p. 182)

tradition (trə dish' ən) a custom or belief that is handed down over the years (p. 308)

Union (yü' nyən) another name for the United States; the Northern states during the Civil War (p. 151)

urban community (ėr' bən kə myü' nə tē) a community that is in the city (p. 67)

V

volunteer (vol ən tir') someone who works without pay (p. 266)

wetlands (wet' ləndz) marshes, swamps, or other kinds of land that are damp or covered with water (p. 41)

wildlife (wīld' līf') animals and plants that live in the wild (p. 99)

Pronunciation Key

a	in hat	ō	in open	sh	in she
ā	in age	ȯ	in all	th	in thin
â	in care	ô	in order	ŦH	in then
ä	in far	oi	in oil	zh	in measure
e	in let	ou	in out	ə	= a in about
ē	in equal	u	in cup	ə	= e in taken
ėr	in term	u̇	in put	ə	= i in pencil
i	in it	ü	in rule	ə	= o in lemon
ī	in ice	ch	in child	ə	= u in circus
o	in hot	ng	in long		

Index

Titles appear in italics or quotation marks. Page numbers in **bold** print indicate vocabulary definitions. An *m* following a page number indicates a map. The terms *See* and *See also* direct the reader to alternative entries.

abundance, 92
Acadia, 134, 136, 136*m*
Acadia Parish, 39
Acadians, 134, 136–137, 285
adapt, 78–79
Africa, 133, 209, 290
African Americans
   artist, 48–49
   business and, 172, 201,
     206–207
   Civil War and, 152,
     158–159
   education and, 268–269
   equal rights and, 154,
     158–159
   festivals and, 316
   music and, 283, 285,
     298–301, 307
   right to vote and, 154
agriculture. *See* farming
Alexandria, 13*m*, 24–25, 259
Allen, Henry Watkins, R24
Allen, Oscar K., R25
alligator, 100
almanac, H4, 270
Amazon River, 36–37, 36*m*
American Revolution, 135,
   138–139
Armstrong, Louis, 283, 285,
   299–301, 323
artists
   African American, 48–49
   Native American, 80–81
   nature, 104–105
Asia, 106, 291–292, 295
astronaut, 11, 263
Atchafalaya River, 41, 182*m*
Atchafalaya Swamp, 28,
   40*m*, 40–41
Athens, 66*m*, 68
atlas, H4, 270

Audubon, John James, 60,
   99, 104–105
Audubon Zoo, 99
Avery Island, 86, 88*m*,
   88–89, 103
Avondale, 176, 188*m*, 191

Baker, 73
Baker, Joshua, R24
bald cypress, 100
banks, 204
bar graph, 294–295
Barry, Daniel T., 11
basket weaving, 79–81
Baton Rouge, 28
   as capital, 32, 234,
     242–243, 248
   economy of, 193, 205
   history of, 139, 146, 152,
     157
   maps of, 13*m*, 38*m*, 248*m*,
     312*m*
   population of, 32, 38, 67,
     73
   state services in, 233
Battle of New Orleans,
   146, 297
bay, R12
bayou, 3, 9, **20**, 42–43, 78
Bayou Sauvage National
   Wildlife Refuge, 96*m*,
   97
Bayou Teche, 29, 42–43,
   134, 182*m*
Beauregard, P. G. T., 118,
   151–152
Beauvais, Armand Julie,
   R24
Beriwal, Madhu, 173,
   192–193

bill, 244–245
biographies
   Armstrong, Louis, 300–301
   Audubon, John James,
     104–105
   Boggs, Lindy, 260–261
   Delhomme, Jake, 320–321
   Fisher-Blassingame, Rose,
     80–81
   Gálvez, Bernardo de,
     138–139
   Hunter, Clementine, 48–49
   La Salle, Robert, 16–17
   Long, Huey, 240–241
   Morgan, Sarah, 156–157
   Prudhomme, Paul, 194–195
   Walker, Madam C. J.,
     206–207
biography (as reference
   source), 271
Birds of America, The, 105
Blanchard, Newton C., R24
Blanco, Kathleen, 231, 245,
   R25
Bodcau Bayou, 8, 19*m*, 20
bodies of water, H15
Boggs, Hale, 261
Boggs, Lindy, 230, 257,
   260–261
border, H13
Breaux, Scholastique
   Picou, 282, 286, 296–297
Breaux Bridge, 286, 296*m*,
   296–297, 320–321
Briarwood, 46–47
Bridges, Ruby, 231,
   267–269
brown pelican, 6–7, 45, 100,
   R26
business, 201, 204–207,
   214–215, 318

Cabildo, 134, 314
Caddo, 126
Cajun, 134, 136–137, 285,
   307, 316
Calcasieu River Bridge,
   233
Cameron Parish, 39
Canada, 9*m*, 16, 290
Canary Islands, 288
canyon, R12
capital, 243
   national, 248*m*, 248–249
   state, 32, 234, 242–243,
     248, 248*m*
capital resource, 190
capitol, 243, 246
   national, 248–249
   state, 242–243, 246, 248
cardinal directions, 96
caring, H2, 46–47
cause and effect, 174–175
century, 128
character attributes
   caring, H2, 46–47
   courage, H2, 268–269
   fairness, H2, 158–159
   honesty, H2, 310–311
   respect, H2, 218–219
   responsibility, H2, 82–83
Chavis, Boozoo, 307
China, 184, 185*m*, 208–209
Chitimacha, 43, 117, 126
Choctaw, 79–81, 126
Chopin, Kate, 298
circle graph, 294–295
cities, 62–63, 67, 73. *See*
   also names of specific cities
   populations of, 67, 73
citizen, 258
   responsibilities of,
     258–259, 265
   rights of, 154, 243
citizenship, 264–267

Index

caring as, H2, 46–47
courage as, H2, 268–269
fairness as, H2, 158–159
honesty as, H2, 310–311
respect as, H2, 218–219
responsibility as, H2, 82–83, 258–259
civil rights, 231
Civil War, 121, **151**–159, 153*m*, 160–161, 262
Claiborne Parish, 68, 179
Claiborne, William, 146, R24
classify, 72–73
cliff, R12
Cloutierville, 5
coast, R12
coastal areas, 101–103
colony, 131–135
community, 67–71
resources, H6
rural, **68**–69, 73
suburban, 64, **70**–71, 73
urban, **67**, 73
compare and contrast, 62–63
comparing sources, 148–149
compass, 14
compass rose, H13, **96**–97
competition, 214
computer, H5, 192, 270
Confederacy, 151–153, 161, 262
Confederate States of America, 151, 151*m*, 262
Congress, United States, 260–261
conserve, 92–93
constitution, 243
Constitution, Louisiana State, 229, 243–244
consumer, 202, 214
continent, 12, 36
cotton, 31, 49, 175, 180, 182, 207
courage, H2, 268–269
Coushatta, 127
Covington, 178
crawfish, 78, 316
Creole, 158, 307, 316
Crowley, 198, 200*m*, 202

culture, 287, **289**–291, 305–307, 309, 316
custom, 307–308
cutaway diagram, 186–187
Cypremort Point State Park, 44*m*, 103

Daily Picayune, The, 310–311
dam, 77
Davis, Jimmie H., 274, R25
De Soto, Hernando, 118, 131
decade, 128
decision making, H3, 216–217
Delhomme, Jake, 283, 319–321
Delta, 172, 206
delta (landform), 21, 34–35
demand, 212–213
democracy, 257–258
Derbigny, Pierre, R24
DeRidder, 264*m*, 264–265
desert, R12
diagram, cutaway, 186–187
dictionary, H4, 270
Dormon, Caroline, 5, 44, 46–47
draw conclusions, 232–233
Driskill Mountain, 20, 29, 40*m*, 44
Dupré, Jacques, R24

earn, 201
East Gulf Coastal Plain, 19*m*, 19–20
economic choice, 211
economy, 179–180, 183, 199, 204, 318. *See also* Louisiana, economy of

education, 192, 238, 268–269
Edwards, Edwin W., R25
elevation, 44
encyclopedia, H4, 270–271
England, 131, 209. *See also* Great Britain
environment, 75–79, 87, 126
erosion, 101–102, 266
"Evangeline," 134
executive branch (state), 244–245
explorer, 15
De Soto, Hernando, 131
La Salle, Robert, 4, 15–17, 131
tools of, 14
export, 182, 184–185

fairness, H2, 158–159
farming, 20, 30–31, 126–127, 136, 180, 202–203, 292
fertile, 31
festival, 316–317, 317*m*
Fiddle Fever, 326–327
Fisher-Blassingame, Rose, 61, 79–81
fishing, 7, 136–137, 292, 318
flag, 121, 262–263, R18–R19
Flanders, Benjamin Franklin, R24
flood, 76–77
floodplain, 31
football, 319–321
foothills, R12
forest, 44, 46–47, R12
Forest Hill, 66*m*, 69
Foster, Murphy J., R25
Foster, Murphy James, R24
France, 16–17, 105, 121, 123, 131–132, 134–135, 145, 158, 290
Fuqua, Henry L., R25

Galveston, Texas, 139
Gálvez, Bernardo de, 118, 135, 138–139
geography, 14–15
themes of, H8–H9
Germany, 132, 290
"Give Me Louisiana," 52–53
Global Positioning System (GPS), 14
globe, H11
Gonzales, 306
goods, 179–**180,** 182, 186, 190, 201, 204, 212
gospel music, 285, 298
Gottschalk, Louis Moreau, 282, 299
government, 236–239, **237**
local, 39, 237
national, 237, 241, 248–249, 257, 260–261
services of, 233, 238, 241
state, 32, 233, 235, 237–239, 242–247
governor, 245, 248
Grand Isle, 7
Grand Isle State Park, 7, 44*m*
graphs, understanding, 294–295
Graves, Todd, 171, 173, 205
Great Britain, 146. *See also* England
grid, H17
gulf, R12
Gulf of Mexico, 9*m*, 11, 17, 21, 31, 33–36, 90, 101, 106
Gumbel, Bryant, 298

Hahn, Michael, R24
Hall, Luther E., R25
harbor, R12
Haughton, 13, 13*m*
Haynesville, 68
Heard, William Wright, R24
Hebert, Paul O., R24
hemisphere, 12
hill, R12
historic site, 315
history map, H18
Holt, Kimberly Willis, 61, 69
honesty, H2, 310–311
Houma, 265
human resource, 190
Hunter, Clementine, 5, 45, 48–49
Hurricane Katrina, 7, 77, 218–219

Iberia Parish, 231
immigrant, 291–292, 294–295
import, 182
Indians. *See* Native Americans
interdependence, 191
intermediate directions, 96–97
Internet search, H5, **270**–271
interstate highway, 238, 312, 312*m*
interview, H6
island, R12
Isleños, 286, 288–289

Jackson, 314*m*, 315
Jackson, Andrew, 146
Jackson, Mahalia, 298
jambalaya, 306–307
Jambalaya Festival, 306
jazz, 284–285, **299**–301, 322–323
Jefferson, Thomas, 145
Jefferson Parish, 64, 66*m*, 70
Jennings, 88*m*, 90
Johnson, Henry S., R24
Johnson, Isaac, R24
Jones, Sam H., R25
judicial branch (state), 244–245, 247

Kellogg, William Pitt, R24
Kennon, Robert F., R25
key, H13
keyword search, 271
King, Alvin O., R25
Kisatchie National Forest, 44, 44*m*, 47

La Salle, Robert, 4, 15–17, 120–121, 131
Lafitte, Jean, 282, 297
lake, R12
Lake Charles, 13*m*, 66–67
landform, H15, **20**
Latin America, 291, 294–295
law, 239, 244–245, 247, 257–258, 265
Le Moyne, Jean-Baptiste, de Bienville, 297
Leche, Richard W., R25

"Legend of Bayou Teche," The, 43
legislative branch (state), 244–245
Lent, 308
levee, 77
library, using the, 270–271
Lincoln, Abraham, 150–151
line graph, 24–25
literature
  "Evangeline," 134
  Fiddle Fever, 326–327
  "Legend of Bayou Teche," The, 43
  "Louisiana," 110–111
  Louisiana State Constitution, 243
  "Moon's Cloud Blanket," 164–165
  My Louisiana Sky, 69
  Nicky the Swamp Dog, 181
  "Why Lapin's Tail Is Short," 290
litter, 94–95, 102
Livingston Parish, 51
Long, Earl K., R25
Long, Huey, 230, 237, 240–242, R25
Longfellow, Henry Wadsworth, 134
"Louisiana," 110–111
Louisiana
  communities of, 66–71
  cultures of, 287, 289–291, 305–307, 309, 316
  economy of, 178–180, 182–183, 188–193, 199, 204–205, 318
  education in, 192, 238, 268–269
  environment of, 74–79, 87, 126
  festivals in, 304–306, 308–309, **316**–317, 317*m*
  geography of, 14–15, 40–45
  history of, 124–127, 130–139, 142, 144–147, 150–159, 297
  immigrants in, 291–292, 294–295
  location of, 10–13

maps of, 13*m*, 19*m*, 38*m*, 44*m*, 126*m*, 182*m*, 312*m*
music in, 299, 322–323
Native Americans in, 17, 43, 79–81, 117, 124–127, 126*m*, 130–132, 164–165, 290, 316
natural resources of, 88–93, 91*m*
regions of, 18–21, 19*m*
sports in, 319–321
wildlife in, 98–101
Louisiana black bear, 98–100, R26
Louisiana House of Representatives, 244
Louisiana Purchase, 145, 145*m*, 314
Louisiana red beans and rice, 222–223
Louisiana State Capitol, 242–243, 246, 248
Louisiana State Constitution, 229, 243–244
Louisiana State Senate, 244
Louisiana State University, 319
Louisiana Supreme Court, 247
Louisiana Tech University, 319

Madison Parish, 51
magazine, 270
magnolia, 100
main idea and details, 6–7
Maine, 102–103, 103*m*
Mamou, 306*m*, 309
map scale, 312–313
maps, H12, 13
  features, H13
  grid, H17
  history, H18

Index

Index

Credits

DORLING KINDERSLEY (DK) is an international publishing company specializing in the creation of high quality reference content for books, CD-ROMs, online materials, and video. The hallmark of DK content is its unique combination of educational content that delights children, parents, and teachers around the world. Scott Foresman is delighted to have been able to use selected extracts of DK content within this Scott Foresman Social Studies program.

22–23 from Eyewitness Pond and River, by Steve Parker, copyright © 2000 by Dorling Kindersley Limited

106–107 from Eyewitness Ocean by Miranda MacQuitty, copyright © 2000 by Dorling Kindersley Limited

160–161 from The Visual Dictionary of the Civil War by John Stanchak in association with the Smithsonian Institution, copyright © 2000 by Dorling Kindersley Limited and the Smithsonian Institution

209 from Money by Joe Cribb, copyright © 2000 by Dorling Kindersley Limited

262–263 from "The United States of America" from Flag by William Crampton, copyright © 2000 by Dorling Kindersley Limited

322–323 from Eyewitness Music by Neil Ardley, copyright © 2000 by Dorling Kindersley Limited

Text

Excerpts from My Louisiana Sky by Kimberly Willis Holt, copyright © 1998 by Kimberly Willis Holt. Reprinted by permission of Henry Holt and Company, LLC

Excerpts from My Louisiana Sky by Kimberly Willis Holt, copyright © 1998 by Kimberly Willis Holt. Reprinted by permission of Henry Holt and Company, LLC

From Louisiana: An Illustrated History by C. E. Richard. Copyright © 2003 by The Foundation for Excellence in Louisiana Public Broadcasting. Reprinted by permission of Louisiana Public Broadcasting.

Reprinted by permission of Louisiana State University Press from Louisiana Sojourns: Travelers' Tales And Literary Journeys edited by Frank de Caro. Copyright © 1998 by Louisiana State University Press.

From America The Beautiful: Louisiana by Deborah Kent. Published by Childrens Press, Chicago, copyright © 1988. Reprinted by permission of Scholastic Library Publishing Company, Inc., a division of Scholastic Incorporated.

Reprinted by permission of Louisiana State University Press from Louisiana Sojourns: Travelers' Tales And Literary Journeys edited by Frank de Caro. Copyright © 1998 by Louisiana State University Press.

Adaptation of The Legend of Bayou Teche as told by the Chitimacha tribe of Louisiana.

Twelve Years As A Slave by Solomon Northup, (Auburn: Derby and Miller, 1853).

"Louisiana" by Jean McGivney Boese, Poet Laureate for the State of Louisiana. Reprinted by permission of Robert Lamar Boese.

Excerpts from La Salle: Explorer Of The North American Frontier by Anka Muhlstein: translated from the French by Willard Wood. Copyright © 1992 by Grasset & Fasquelle. Translation copyright © 1994 by Arcade Publishing, Inc.

From "Parish launching anti-litter campaign through fast-food outlets" by William Johnson/Louisiana Gannett News, posted March 21, 2004 at http://www.dailyworld.com. Reprinted by permission of The Advertiser/Gannett.

Reprinted by permission of Louisiana State University Press from Louisiana Sojourns: Travelers' Tales And Literary Journeys edited by Frank de Caro. Copyright © 1998 by Louisiana State University Press.

"Give Me Louisiana", words and music by Doralice Fontane.

From Moon's Cloud Blanket by Rose Anne St. Romain, illustrated by Joan C. Waites copyright © 2003. Used by permission of the licenser, Pelican Publishing Company, Inc.

From "Trash Bash volunteers fill 70 trash bags" by Jacqueline Cochran, posted March 21, 2004 at http://www.dailyworld.com. Reprinted by permission of The Advertiser/Gannett.

From Choctaw Split Cane Basketry, Louisiana Regional Folklife Program, http://www.nsula.edu/regionalfolklife/researchProjects/splitbasket/rose.htm. Reprinted by permission of Dayna Bowker Lee.

Excerpts based on information from Clementine Hunter: American Folk Artist by James L. Wilson. Copyright © 1988 by James L. Wilson, (Pelican Publishing Company, Gretna, Louisiana).

From the journal of John James Audubon, Louisiana, 1821.

Excerpt of 1862 diary entry from A Confederate Girl's Diary by Sarah Morgan Dawson. Edited by Warrington Dawson (Boston: Houghton Mifflin Company, 1913).

From Life On The Mississippi by Mark Twain, (Boston: James R. Osgood and Company, 1883).

Excerpt from Evangeline by Henry Wadsworth Longfellow, 1847.

From Every Man A King: The Autobiography Of Huey P. Long by Huey P. Long (New Orleans: National Book Co., 1933)

Excerpt from "Preface" in Washington Through A Purple Veil: Memoirs Of A Southern Woman by Lindy Boggs, copyright © 1994 by Corinne C. Boggs, reprinted by permission of Harcourt, Inc.

"You Are My Sunshine", Words and Music by Jimmie Davis and Charles Mitchell. Copyright © 1930 by Peer International Corporation. Copyright Renewed. International Copyright Secured. All Rights Reserved.

Excerpt of Press Release from Office of the Governor of the State of Louisiana, "Governor Blanco celebrates 100th day in office", April 20, 2004.

From Article I, Section 1 of Louisiana Constitution of 1974, Baton Rouge, Louisiana.

From Article I, Section 1 of Louisiana Constitution of 1974, Baton Rouge, Louisiana.

Excerpt of quote by writer Ernest Gaines, from Introduction, Louisiana: An Illustrated History By C.E. Richard (The Foundation for Excellence in Louisiana Public Broadcasting, 2003).

From "Perseverance: Delhomme never says die" by Skip Wood (usatoday.com, posted Jan. 29, 2004).

From Why Lapin's Ears Are Long And Other Tales From The Louisiana Bayou adapted by Sharon Arms Doucet. Published by Orchard Books, a division of Scholastic Inc. Copyright © 1997 by Sharon Arms Doucet. Reprinted by permission of Scholastic Inc.

Excerpt from Fiddle Fever by Sharon Arms Doucet. Copyright © 2000 by Sharon Arms Doucet. Reprinted by permission of Clarion Books, an imprint of Houghton Mifflin Company. All rights reserved.

From Satchmo: My Life In New Orleans by Louis Armstrong (New York, Prentice-Hall, 1954).

Maps

MapQuest, Inc.

Illustrations

LA12, LA13, LA16 Marty Martinez
4, 16–17 Eric Fortune
5, 48, 119, 131, 158, 164, 310 Yoshi Miyake
12–13, 122–125 Albert Lorenz
33, 91, 246, 317 Susan J. Carlson
43, 300 Donna Perrone
60, 104 Steven Dittberner
96 Geoff McCormack
110, 186 Robert Lawson
118, 129, 138 Karel Hayes
153 Elizabeth Wolf
157 Maria Teresa Aguilar
178 Cortney Skinner
194-195, 321 Mary Teichman
203 Elizabeth Wolf
214 Mike Hortens
222 Ken Tiessen

Credits

274 Drew-Brook Cormack
297 Tony Crnkovich
300 Laura Normandin
326 Beata Szpura
R12 Leland Klanderman
R34 Yoshi Miyake

Photographs

Every effort has been made to secure permission and provide appropriate credit for photographic material. The publisher deeply regrets any omission and pledges to correct errors called to its attention in subsequent editions.

Unless otherwise acknowledged, all photographs are the property of Scott Foresman, a division of Pearson Education.

Photo locators denoted as follows: Top (T), Center (C), Bottom (B), Left (L), Right (R), Background (Bkgd).

Cover

(BR) ©Peter Smithers/Corbis, (Bkgd) ©MAPS/Corbis, (C) Philip Gould Photography

Front Matter

LA1 (T) Eastcott Momatiuk/National Geographic/Getty Images, (CL) Sydney Byrd, (BL) ©Bettmann/Corbis; LA2 (BR) Philip Gould/Corbis, (C) ©Royalty-Free/Corbis, (L) C.C. Lockwood/DDB Stock Photography; LA3 (CR) ©C.C. Lockwood 2006, (C) Eastcott Momatiuk/National Geographic/Getty Images, (BR) ©Royalty-Free/Corbis, (CL) Alex Demyan; LA4 (B) ©Bettmann/Corbis, (BC) Farrell Grehan/Corbis, (TR) Chicago Historical Society, Chicago, USA/Bridgeman Art Library; LA6 (BL) Andrew Putler/Redferns, (BC) Sydney Byrd; LA7 Philip Gould/Corbis; LA9 (BL) Arthur D. Lauck/AP/Wide World Photos, (BR) Bill Feig/AP/Wide World Photos; LA10 (B) Courtesy of the Ville Platte Gazette, (CL) ©Charles Bush; LA11 (CR, B, BL) ©David McGuire; LA14 Photograph Collection, Archives & Special Collections Department, Frazar Memorial Library, McNeese State University/McNeese State University Library; LA15 (BL) David Mendelsohn/Masterfile Corporation, (CR) Photograph Collection, Archives & Special Collections Department, Frazar Memorial Library, McNeese State University/McNeese State University Library; LA16 (T) ©Royalty-Free/Corbis, (TL) Farrell Grehan/Corbis, (CL) Philip Gould/Corbis, (B) Photograph Collection, Archives & Special Collections Department, Frazar Memorial Library, McNeese State University/McNeese State University Library; H2 Getty Images, ©Bard Martin/ Getty Images, ©Stephen Wilkes/Getty Images; H3 ©Ed Kashi/ Corbis, ©O'Brien Productions/ Corbis; H8 (BC) ©Stephen J. Krasemann/Photo Researchers, Inc., (BR) ©Joel Sartore/NGS Image Collection, (CC) Alex Demyan; H9 (BL) Alex Demyan, (BR) ©George D. Lepp/Corbis

Unit 1

1 Louisiana State Museum; 2 Louisiana State Museum; 4 The Granger Collection, NY; 5 ©Alexandria Town Talk/AP/Wide World Photos; 7 (T) ©C. C. Lockwood; 8 (B)©Brian Miller/DDB Stock Photography, (T) Photri-Microstock; 10 NASA Image Exchange; 11 (T) Photri-Microstock (BR) JSC Digital Image Collection; 14 (CL) ©National Maritime Museum, London, (TR) ©Magellan RoadMate 500 GPS/Courtesy of Thales Navigation, (BL) John B. Senter III/Omni-Photo Communications, Inc.; 18 Getty Images; 19 Alex Demyan; 20 (TL) ©C. C. Lockwood (BL) ©Brian Miller/DDB Stock Photography (CR) ©Jeff Greenberg/PhotoEdit (BR) DDB Stock Photography; 22 (CR) ©Richard Vaughan/Ardea, London; 23 (TL, TR, CR, BL, BR) DK Images; 25 (B) Courtesy of the City of Alexandria and Pineville Convention and Visitors Bureau/Marcus Campkin; 26 NASA Image Exchange; 28 (T) John Elk III, (B) ©Eastcott Momatiuk/Getty Images; 30 ©Richard Cummins/Corbis; 31 (BR) Getty Images (BC) ©Philip Gould Photography; 32 John Elk III; 34 (TC) Corbis (BL) ©Rud Plank/ Photo Researchers; 36 (B) ©C.C. Lockwood, (CL) ©John B. Senter III/Omni-Photo Communications, Inc.; 37 (T) ©Ricardo Funari/Latin Focus, (B) ©Paulo Santos/AP/Wide World Photos; 39 ©C.C. Lockwood; 40 ©Kevin Leigh/Index Stock Imagery; 41 (B, CR) ©Eastcott Momatiuk/Getty Images; 42 (B) ©C.C. Lockwood/Animals Animals/Earth Scenes, (CL) ©Neil Johnson; 44 Alex Demyan; 45 Alex Demyan; 46 Sydney Byrd, (C) ©Alexandria Town Talk/AP/Wide World Photos; 48 Shelby R. Gilley; 49 ©Collection of Thomas N. Whitehead; 50 ©Richard Cummins/Corbis; 52 (Bkgd) ©C. C. Lockwood (TL) ©Philip Gould/ Corbis; 53 (BR) ©Gladden William Willis/ Animals Animals/Earth Scenes; 54 ©David Muench/Corbis

Unit 2

57 ©Arthur Roger Gallery; 58 ©Arthur Roger Gallery; 60 (TR) ©Eric J. Brock; 61 (TL) ©Fuqua Photography, Inc./Courtesy of Henry Holt and Company, (TR) ©Philip Gould Photography; 63 (TR) ©John Elk III (TL) ©Joseph Sohm/ Chromosohm Inc/Corbis; 64 (T) ©Douglas Keister Photography, (B) Robertstock; 67 ©D. Donne Bryant/DDB Stock Photography; 68 (CL) ©Leroy Simon/Visuals Unlimited (TR) ©Joel S. Ponder; 70 (T) ©Douglas Keister Photography (CL) ©Robert Holmes/Corbis; 74 Bruce Coleman Inc.; 75 (B) Robertstock, (CR) ©Peter Blakely/ Corbis; 76 (L,R) ©US Army Corps of Engineers-New Orleans District; 77 (B) Tom Pantages, (TR) AP/Wide World Photos; 78 (TL) ©C. C. Lockwood (B) ©John Elk III; 80 (BL)(BR) ©Dayna Bowker Lee (Bkgd) Louisiana Regional Folklife Program, NSU (CL) ©Philip Gould Photography; 81 (TR) ©Dayna Bowker Lee (BR) ©Philip Gould Photography (TR) ©Philip Gould

Photography; 82 (B) ©Captain Henry M. Shreve Clearing the Great Raft from Red River, 1833– 38, painted by Lloyd Hawthorne, and Courtesy of The R.W. Norton Art Gallery-Shreveport, LA; 84 Bruce Coleman Inc.; 86 (T) ©DDB Stock Photography (B) ©C. C. Lockwood; 88 ©Philip Gould Photography; 89 (B) ©D. Donne Bryant/ DDB Stock Photography, (CR) ©Philip Gould/ Corbis; 90 (TL) ©W.D. Morse/Jennings Carnegie Library Archival Collection, Jennings, LA, (B) ©C.C. Lockwood/DDB Stock Photography; 92 (CL) ©Philip Gould Photography, (T) ©Peter Blakely/Corbis/SABA; 93 ©David B. Grunfeld/ The Image Works, Inc.; 94 (BC) ©David Young Wolff/PhotoEdit, (BR) ©Lisa Allison Parr/DDB Stock Photography, (Bkgd) ©David B. Grunfeld/ The Image Works, Inc.; 95 ©David Young-Wolff/PhotoEdit; 98 ©C.C. Lockwood/DDB Stock Photography; 99 (CR) ©Sarah Leen/NGS Image Collection (B) ©C. C. Lockwood; 100 (TR) ©Alex Demyan (TL) ©C. C. Lockwood/ DDB Stock Photography (CR) ©D. Donne Bryant/ DDB Stock Photography (BL) Dorling Kindersley LTD (BR) ©Gladden William Wills/Animals/Earth Science; 102 (B) ©SPCP4/Alex Demyan, (B) ©Joseph Sohm-ChromoSohm Inc/Corbis, (CR) ©Raymond Gehman/Corbis, (TL) ©Theresa Wiper; 103 (B) SPCP4/©Alex Demyan (CR) ©C. C. Lockwood; 104 ©Engraved by Robert Havell (1793–1878) 1834 (coloured engraving) Audubon, John James (1758–1851) (after)/Private Collection/Bridgeman Art Library; 105 (BR) ©National Audubon Society, (TR) ©Arthur Morris/Visuals Unlimited; 106 (BL) Katz Pictures Limited, (BC) ©DK Images, (TL) Mary Evans Picture Library; 107 (TR) Ocean Works International Inc (BR) ©Keith Danne Miller/Alamy Images; 108 ©DK Images

Unit 3

115 (Bkgd) Chitimacha Tribe of Louisiana; 116 (Bkgd) Chitimacha Tribe of Louisiana; 118 (TL) The Granger Collection, NY, (TR) Corbis; 119 Duke University, Rare Books, Manuscript & Special Collections Library; 121 (T) ©Philip Gould Photography, North Wind Picture Archives; 122 (B) ©Philip Gould Photography; 124 ©Robert Buquoi/Poverty Point State Historic Site; 125 Alex Demyan; 126 (BL) Northwestern State University of Louisiana, Cammie G. Henry Research Center; 128 (BL) Northwind Picture Archives (CL) ©Philip Gould Photography/North Wind Picture Archives; 129 ©Comstock Inc.; 130 North Wind Picture Archives; 132 (CR) ©Philip Gould Photography, (BL) ©Sonny Carter Photography, (TL) Alex Demyan; 133 (T) North Wind Picture Archives, (CR) ©Richard Cummins/Corbis; 134 (TR) ©Bettmann/Corbis, (BL) ©Robert Holmes/Corbis; 136 (BL) ©Owen Franklin/ Corbis, (BR) ©Brian Miller Photography; 137 (B) ©Richard T. Nowitz/Corbis, (TR) ©Robert Dafford/Acadi-

an Memorial; 139 ©Greg Smith/Corbis; 142 (T) Stock Montage/SuperStock, (B) ©Randal Sanders Photography; 144 ©Richard Cummins/Corbis; 145 The Granger Collection, NY; 146 (CR) ©Charlie Borland/Index Stock Imagery (TL) Stock Montage/Superstock (CL) Bettmann Corbis; 149 (C) ©Bettmann/Corbis, (BR) The Granger Collection, NY; 150 Stock Montage Inc.; 151 Corbis; 152 (BC) Corbis, (BL) The Granger Collection, NY; 154 (T) Corbis, (BL) ©Randal Sanders Photography; 155 ©Tria Giovan/Corbis; 156 Duke University, Rare Books, Manuscript & Special Collections Library; 157 (Bkgd) Corbis; 159 ©Louisiana State University Libraries; 160 (CR)(BL)(TR) Confederate Memorial Hall (TR) 161 (TR) Confederate Memorial Hall (B) Gettysburg National Military Park/Dorling Kindersley

Unit 4
169 (C) ©Courtesy of Louisiana State University Museum of Art, Gift of the Lafourche Parish School Board; 170 (C) ©Courtesy of Louisiana State University Museum of Art, Gift of the Lafourche Parish School Board; 172 (TR) AP/Wide World Photos, (TL) The Granger Collection, New York; 175 ©Philip Gould Photography; 176 ©Cindy McCleish Ingram; 179 (B) ©Webster Fair Collection, donated by A.D. Martin, (TR) ©Syndey Byrd; 180 (BR) ©Syndey Byrd, (CL) ©Bill Aron/PhotoEdit, (BL) ©Cindy McCleish Ingram; 181 (BL, CR) ©Charles Jackson; 183 Alex Demyan; 184 Alex Demyan; 185 (T) ©Liu Liqun/Corbis, (BL) ©Syndey Byrd; 188 ©Syndey Byrd ; 189 (BL) ©Bill Aron/PhotoEdit, (TR, CR, BR) AP/Wide World Photos; 190 (BL) ©Debra L Ferguson/Southern Images, (BR) Alamy Images, (CL) AP/Wide World Photos; 192 (CR) ©Neil Johnson, (CL) ©Department of Education/Louisiana State Archives; 193 ©D. Donne Bryant/DDB Stock Photography; 194 (BL) AP/Wide World Photos, (Bkgd) ©Robert Holmes/Corbis; 195 ©Owen Franken/Corbis; 198 (T) ©Mark E. Gibson Stock Photography, (BC) ©Cindy McCleish Ingram; 200 Getty Images; 201 (BC) ©Tony Anderson/Getty Images, (CR) ©Comstock Inc.; 202 ©Mark E. Gibson Stock Photography; 204 (T) ©Neil Alexander Photography, (BL) ©Steve Smith/SuperStock, (BL) The Granger Collection, NY; 206 (BL) The Granger Collection, New York; 207 (C) From the Walker Collection of A'Leila Bundles (TR) Photograph by Madam Walker Collection/Indiana Historical Society; 208 (CR) (CL) (TR) (BR) (BR) (CR) The Trustees of the British Museum; 209 (TC) (T) (TR) (CL) (CC) (BC) (BL) The Trustees of the British Museum (BR) Dorling Kindersley; 210 AP/Wide World Photos; 211 ©Cindy McCleish Ingram; 212 (BR, BL) ©Spencer Grant/PhotoEdit; 214 ©Myrleen Cate/Photo Network/ Alamy Images; 216 (B) ©Carin Krasner/Stone; 218 ©Ferrara Fire Apparatus Inc.; 219 ©Chris Mickal/911 Pictures;

220 AP/ Wide World Photos; 222 ©Robert Holmes/ Corbis;

Unit 5
230 (TL) Corbis, (TR) ©George Long Photography, Inc.; 231 (TL, TR) AP/Wide World Photos; 233 AP/Wide World Photos; 234 (T) AP/Wide World Photos, (B) ©DDB Stock Photography; 236 ©Joe Sohm/Alamy; 237 ©DDB Stock Photography; 238 (TR) AP/Wide World Photos (BR) ©Neil Johnson (TL) ©Alex Demyan (BL) ©Eric J. Brock; 240 (BL) Corbis (Bkgd) ©Didier Dorval/Masterfile Corporation; 241 (TR) ©Syndey Byrd (BR) Getty Images; 242 ©Andre Jenny/Alamy Images; 243 (TR) ©Syndey Byrd (BR) ©Andre Jenny/Alamy Images; 244 (TR) ©Senator James David Cain (BC) ©Nancy P. Alexander/PhotoEdit (BR) AP/Wide World Photos (BL) DDB Stock Photography; 245 AP/Wide World Photos; 248 (BC) ©Roy Ooms/Masterfile Corporation (TL) ©Dennis O'Claire/Stone/Getty Images (CR) ©Dennis Brack Photography; 249 (BC) ©Roy Ooms/Masterfile Corporation, (TL) ©Dennis O'Clair/Stone/Getty Images; 250 ©Mark Saltz/The Advocate; 252 Alex Demyan; 254 (BC) ©Neil Johnson (TC) Thibodaux Volunteer Fire Department; 257 (BC) ©Bruno Torres/Corbis, (TR) AP/Wide World Photos; 258 (CL) ©Gloria F. Hamilton, (TC) ©Thibodaux Volunteer Fire Department; 260 (Bkgd) AP/ Wide World Photo (BL) ©George Long Photography Inc; 261 ©cmarl/Alamy Images; 262 (BR) Public Building Service/National Archives (TL)(BL)(TR) Dorling Kindersley; 263 (BR) NASA (T) Dorling Kindersley (BL) ©Denis McDonald/ PhotoEdit; 265 (B) ©Eric J. Brock (CR) ©Willaim A. Dunckleman; 266 (BL) Louisiana Department of Natural Resouces (T) ©Neil Johnson; 268 (BL)(BR) AP/Wide World Photos; 269 AP/Wide World Photos; 270 ©Jose Luis Pelaez, Inc./Corbis; 272 ©Roy Ooms/Masterfile Corporation; 274 AP/Wide World Photos

Unit 6
279 (Bkgd) ©Paul Schexnayder; 280 (Bkgd) ©Paul Schexnayder; 282 (TC) ©Charles Bush, (TR, TL) The Granger Collection, NY; 283 (TR) Acadiana Profile Magazine; 285 AP/Wide World Photos; 286 (BC) ©Charles Bush, (T) ©Sydney Byrd; 288 Sydney Byrd; 289 (CR, TR) ©Sydney Byrd; 290 (BL) ©Bob Krist/Corbis (CR) Getty Images; 292 (CR, BL) ©Sydney Byrd, (TL) ©R. Lynn Hadley; 293 (TR) ©Owen Franken/ Getty Images, (B) ©Thomas Schmitt/Getty Images, (BL) ©Oliver Benn/Getty Images; 296 ©Charles Bush; 297 (TR) Louisiana State Museum; 298 (BL) ©David Redfern, (TL) ©Photo by Nancy Kaszerman/Zuma Press, (TR) The Granger Collection, New York (CR) ©Philip Gould Photography; 300 (BC) Corbis (R) Getty Images; 301 (TR) AP/Wide World Photos, (BR) ©Blank Archives/Getty Images; 302 ©Bob Krist/Corbis; 304 (BC) ©Philip Gould Photogra-

phy, (TC) ©Syndey Byrd; 306 (BL) ©C. C. Lockwood; 307 (BL) ©Sydney Byrd, (TR) ©Mark Andresen, (BR) ©D. Donne Bryant/DDB Stock Photography; 308 (TR) Corbis, (CL) ©Philip Gould Photography, (BL) ©Comstock Inc., (TC) ©Syndey Byrd; 311 ©Widener Library/Harvard University; 313 Alex Demyan; 314 ©Robert Holmes/Corbis; 315 (B) ©Richard Cummins/ Corbis, (CR) ©Syndey Byrd ; 316 (TL) ©Philip Gould Photography, (BR) ©Sydney Byrd; 318 (TR) ©Cindy Charles/PhotoEdit, (BL) AP/Wide World Photos (C) ©Neil Alexander Photography; 320 (L) Acadiana Profile Magazine (Bkgd) ©C. C. Lockwood; 321 (CR) Acadiana Profile Magazine; 322 (BL, BR) ©Sefton Samuels Photography, (CC, CR) Getty Images; 323 (L) Silver Burdett Ginn (TR) Getty Images (BR)(CR) Redfern Music Picture Library; 324 ©Comstock Inc.

End Matter
R2 Earth Imaging/Stone; R24 Bettmann/ Corbis; R25 Getty Images, (CC) Philip Gould Photography, (BR) AP/Wide World Photos; R26 (TR) Joe Sohm/Alamy, (TR) Joe McDonald/ Corbis, (CC) Peter Smithers/Corbis, Larry Miller, (BR) Bill Curtsinger/NGS Image Collection; R27 (TL) ©Henry Robison/Visuals Unlimited, (TR) ©Tara Darling, (CC) John Pickles/Alamy, (BL) David Maitland/Getty Images, (BR) Millard H. Sharp/ Photo Researchers, Inc.; R33 AP/Wide World Photos; R35 (TL) The Granger Collection, NY, (CL) Duke University, Rare Books, Manuscript & Special Collections Library; R36 The Granger Collection, New York; R38 Owen Franklin/Corbis; R40 Corbis; R41 ©Comstock Inc.; R42 ©C.C. Lockwood/Animals Animals/Earth Scenes; R43 ©Douglas Keister Photography ; R44 ©Eastcott-Momatiuk/The Image Works, Inc.